THE
GREY PARROT

The Grey Parrot is an unabridged translation, with minor emendations by the author, of the German text of the Fifth, Enlarged Edition of *Der Graupapagei: Pflege, Zucht und Zähmung—Eine Chronik aus 100 Jahren,* © 1976, 1982 by Eugen Ulmer GmbH & Co., Stuttgart, FRG. English translation © 1987 by T.F.H. Publications, Inc. Photographs and captions have been added for this English-language edition; copyright is also claimed for this additional material.

Photographs: Dr. Herbert R. Axelrod; Glen S. Axelrod; S. Bischoff; W. de Grahl; Duett-Werk; Wilfriede Adhi Karg; Harry V. Lacey; Lobback-Voliere; E. J. Mulawka; Max Mills; Frank Nothaft; B. Roth; St. Langberg, Lind, Denmark; Courtesy of San Diego Zoo; H. Stock; Theiling-Voliere; Courtesy of Vogelpark Walsrode; Louise Van der Meid; Wöllhaf; ZDF/A. Grimm, Berlin.

t.f.h.

© 1987 by T.F.H. Publications, Inc.

Distributed in the UNITED STATES by T.F.H. Publications, Inc., 211 West Sylvania Avenue, Neptune City, NJ 07753; in CANADA to the Pet Trade by H & L Pet Supplies Inc., 27 Kingston Crescent, Kitchener, Ontario N2B 2T6; Rolf C. Hagen Ltd., 3225 Sartelon Street, Montreal 382 Quebec; in CANADA to the Book Trade by Macmillan of Canada (A Division of Canada Publishing Corporation), 164 Commander Boulevard, Agincourt, Ontario M1S 3C7; in ENGLAND by T.F.H. Publications Limited, 4 Kier Park, Ascot, Berkshire SL5 7DS; in AUSTRALIA AND THE SOUTH PACIFIC by T.F.H. (Australia) Pty. Ltd., Box 149, Brookvale 2100 N.S.W., Australia; in NEW ZEALAND by Ross Haines & Son, Ltd., 18 Monmouth Street, Grey Lynn, Auckland 2, New Zealand; in SINGAPORE AND MALAYSIA by MPH Distributors (S) Pte., Ltd., 601 Sims Drive, #03/07/21, Singapore 1438; in the PHILIPPINES by Bio-Research, 5 Lippay Street, San Lorenzo Village, Makati Rizal; in SOUTH AFRICA by Multipet Pty. Ltd., 30 Turners Avenue, Durban 4001. Published by T.F.H. Publications, Inc. Manufactured in the United States of America by T.F.H. Publications, Inc.

THE
GREY PARROT

Wolfgang de Grahl

Translated by
William Charlton

DEDICATION

To Herr Doctor Joachim Steinbacher,
director of the Ornithology Department
of the Natural History Museum and Senckenberg
Research Institute in Stuttgart for thirty years;
editor for forty-four years of *Die Gefiederte Welt*,
specialty journal with a hundred-year tradition.

*Dr. Joachim Steinbacher on the German television program
"Großen Preis," judging the competition in which the Grey
Parrot named Lora Eston participated.*

Contents

Preface

In the family of large parrots, the Grey Parrot is the most talented mimic. Its considerable imitative ability, as well as the ever more frequent successes in breeding, make it an extremely interesting bird. This is demonstrated by the publication of this fifth edition in so short a time.

Besides the genus description and the information on care and breeding, the numerous reports and experiences of readers show time after time that each Grey Parrot is a unique individual. The important chapter on illnesses has in each edition been reviewed by veterinarian Siegfried Mundt and, where necessary, has been revised.

The warning I stated in the preface to the first edition will become increasingly significant in the future: the environmental conditions for Grey Parrots in their homeland are deteriorating at an alarming rate, so that we can no longer afford to reduce their numbers in the wild. We must place special emphasis on breeding the Grey Parrot in captivity to preserve and increase the numbers of this valued and beloved species of parrot. Anyone who owns Grey Parrots should accept this responsibility by providing them with the best possible care.

Hamburg, 1982   WOLFGANG DE GRAHL

Description of the Genus

Genus: **Grey Parrots,** *Psittacus erithacus* **Linnaeus 1758**
One species, two races, 31–37 centimeters in length.

Grey Parrot, *P. erithacus erithacus* **Linnaeus 1758**
Range: Southeastern Ivory Coast, Ghana, Togo, Dahomey, Nigeria, southern Chad, to approximately 10 degrees north latitude; Cameroon, Central African Republic, Zaire, Uganda, western Kenya, Rwanda, Burundi, northwest Tanzania, northern Angola, Congo Republic, Gabon, Equatorial Guinea, and the islands of Principe and Fernando Po [now called Bioko— *Ed.*]; to the south, the range extends to approximately 10 degrees south latitude.

According to information provided in 1973 by Dr. Martin Eisentraut of the zoological research institute and museum in Bonn, the island form *P. e. princeps* can no longer be recognized as a third race, since it is also found locally on the mainland and the differentiating characteristics are too slight—variations in coloration and size are also found in other regions.

Size: 33–37 centimeters in total length; wings: in males, the average length is 24.2 centimeters, in females, 23.4 centimeters; tail: 8.6–9.4 centimeters in length.

Male: The entire plumage is grayish overall, the edges of the feathers of the nape and breast are dark. The bare cere and the broad, elliptical orbital ring are grayish white. The rump is gray to light gray. The tail feathers are bright red. The head and neck feathers are edged light gray. The bill is black, the feet are gray, and the iris is light yellow to maize yellow.

7

Female: The skull is somewhat narrower, the upper mandible is less hooked, the underparts are usually lighter.

Young: The iris is at first dark, then gray after a few months, and finally whitish yellow to maize yellow; the under tail coverts are spotted with gray, the wing coverts and back are light brownish gray, the tail feathers are somewhat speckled; the first molt occurs after about twelve months.

P. erithacus timneh Fraser 1844

Range: Southern Guinea, Sierra Leone, Liberia, and western Ivory Coast.

Size: 31–32 centimeters in total length; wings: an average length of 21.5 centimeters in males, 20.8 centimeters in females; tail: 8 centimeters in length.

Male: The top of the upper mandible is light pink, becoming blackish toward the tip. The tail feathers are rust brown to gray brown. The plumage is dark gray overall; the neck and breast feathers are almost without a different edge. The iris is whitish yellow.

Female: The skull is narrower.

Young: The iris is black to gray; the tail feathers are very dark.

1.   Life in the Wild

The Swiss naturalist Konrad Gesner (1516–1565) compiled the best animal book of his time. He was, in fact, one of the earliest authors to describe the homeland of the Grey Parrot. He wrote the following: "I also saw a parrot whose entire body is ash color or light blue; only on the tail does it have red feathers, and around the eyes it is white . . . ."

It was over 100 years ago, in the years 1872–1873, that Dr. Anton Reichenow was able to observe the habits of the Grey Parrot in the wild. He explored Guinea, the Gold Coast, Cameroon, and Gabon. In those days these parrots were found in large numbers. They were impossible to overlook, since in large flocks, and with considerable screeching and croaking, they flew along rivers and roosted in the thick mangrove forests. Their flight looks heavy and resembles that of ducks; they beat their wings rapidly, as if afraid of falling out of the sky. Before they land on a branch, one can often observe a peculiar trait: they hover like a kestrel, with the body almost vertical. It appears as though the birds are deciding where they are going to alight. They choose the tallest trees for roosting at night, and they fly to the same trees every evening. The flock arrives punctually each evening, and the next morning they fly off as a group to their feeding sites. This flocking behavior is only observed outside the breeding season; during the breeding season Grey Parrots split up by pairs. The flock always assemble at sunset, and only when it is completely dark do their noise and restlessness subside. Since the feeding sites inland are usually located on plains at higher elevations, different flocks always use the same flight routes. They are particularly fond of feeding in

9

fields of half-ripened maize, where they can do considerable damage. They also fly from tree to tree to find fruits, nuts, and berries. They are particularly attracted to the fruit of the oil palm (*Elaeis guinesis*).

Mankind is the principal enemy of the Grey Parrot. In earlier times, natives killed them for food, though the flesh is said to be tough by European standards. They were also frequently killed for their red tail feathers. These were used for head-dresses, and in some tribes they were considered to have magical properties. But since more money is paid for live birds, even a century ago the birds were brought into ports to be sold. In those days young birds were usually taken from nests, reared, and sold, because they commanded the highest prices. Furthermore, Grey Parrots are extremely shy and wary, and in earlier times it was hardly possible to capture them with nets or snares. It was much easier to find fledged youngsters that only occasionally flew to and from their nest holes, or to climb up the tree at night to fasten a net or sack in front of the hole. After beating on the tree with a cudgel, the frightened birds flew from the cavity and were caught in the net or sack. The adults were usually released (in earlier times), because they were too wild to tame. The natives captured birds only to be sold; they did not keep them as pets. It was often possible to see whole rows of tame birds with clipped flights sitting on the roofs of huts. In Ghana, posts with several perches were used, and approximately fifteen Grey Parrots were chained to such a "tree" to get them used to the presence of humans.

Another enemy of the Grey Parrot is apparently the Palm-nut Vulture (*Gypohierax angolensis*), which is also called the "Vulture Eagle." Systematically, this bird of prey was first placed with the vultures, then later with the eagles. This approximately 55-centimeter-long bird feeds primarily on the fruits of the oil palm and the raffia palm, but also feeds on fish, crabs, and molluscs. Frequently found in mangrove forests, it is distributed through Angola, Zaire, Gabon, and Cameroon. This predator has been observed chasing Grey Parrots, which fled in panic from it. Perhaps this is only a kind of territorial defense, or a behavior similar to the mobbing of crows, since

Distribution of the Two Races

Psittacus erithacus timneh: Southern Guinea, Sierra Leone, Liberia, western Ivory Coast.

Psittacus erithacus erithacus: Southeastern Ivory Coast, Ghana, Togo, Dahomey, Nigeria, southern Chad, Cameroon, Central African Republic, Zaire, Uganda, western Kenya, Burundi, northwestern Tanzania, northern Angola, Congo Republic, Gabon, Equatorial Guinea, the islands of Principe and Fernando Po.

11

the Palm-nut Vulture is not nimble enough to catch a Grey Parrot easily.

Martin Eisentraut of the zoological research institute in Bonn was able in 1973 to confirm that Grey Parrots occur only up to an altitude of 1200 meters. The *timneh* race is found only from the Ivory Coast to Guinea.

The breeding season varies a great deal over the species' extensive Africa range, depending on whether the Greys live north or south of the equator. Eggs were found in eastern Nigeria in January, even though it was the dry season. Young birds were seen in Liberia in April. In Uganda, they breed from July to September, and in Zaire eggs were found in August. On Principe Island, young were found in nests in December, just after the end of the rainy season. In other regions, they are believed to nest during the rainy season as well. Their nests are found in deep holes in tree trunks, but they also nest in holes in branches. They use their bills to enlarge natural holes. Frequently, many pairs nest in a relatively small area, but only one pair nests in each tree. Approximately 60 centimeters below the entrance hole, three or four eggs, but occasionally as many as five, are laid on the wood mold. The nests are usually quite difficult to find, since they are situated in impenetrable thickets. The round-to-oval eggs have an average size of 39×31 millimeters, and an average weight of approximately 13 grams. Nesting trees inherited by those born in them once existed, and perhaps still do in certain areas, as is the case in South America with the macaws.

2.

Races, Variants, and Coloration

Until the year 1886, the situation with the juvenal plumage (the tail feathers) was unclear. It was assumed that birds with red tails were males and those with dark tails (*timneh*) were females. Even Reichenow (*Journal für Ornithologie,* 1875) wrote that "even though I never had the opportunity to examine nestlings, I believe that, according to my observations and inquiries, I can claim that the tail feathers of young birds are originally dark gray, which contradicts the previously held belief. This was confirmed by the Negroes who take the young birds from their nests and sell them to Europeans. I myself frequently saw younger individuals on which the basal parts of the tail feathers were dark gray and the tips were red, but not as pure as those of adults, which were brownish red. This is proof that the coloration gradually changes from gray to red." This passage clearly deals with the other race, *P. e. timneh.* Only in the year 1886 did the various researchers learn the correct explanation from a sailor: "I was greatly surprised when I opened the reed basket which is frequently used by the natives as a cage for Grey Parrots and found, next to an impeccable jocko, a little bird that was still almost completely covered in down. This little bird did, however, have most of its flights as well as most of its tail feathers, and these were completely red. A half dozen of the latter were still pin feathers; they were still covered by their sheaths, and only a part of each feather had broken out, but these were as red as the others." Here was the indisputable proof that the tail feathers of the Grey Parrot are red even in the youngest birds.

By 1896, it had also been determined that the Grey Parrots on the island of Fernando Po were somewhat darker in coloration than normal. Even until the present day these Grey Parrots have been considered to be a third race. In 1973, a group from the research institute in Bonn under M. Eisentraut determined that the birds found on Principe Island and Fernando Po (the race *P. e. princeps* Alexander 1909), could not be said to constitute a separate race. Specimens collected on these islands are virtually indistinguishable from animals taken from the area surrounding Mt. Cameroun on the mainland. On the islands, they were found to an altitude of 1200 meters in Mocatal and at the same elevation at Buea on Mt. Cameroun. They were not found at higher elevations.

There are also other variations in the coloration of Grey Parrots. Finsch reported, as early as 1868, that Levaillant had made a drawing of a specimen in which the upper wing coverts, some of the secondaries, and the thighs were red. Birds speckled with red were also found from time to time. They were called "king birds" or "king jockos" by dealers and were coveted because of their unusual coloration.

Herr Linek, of Altausee in Austria, notified me early in 1976 that a king jocko, which was not for sale, was in the possession of the firm of Holler in Tobelbad. Several photographs showed that the belly was rose red down to the legs and that it also had several similar feathers on the nape. According to the photographs, it must have been a male. Herr Linek wrote: "I was astounded by the bird's beauty. The son of a Negro chieftain demanded a whole basket of other jockos from Frau Holler in exchange." Gierke, the Hamburg importer, indicated that in his entire long career in the business he had imported only four birds with red feathers in their plumage; only one bird's belly was completely red. He also confirmed that this red coloration had not disappeared after molting; therefore, the birds had not been dyed.

Many years ago (1882), a Grey Parrot with a pure white tail was brought to Rotterdam. Also in August of 1894 a gray-eyed, normally colored bird was purchased; after molting the next year, it was completely speckled with red. These changes in

The breeding pair of Grey Parrots from Heide/Holstein, so prolific for so many years. The hen exhibits a somewhat lighter-colored breast and belly and a more slender head.

coloration can sometimes be effected by altering the living conditions of the bird, such as by changing the diet or the climate. This is probably the reason why a gray bird that Dr. Hennicke bought in Gabon had several red feathers on the breast and at the bend of the wing after molting, and therefore became a king bird. A white bird with red feathers was shown at the Aegintha Exhibition in Berlin in 1890. Such animals are extremely rare. In the 1950s the firm of Gustav Müller in Hamburg owned a nearly black Grey Parrot with a red tail; a black parrot was also advertised at that time.

As was previously mentioned, there is considerable variation in coloration and size even in the nominate form of the Grey Parrot through its large range. These variations may be caused by differences in climate and dietary habits. It was already mentioned that the birds found on the islands off Guinea and in the area of Mt. Cameroun have unusually dark backs. In other areas, the backs of Grey Parrots are somewhat lighter than normal. Nevertheless, it seems certain that females have the lighter and males the darker underparts. The author was also able to confirm this in breeding pairs. But this cannot safely be used to distinguish between the sexes, because at some collection points the birds are brought together from widely separate areas. Certainly this was done more often in the past than today, since the birds are now transported by airplane instead of by ship. Even so, it is possible that Grey Parrots could first be brought from Sierra Leone to Guinea, for example, from whence they are shipped to Europe, along with birds from Guinea.

P. e. timneh is smaller, and its plumage is darker overall. The upper mandible remains rose red, and the tail feathers are dark brownish red in the adults. Apparently, very young *timneh* Grey Parrots always have gray black tail feathers, which become brownish red only after the first molt. It is also possible, however, that the color of the tail feathers varies in adult birds from different areas.

The name *timneh* seems to have been derived from the inhabitants of Sierra Leone (which is one of the areas where the *timneh* Grey Parrot is found). One of the tribes found there is the "Temme." One also speaks of the "Timmani," who live in "Timmanee country."

3.

Trade, Past and Present

The Egyptians apparently did not keep parrots, since no trace of them can be found in hieroglyphics. In Roman times, a kind of trade in parrots probably existed, since Marcus Portius Cato censured the fashion for carrying parrots about on the hand. Emperor Antonius Heliogabalus, in Rome, received a large shipment of parrots from Africa, which were served at banquets; they were even fed to lions. It cannot be proved that any Grey Parrots were among these, but it seems reasonable to assume that they were. The naturalist Ulysses Aldrovandi (born in 1522 in Bologna, Italy) mentioned the Grey Parrot in his zoological work, so that we can say with certainty that it was known and traded by that time. In 1843, it was reported that President Kleinmayrn in Vienna owned a Grey Parrot.

The sailing ships and steamers that used to call at the ports of West Africa were immediately loaded with booty from the native peoples; Grey Parrots were included. In some ports, virtually all the birds offered for sale were tame birds that had been taken from their nests and raised by hand. These were understandably coveted, even though they cost more than captured adult birds. The containers (cages) in which the birds were transported were cylindrical and made of reeds. They were 50 centimeters long, with a diameter of 20 centimeters, and had a handle for carrying. The prices varied in the different harbors and were determined by supply and demand. The price fluctuated between 4 and 15 shillings, and after the breeding season in 1890, when the supply was particularly large, the price decreased by 1.5 shillings. In Accra, the port of Ghana, and in Gabon (and to some extent in Nigeria) the supply was large in those days, while in Cameroon and Liberia the birds were seldom available. In the port of Freetown (Sierra Leone), *timneh* Grey Parrots were occasionally offered for sale. These birds had already been obtained secondhand. Even in those days, buyers traveled along the coast and inland to buy the birds from trappers. At this time, it was also mistakenly believed that the birds were also found on the Cape Verde and Canary islands, since they were offered for sale there; but these birds had been brought from the African mainland. Almost all sailing vessels and steamers carried the so-called jockos to the major ports of Europe. In England they were brought mainly to Liverpool, in Belgium to Antwerp, in Holland to Rotterdam, and in Germany to Hamburg. Untamed birds were offered for 15 to 20 marks, but birds that could whistle or mimic other sounds were sold, even in those days, for 200 to 300 marks. Here in Hamburg, the steamers and sailing ships from West Africa were met by importers. The birds from sailing ships commanded higher prices, because experience showed that these birds became acclimated more rapidly and were less likely to die, since they had been kept in better accommodations on board (oxygen, light, and care). In the cabins of the steamers, the temperatures were usually as high as 30–40 C., and not only were many parrots confined in those cramped quarters, but monkeys and other animals as well. While at sea, the portholes remained closed, and when the captain or an officer appeared, the animals were hidden or covered with blankets. In those days, the cabins had little light and no ventilation.

Another evil practice of the day was the result of the widespread belief that the parrots should not have any water during the journey! They were fed only dry bread and cooked rice, which led to the expected result; the death rate in Europe was high. Even Dr. Reichenow warned, in 1874, that it was unwholesome to give Grey Parrots a constant supply of water. Even so, Reichenow was one of the "progressive" fanciers, since there were others who felt the birds should be given water only once a day. There were disputes concerning whether the water should be boiled, whether the importers should feed them hemp after their arrival, and whether the birds should be kept very warm or not so warm. Most of the birds died with swollen livers and constipation, and some had tuberculosis of the lungs. The death rate was considerably higher in young birds (those with dark eyes) than in older birds. Some believed that the birds were diseased before they left their homelands. Parrot fanciers, however, who brought with them a few birds from Africa (even some very young ones), had few losses, while sailors who brought back birds on the same trip lost a greater number of birds. Others believed the birds could not stand the condensation from the boilers on steamships. A steamer took five weeks to sail from Lagos (Nigeria) to Liverpool (England) in 1880. By 1900, Grey Parrots were transported only on steamships, because sailing vessels were too slow. A German who had to inspect every German ship that arrived in Liverpool wrote that parrots were kept in small rooms, not in cages or allowed to fly free, but chained to wooden perches. The animal importer Gros, "the king of the wild beasts," always used cages to house large numbers of Grey Parrots. This parrot was also common in the other coastal cities of England, especially the ports. Young and old alike spared no expense when buying one of these birds. Finally, some years later, large transport boxes were used to ship the birds. There was room for about a dozen Grey Parrots in these boxes (1 meter long, 60 centimeters wide, and 40 centimeters high), which were covered with wire mesh on one side. The boxes were placed on the decks of the ships, so that the animals now had good air and sufficient oxygen. The birds were usually imported in spring and summer in those days, so the birds would not have to face such severe changes in climate.

Before World War II, the importers in Hamburg went directly on board the ships to buy the birds. Many had contracts with sailors who always took the same route to West Africa. These birds were frequently confiding or already tame, and the sailors frequently taught the birds profanity for fun. Among these birds there were few losses during transport; only young birds presented difficulties to those who did not look after them with much affection. It was said that the most beautiful and largest Greys came from the Congo; these birds were also considered to be the best mimics. Some importers also traveled as far as Marseille to buy Grey Parrots.

The trade in Grey Parrots has become more difficult today because they are not available in the same numbers as in the past. This may be caused partly by the natives, who no longer work at capturing the birds, partly by the destruction of habitat from cutting down trees, partly because of the high prices (Nigeria, for example, places a tax on each bird leaving the country), and finally, it is almost certain that the populations in the coastal regions have declined. It is understandable that more trapping is done in areas close to ports, railroads, or roads; few trappers venture deep into the forests.

Today, Grey Parrots from Cameroon or Gabon can be in the hands of European importers within twenty-four hours. In spite of this, it is no easy task for shippers to keep young, dark-eyed birds alive. The required quarantine with its medication, necessary as it may be, also places a great strain on the birds. Other difficulties are arise from changes in diet and climate. So, even though veterinarians and importers spare no effort, the losses can be high in some shipments. Despite investigations, some illnesses still cannot be explained. The greatest losses are caused by fungal infections and salmonellosis (*Salmonella typhimurium*); on the other hand, psittacosis is extremely rare.

4.

Recommendations Prior to Purchase

As was previously mentioned in the Preface, every prospective owner of a bird must ask himself if he is willing and able to provide the care it demands. A Grey Parrot should be viewed as a "child in the household," a member of the family. Next, accommodations must be considered. Is there a well-lighted place available with room for a cage at least 60 centimeters long? Once a location has been chosen, the cage should be moved as little as possible, since this parrot is particularly sensitive to change. Man is not the only creature of habit!

It is also important to keep in mind that a singly kept Grey Parrot should not be left alone the whole day with no people around. If this cannot be avoided, it is better to buy two Grey Parrots or to keep the bird with another parrot of approximately the same size.

Buying the parrot involves a great deal of luck and sensitivity. The seller can, of course, say which bird is or is not tame, but he cannot know how a particular bird will develop under someone else's care. The buyer must have a "feel" for whether a particular parrot is receptive to him, since parrots have likes and dislikes when it comes to people. It is not advisable to have a Grey Parrot sent. In the first place, this is not good for the bird's health, and at the very least a tame bird could become frightened. It is much better to make the effort to pick up the bird, even though one runs the risk of returning home without a Grey Parrot, because one did not like the bird in question.

Unfortunately, buying and selling animals is never free of problems. Not only the buyer but the seller as well can be displeased. This point cannot be overemphasized. If possible, the buyer should ask for certain information from the seller: Does the bird eat properly (and what does its diet consist of)? Are there any visible signs of illness? Does the bird behave calmly, or is it constantly nervous and afraid? The breastbone should not be sharp edged; it should be possible to feel flesh on both sides of it. A bird that is too thin can have diseased internal organs. While observing the bird, the buyer and the seller should not stand too close to the cage, since the bird could be frightened and would not then behave normally. Fluffed plumage, apathetic behavior, and closed eyes indicate that the bird is in poor condition. Sick birds always seem tamer because they are weak and listless. From a reasonable distance it is still possible to tell whether a Grey Parrot has sleek plumage and is lively. The condition of the flights and tail feathers is not that important. In a healthy bird, such cosmetic shortcomings will be rectified at the next molt. A so-called feather plucker is another story. If the feathers have been bitten off or if the breast has been plucked bare, the bird should not be bought under any circumstances.

Every imported Grey Parrot must spend several weeks in quarantine. During this time, the droppings and sometimes the blood are tested. In addition, the birds are given various obligatory courses of medication under the supervision of government veterinarians. The purpose of the quarantine is to make sure that any parrot sold is free of communicable diseases, so that there is no danger of infecting other birds or people. The quarantine does not guarantee that the parrot is free of liver disease, for instance, or other undetectable diseases. But the buyer should not be concerned about this possibility, because the Grey Parrot is an extremely robust bird which can live longer than a person, once it has become acclimated to its new surroundings. The bird, in fact, becomes acclimated during the weeks spent in quarantine. The seller should not be held responsible for every illness the bird might contract, because it is impossible to see inside the bird. Surviving quarantine offers no guarantee, unfortunately, that the Grey will not become ill at a later date. For this reason, the reader should become familiar

When a dealer has a number of Grey Parrots available for sale, the prospective buyer has the opportunity to select one suitable to the purpose he has in mind. Observing the birds will reveal differences that may allow an estimation of their sexes, talking abilities, or tameness.

with the following symptoms of illness, which could help to detect a disease at an early stage:

a) Frequently tucking the head in the feathers during the day.
b) Sitting listlessly with partially or fully closed eyes and ruffled plumage.
c) Wet, runny, or swollen eyes.
d) Repeatedly opening the bill as if yawning.
e) Noisy breathing, accompanied by raising and lowering the tail feathers.
f) Smacking noises, accompanied by frequently opening and closing the bill.
g) Lack of appetite and the breastbone sticks out (the breast should be fleshy).

h) Are the bill and feet normal, or do they have growths or white encrustations?

i) Liquid or foamy droppings, compared to what is normal.

The age of the bird should be carefully considered before purchase. It is understandable that younger Greys become accustomed to their new owners more quickly than older birds. On the other hand, the younger bird is more sensitive to change, and altering its diet can present difficulties. This is particularly true of black-eyed birds, which sometimes are not yet able to feed themselves. In young birds, the iris changes from black to gray, and then to white and whitish yellow. Such birds are all youngsters that can more easily stand changes in diet. They are the ideal birds to buy, but they seldom come on the market. The situation today is such that a buyer should feel fortunate to be able to choose among several Grey Parrots, since fewer are being offered for sale than in the past and it is difficult to find a large selection anywhere. More clearly stated, this means that a buyer will probably have to settle for a bird with yellow or maize yellow eyes. But, with patience, these birds can become just as attached to the owner as a younger bird.

The color of the iris changes rapidly. In the Grey Parrot, the transition from ash gray to maize yellow can take place in only eight months. However, there are reports of birds with pearl gray eyes even at an age of one to two years. Another fancier reports that the iris began to turn yellow only during the third year. Observations of birds bred in captivity indicate that the iris starts to become lighter at an age of three and one-half months. The duration of the grayish stage can vary, before the iris starts to turn light yellow and gradually becomes more yellow. The time needed for this change may be affected by diet.

Additionally, the author has been able to determine that the skull of the male is wider and more massive than the female's when viewed from above, and the bill is larger. In contrast, the female's skull is narrower and the bill is smaller. Even so, it is not always easy to ascertain the sex of certain animals.

There are fanciers who claim the male has red feathers around the vent, which contrast sharply with the light gray or even white feathers around them. At one time sailors even insisted that the nostrils of males were round and those of females were more elongated. The theory claiming that the wings of males extend beyond the tail, while those of females are even with the tail feathers, cannot be demonstrated in all cases; however, this does not mean that the theory is incorrect. The author was able to confirm it by examining a number of specimens in museums. Unfortunately, not all of the skins were labelled as to sex, so these could not be used. By examining the measurements given in foreign books, it is possible to conclude that the males have longer wings, at least in the previously recognized race *P. e. princeps*. The birds found around Mt. Cameroun are considered to be the same as these.

There is no difference in tameness or mimicking ability between the *timneh* Grey Parrot and the nominate form. The author has seen a *timneh* that was as tame as anyone could hope for. This was also noted in earlier times. Since it ordinarily appears on the market much less frequently, there has been correspondingly less written about this race. There are also buyers who prefer bright red tail feathers to the dark ones of the *timneh*. Others find both the smaller size of the *timneh* and the fact that most people own only the "usual Grey" more appealing.

It is interesting to examine the evolution of the language of sales advertisements for Grey Parrots over the past century (prior to 1875 these were rare)—these are given verbatim.

1875: Grey Parrots, overwintered birds, well cared for, are beginning to talk, 36 marks each, recommended . . .

1875: Grey Parrot whistles two songs, sings, talks a great deal, including *One, two, three, hurrah—Bismarck, hurrah—again, hurrah.* Offered at 300 marks . . .

1876: Talking Grey Parrot for sale, very confiding, young; laughs, sings, and whistles melodies; talks a great deal, including complete sentences, price 100 marks . . .

1878: A tame, young, talking Grey Parrot, accustomed to drinking water, is for sale for 100 marks, including a large cage . . .

1880: A splendid Grey Parrot, two years old, talks and whistles, learns something new every day, lets itself be handled by anyone, is

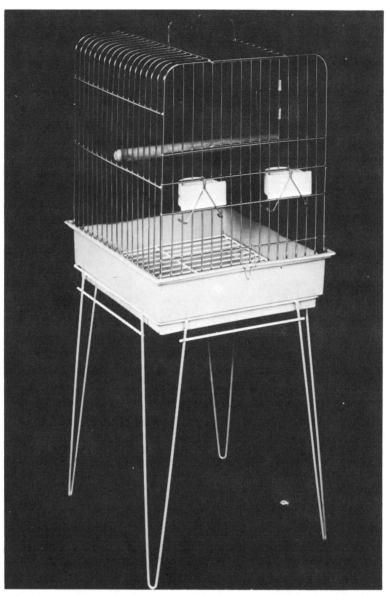

The wire top of this cage fits into a sturdy plastic tray. The latch on the door cannot be opened by the bird.

completely finger tame. For sale for the firm price of 100 marks . . .

1882: Jocko, owned three years, accustomed to hemp seed and water, able to say numerous words and sentences and use them appropriately, usually; offered for sale for the firm price of 140 marks . . .

1883: Chs. Jamrach, naturalist and animal dealer in London, offers Grey Parrots for 12 marks . . .

1883: Christiane Hagenbeck, Hamburg, Spielbudenplatz, has received a shipment of splendid, very good jockos, or Grey Parrots, sailing-ship birds, very teachable, accustomed to hemp seed, maize, and water, for 36 marks; young, well-feathered Grey Parrots, not completely acclimated but completely healthy, for 18 marks . . .

1884: Wilhelm Bandermann, Hamburg, obtained 30 Grey Parrots from the German bark *Kanton* on October 3—these are therefore authentic sailing-ship birds for 24 marks apiece. They are young, nicely feathered, accustomed to hemp and water, and are 3.5 months old, according to the testimony of the people on ship. One thousand marks reward to anyone who can prove the jockos described above were not purchased by me or are not sailing-ship birds. Two Grey Parrots, talk a great deal, very tame, 120 marks apiece; five that can speak a few words for 75 marks apiece . . .

1887: One Grey Parrot, rarity, talker of the first rank, can speak 200 words as clean and clear as a person, sings one song, whistles two songs, all guaranteed, 250 marks . . .

1892: King Grey Parrot, a most unusual rarity with bright red back and wings, one-half-year old, completely finger tame, can already speak a few words, flawless plumage, and fit as a fiddle for 100 marks . . .

1952: Grey Parrot, A-1 Congo bird, price 450 marks . . .

More advertisements from more recent times:

Five Grey Parrots and amazons talk for your parrot, half an hour on audiocassette . . .

Rarity: very young, black Grey Parrot, plumage like velvet . . .

Grey Parrot, speaks only English, bites women and children . . .

Grey Parrot, coughs, laughs, likes women and young people in particular, gentle, likes to cuddle, pretty, good plumage . . .

Young Grey Parrot, can speak entire sentences, with a new cage . . .
Voices of Grey Parrots, talking, singing, without one harsh whistle or screech, for playing in front of your own bird, one-half-hour long on audiocassette . . .
Speech laboratory, five talking parrots . . .
Congo Grey Parrot, large, tame, beautiful plumage, sits free on a stand, must sell due to circumstances . . .

Prices. Even in their homeland, Grey Parrots can no longer be brought cheaply. People there also know that half-tame or completely tame birds command markedly higher prices. Air freight has steadily increased, and today virtually no birds are transported by ship. There are also a few African nations (such as Nigeria) that impose a kind of export tax on each bird shipped. The demand is greater than the supply, and this, along with the previously mentioned factors, has led to an increase in prices.

A Grey Parrot that is still shy is cheaper than an already confiding bird. A completely tame bird that possibly may become hand tame will be even more expensive. With Grey Parrots, however, mimicking ability is just as important. Some bird keepers, however, place particular emphasis on taming or teaching the birds to talk. Tape recorders are used to teach the birds what they are supposed to learn. Tame Grey Parrots that are also good mimics are therefore justifiably sold at high prices. It is important to be careful when buying and paying for such birds. Only those birds that can demonstrate their accomplishments on the spot are worth so much money. A bird of this kind cannot be bought like a "pig in a poke."

5.   Care

Cages. A cage can never be too large, but one less than 60 centimeters is too small. The shape is also important; it should be rectangular, if possible. Round cages may seem to be attractive, but they are certainly not ideal for birds, because they can, for example, cause so-called turning sickness: the animal constantly looks up and moves its head in circles. As a rule, placing unnecessary ornaments in the cage is also impractical. It is important to have large food bowls that are stable and easy to remove from outside the cage. Heavy porcelain is still the best material. At least four bowls should be used so that various foods can be given separately, since one bowl must be reserved for water. The bowls should be placed at the level of the first perch if possible, even though this arrangement has the disadvantage that food can easily be spilled from the cage. If the bowls are placed lower, they could easily be fouled with droppings. Ideally, the bowls should be placed in the upper part with a guard arrangement to prevent food or empty seed hulls from falling out of the cage.

The perches should always be arranged so droppings cannot fall onto a lower perch from a higher one. A swing can be hung inside, so long as it does not interfere with the flapping of the bird's wings. Depending on the size of the cage, three to five perches can be installed. All perches on the market are made of birch, because this wood is very hard. Of course, oak would be an even better choice. These "normal" perches notwithstanding, it is advisable to give the Grey Parrot a fresh piece of wood (branch) at least once a week, which should be put near the top, if possible. This also gives the bird's feet the opportu-

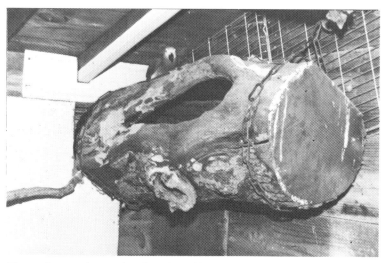

To simulate conditions found in the wild, a section of a tree trunk containing a natural cavity has been hung in an aviary as a nesting site.

nity to grip different thicknesses of wood. Fresh branches will also be discussed in the chapter on diet. Anyone who is handy can also modify a perch so its shape is conical. A conical perch is simply one that tapers from a thick end to a thinner one. In the wild, the birds do not sit on branches of the same thickness all the time. This also helps the claws to wear better. With very thin perches, the ends of the claws almost hang in the air! If the perches are thick, the claws will grip into the wood.

The different thicknesses of the perches have already been mentioned. What follows is a very old report from a parrot fancier, which is still as valid today as when it was written.

I have always kept parrots and have a passionate love for them, and I try to make life as comfortable for them as possible. I have a Grey Parrot (for over five years) who in intelligence, talking ability, and unfathomable maliciousness exceeds everything I have ever heard, read, or experienced concerning these birds. The number of words he can repeat and the apt usage and sense of what he can say is simply unbelievable. But even so, his sole object seems to be to bite, throw sand, and splash with water anyone who comes within range. No one has ever done anything to hurt him, and he has always been given the gentlest care and handling. Even so, he gets more malicious all the time. But this is incidental. I wanted to determine experimentally which perch thickness this animal prefers. Using a variety of perches does not prove anything, because every parrot always stays on the highest perch. I therefore made a rough, conical perch about 50 centimeters long, which had a diameter of 1.5 centimeters on one end and gradually increased to a diameter of 5 centimeters at the other end. I wanted to observe (by varying the position of the cage) on which part of the perch the bird preferred to spend his time, so I could give him perches with a thickness he himself had chosen. The result was unexpected, if also completely natural: the parrot sat here for a while, there for a while. He perched for hours on the thinner part (1.5 centimeters), then just as long on the thicker part (5 centimeters); in short, the bird wanted variety. This is quite understandable; in the wild he would have branches of different thicknesses to perch on. When his muscles grew tired from perching in one position, he could simply move to another perch. Our muscles also need variety. I therefore believe that a conical perch with a diameter that tapers from 5 centimeters to 1.5 centimeters is the appropriate perch that normally should be used for Grey Parrots. In this way, perhaps one performs a deed of great kindness to the captive bird; and foot diseases may also be prevented. I often observe my bird sliding slowly and comfortably along the perch, particularly when he is digesting a meal. He certainly appears to be content.

Modern cages usually come equipped with pans on which the cage stands. These are usually made of strong plastic. If the material is not thick enough, a Grey Parrot will not find it difficult one day to bite through it. The cage should also be equipped with plastic panes around the base, particularly when the food dishes are placed down low. There are also cages with a type of grid which is placed a few centimeters above the cage tray. This grid is supposed to allow seed hulls, food, and droppings to fall through. In practice, however, the necessarily heavy metal wire of the grid also becomes soiled. Cleaning the grid is much more tedious than cleaning the smooth cage tray. Since cleanliness is of the utmost importance, the floor of the cage should be covered with sand in the traditional way, and this sand should be changed every second day. In the chapter on diet another important reason for using sand will be mentioned.

Special attention must be given to the latch for the door of the cage. This must be cleverly constructed, or one day our Grey Parrot will certainly learn how to open it. The door should not be too small, and should open to the side, so that one can easily put his hand inside, not to mention the Grey. A flat tray with a climbing tree should be placed on top of the cage, if possible, so the parrot can leave the cage and use the climbing tree as a roost. From there, the parrot can also be quickly and easily placed back in the cage.

A short, heavy chain can provide the parrot with a great deal of amusement and pleasure. The bird can climb up and down it, and it rattles too. A heavy cord can serve the same purpose. The bird will chew on it incessantly, and this occupation also has therapeutic value. We will return to this subject when we discuss feather plucking in a later chapter. Any fancier who is handy can construct a metal frame, to be placed over the cage at night. A thick, dark cloth can then be draped over this wire frame. The bird should not be allowed to reach the cloth, or it will bite holes in it. At night, or at any other time, the bird can then be covered (while watching television, for example). A disadvantage of this accessory is that it takes up space when it is not in use.

Large cages, indoor flights, and the aviaries mentioned in the next section are manufactured, for example, by these German firms: Theiling of Melle, R. K. Lobback of Dannenberg/Elbe, and S. Wunnig of Hahn bei Bad Marienberg, Westerwald. The large cages are on casters and can easily be pushed out into the fresh air.

Aviaries. An aviary can also be called a flight cage. A prefabricated flight can easily be erected in a room or on a veranda. There are a number of companies that can build them to one's

Facing page: A freestanding outdoor flight of this sort is suitable for Grey Parrots. Of course, outdoor accommodations must always be evaluated in terms of the prevailing climate.

own specifications. Or one can build his own flight cage using thin metal tubes or rods (which can be found in hardware stores). One should always make sure that the flight is practical. A large entrance door is indispensable for cleaning. The wire mesh must be strong enough that it cannot be bitten through. The author recommends rectangular galvanized wire mesh, with either 19 millimeters or, better yet, 25 millimeters between strands, so the birds can be seen easily. The 25-millimeter mesh is also stronger, which would make it possible to add another bird such as a cockatoo, which has a very strong bill, to the flight. The mesh and frame should never be coated with plastic, because this would quickly be chewed. Flights are, of course, ideal for breeding parrots, and this subject will be covered in the chapter on breeding.

It is certainly possible to erect a summer flight on a balcony. One must be careful that the bird does not escape while being transported from its cage to the flight. This transfer should be attempted with tame birds only, since catching the bird forcibly would be resented. The Grey Parrot must be at least tame enough that it can go from its cage to the flight on the balcony without struggling. It would be ideal, of course, if some kind of small flight or cage were situated in the room in such a position that the bird could climb through a small door or window into the balcony flight. A similar arrangement could also be used between indoor and outdoor flights. Unfortunately, these are ideal arrangements that only a few of us can manage.

A freestanding outdoor flight is suitable, even during warmer months, only if the Grey Parrot can go into a shelter room (which need not be large) where it can safely avoid rain, wind, or sudden weather changes. Grey Parrots which have been acclimated over several months are not delicate animals; they can even stand some frost if they have been kept in an outdoor flight for some time. Of course, birds should not be suddenly moved from an indoor temperature of 22 C. to an outdoor flight with a temperature of 14 C. or less.

A freestanding outdoor flight must have a foundation so vermin cannot burrow into it. It is best to use finished 50 × 50-centimeter concrete paving stones, and to bury these 30 to 40

Chain is useful in an aviary because it withstands gnawing, yet the parrots enjoy climbing on it.

centimeters in the ground. The frame can be erected on this base. If the wire is, say, 1 meter wide, the foundation should be planned according to this dimension. Since the mesh is expensive, none will be wasted if the flight is 1 meter wide by 2 meters high. Iron T-bars 2 to 3 centimeters wide (depending on the size of the aviary), or galvanized water pipes of 1.0 to 1.5 inches can be used. Tubes will require threaded joints at the corners. When using T-bars, many holes have to be drilled so everything can be screwed together and the mesh can be wired to the frame.

Of course, it is easier to build a flight from wood. So-called roofing laths (4 × 6 centimeters) should be used. Whether these are planed or unfinished depends on the price one wants to pay. It is important to fasten the mesh on the inside, not the outside, using large staples; in this way the Grey Parrot will have less opportunity to gnaw the wood. Wire with a mesh size of 16 or 19 millimeters is best, as long as the wire itself is at least 1 millimeter thick.

After a mimimum of six months, the mesh should be painted black. Bitumen lacquer, which can be obtained cheaply from a plumber, works very well. Painting every two years pays off in the long run for two reasons: first, the mesh no longer glitters; second, it is a good way to prevent the mesh from rusting in later years. Painting is done most easily with a roller on a short handle; in this way, one does not splatter himself. The roller should be stored in mineral spirits so it does not harden. The wood should be preserved by coating it with carbolineum or the like. This protective coating should be renewed every two years. Those who lack patience should use a zinc or plastic paint, so the mesh can be painted at the same time.

A flight can also be built in a basement, particularly when attempting to breed the birds. Otherwise, this is not recommended because the human contact with the birds is lost and they become shy. A garage can also be used for breeding, if one can spare it; but remember, contact is lost here too! More information on this subject is provided in the chapter on breeding.

Above: *With toys and food available, a Grey Parrot will likely remain on its playground and occupy itself there.*

Liberty. The author does not know of any tame Grey Parrots that are kept at liberty. Unfortunately, birds with trimmed flights have a limited amount of freedom. Even very tame birds usually do not return directly to their owners after escaping. In the cases known to me, most simply flew away! Only a few Grey Parrots stayed close by and, because they were driven by hunger, eventually were recaptured. This is illustrated in the following report from a fancier:

My friend Maurle had over the years owned and cared for about thirty Grey Parrots and amazons, which he taught to talk. But the event that took place in the summer of 1959 gave him quite a fright. His best jocko thus far, seeking the bright sunshine, was apparently startled by a sudden movement and flew out an open window. He flew to the top of the tallest tree, took up with some crows, and stopped the people passing below with his rich vocabulary. He was seen continually in the neighborhood for four weeks, but could not be persuaded even by the sweetest enticements of his lord and master to fly down to his finger, as he had been accustomed to do. Jocko obviously felt quite comfortable in the certainly unfamiliar surroundings. There was no sign that he was concerned about either hunger or danger. The entire population of Sigmaringen, alerted by a notice in the newspaper, took an interest in the fate of this unusual traveler. Finally, four weeks later, neighbors told Herr Maurle that his jocko was nearby in a very small tree. This time, he could not resist the food offered on the extended hand, allowing his head to be scratched and then to be carried home. My friend cried tears of joy, because this fine bird was worth a small fortune.

Unfortunately, it frequently happens that a Grey Parrot escapes through carelessness. The following took place in my hometown of Hamburg, and was related to me as follows:

We have a Grey Parrot named Koko. With my wife he is affectionate to a fault; with everybody else he is a consummate rogue. My wife can do anything she wants with him: he lets her scratch his head, and she can stroke him to her heart's content, take him in her hands, lay him on his back, and, in a manner of speaking, knead him. In short, she can do anything she wants. But if our nephew Fritz or I approach him (and he sees us both every day), he holds his head out, ostensibly to be scratched, and then suddenly, quick as a flash, pecks at the offending finger before it can be pulled away. We consider ourselves lucky if no blood is drawn.

One day my wife was puttering around in the kitchen and Koko was sitting as usual in his favorite place, on my wife's shoulder. Suddenly, to her alarm, she noticed that the window was open. Instead of first putting Koko back in his cage, she went to close the window with him still perched on her shoulder. Before she knew it, Koko fluttered out the window into the wide world beyond. First he landed on the roof of the house next door. My wife, who had been paralyzed with fright until now, called to him in the most frightened and sweetest tone of voice. Useless! Koko would no longer see or hear. He was a changed bird. He took off and flew farther away. She spotted him in the neighbor's garden where, using a combination of flying and walking, he quickly went down the steps of the neighbor's house. She saw him again in the next garden over, but he soon disappeared from sight. Everyone was soon alerted; the fugitive was sighted here and

Another alternative to a cage is the hanging perch, particularly if the Grey has trimmed wing feathers.

there, but each time he was approached he flew away to avoid capture. Finally, he disappeared for good.

What a terrible surprise awaited our nephew Fritz and me when we came home from work that afternoon. After hearing the sad story, the search started anew. But all our efforts were to no avail: Koko had disappeared without a trace! Of course, I immediately placed a notice in a dozen papers in Hamburg and the surrounding area: "Ten marks reward for the person who returns our lost Grey Parrot." Now it was simply astounding to find out how many ostensibly lost Grey Parrots were captured while flying around Hamburg that week. In the next eight days the doorbell of our house hardly ever stopped ringing; every moment somebody came with "the lost Grey Parrot," to collect my ten marks, of course. Despite our miserable situation we almost had to laugh at all these offers. Had all of these good animals brought to us really been lost and captured? Unfortunately, only one thing was certain: none of them was our Koko. With each passing day the barometer of our hope sank lower and lower, until, after eight days, we had finally lost all hope of ever seeing our little darling again.

But what should happen next?—on the fourteenth day after the loss of our Koko, the doorbell of our house rang, and there at the door stood two farmer's wives, whose clothing, and particularly their shoes, suggested that they had been on a long trip on foot. One of them, who was carrying a sturdy wooden box under her arm, immediately asked my wife, "Didn't you place a notice in the paper saying you lost a bird? My husband found one, and we wanted to find out if this parrot belongs to you." My wife asked, "Where are you from?" "From Volksdorf," was the answer. "But that's almost four hours from here," replied my wife; "the animal could not possibly have flown that far. Keep the box closed, for it is certainly not our Koko." My wife was almost annoyed by this, as it seemed to her, unnecessary intrusion. She thought the women were just after the ten-mark reward, like everyone else who had stopped by. Her suspicion seemed to be confirmed when the women answered the question about whether the animal had spoken. "Our Koko," my wife had said proudly, "speaks very well." "No, the bird didn't talk, and it didn't eat either; it only shrieked and bit! It bit a piece out of my husband's finger!"

But the women refused to give up—I will now allow my wife to tell the rest of the story—"and they said to me, 'But won't you at least have a look? Maybe it is your bird after all.' They had already raised a corner of the lid; more to get rid of the intruders than out of hope, I looked through the crack, and what did I see? A Grey Parrot whose

Above: *A tame Grey Parrot is often allowed out of its cage to sit on its climbing tree.*

head at least reminded me a bit of Koko, but who looked so wretched, so mangy, so dirty, so shabby and unkempt that I emphatically and with the greatest disappointment cried out, 'No, that animal could never be my Koko!' But I had barely finished, when out of the box came a plaintive but clear and, for me, infinitely sweet voice, saying, *My very best sweet child.* I still do not remember how I managed to open the box in my excitement. The next thing I knew, Koko climbed out of it and onto my shoulder. The tears of joy ran down my face, and both women cried with me and kept repeating, 'Yes, that is your bird, that is your bird!' With indescribable bliss I·returned him to his cage, which had been deserted for fourteen days."

Only now was it possible to see how he had suffered during his unfortunate excursion. How quickly he jumped down to the water dish and to the food! He had been reduced almost to a skeleton. The bird had been found sitting quietly in a cherry tree. He had been shaken to the ground and picked up easily but not without biting the farmer's hand until it was bloody. The good people had put bread and hemp seed before the starving bird, but he touched nothing. To make up for this, he did nothing but eat and sleep for the three days after he was returned to us.

When I came home with my nephew Fritz, we did not at first believe that the wretched, unkempt creature in the cage was really our Koko. Only after he had made a bow upon hearing our voices, and said, *Morning, Herr Fischer,* did all our doubts vanish, and we joined in the jubilation.

Two weeks later, my wife traveled to the Rhine. I had to stay behind in Hamburg, but my wife did not want to be separated from her so recently lost-and-found Koko under any circumstances. After his nearly disastrous vacation through Hamburg, which was, after all, caused by his own stupidity, Koko now had to endure an involuntary but carefully prepared journey down the Rhine River. This time though, the journey would be planned by human intelligence and he would be protected by human love and attention. He was placed in a transport cage, which was covered with a cloth, and my wife brought him along in a compartment of the Hamburg-Cologne express train, where he was placed on the baggage rack. She had folded back a corner of the cloth, so the little fellow could get light and air and could look around a bit during the journey, which would keep him from getting bored. After the train got underway, two women sat down in the compartment across from my wife. Their tongues were quite busy for a while, engaged in more or less weighty conversation. Then, when there was finally a pause in the chatter, a gentle voice was suddenly heard, speaking tender, loving words. The women were thoroughly astonished, and they suddenly grew quiet, looked at each other, looked at my wife, and then looked over the entire compartment, until they finally realized that the voice was coming from the luggage rack above their heads. But such indignation! "What? You dare to leave your poor child up there on the luggage rack instead of taking it on your lap? Well, I never—!" My wife couldn't stop laughing; but the women joined in heartily when the "child" was brought down and turned out to be a parrot, our Koko!

6.   Acclimation

Acclimation is an important part of care, because the Grey Parrot is such an intelligent bird. Often the bird is brought home in the same cage it will be occupy in its new home. If this is not possible, the bird can be transported in a wooden box or something similar. Any unnecessary handling should be avoided, or the bird will become even more shocked and afraid. How often, dear reader, do you think a Grey Parrot is handled on the way from its homeland to its final destination? That is a difficult question to answer, but it is certainly more than the number of fingers on your hands. This is the reason why the Grey is so afraid of being handled. Since this fear becomes ingrained, in large parrots particularly, and is not easily forgotten, the owner must first gain the bird's confidence. This point must be clearly understood. Such confidence will only come slowly, and, especially with older and more experienced parrots, this process can take a long time. I cannot even remember how often I have heard over the telephone, "I've already had my Grey Parrot three months, and it still won't come to my hand!" But this is certainly not a long time!

The process of acclimation frequently requires a year; it sometimes takes longer, and occasionally requires much less time. Every Grey Parrot is an individual; for this reason, it is impossible to make generalizations. The older a Grey Parrot is, the longer acclimation usually takes; a younger bird usually adjusts more quickly. Impatience in any shape or form does not speed the period of adjustment, but slows it down instead, and can even undo what one has already accomplished. Granted, from time to time a great deal of patience is needed, particu-

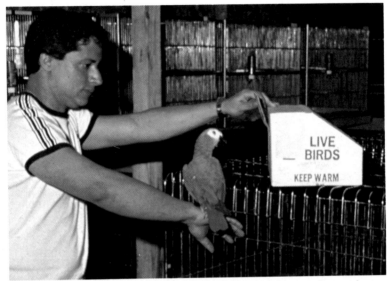

Cardboard cartons for transporting birds are designed to provide ventilation and to keep the bird calm by restricting light.

larly when the Grey Parrot, out of fear, starts gurgling and screeching in the most horrifying fashion, so that it sounds almost as if it has severe bronchitis. The birds do not all have the same disposition; some are quite stubborn, so some luck is needed to obtain a bird that will adjust rapidly. One fancier once gave me this sound advice:

It is better to pay no attention whatsoever to the new arrival during the first week. Do not stand in front of the cage, and act as if no bird is even in the room. In this way it learns to view its surroundings without fear and shyness. During this time one can easily tell if the bird is talented or not. I have learned from experience that all jockos that later develop a good talent for talking were very lively during the first weeks after their arrival and always screeched and whistled a great deal, particularly in the morning and evening but also throughout the day, whenever they heard noises, music, or even the song of another bird.

The animal dealer or importer can say only how long he has had the bird, which will allow one to get a sense of its progress. In this, one must trust the word of the seller. There are some

Grey Parrots that adjust very well at first and quickly get used to their surroundings, but a time comes when they make little or no further progress. Frightened fluttering in the cage occurs less frequently, but young birds still go to the farthest corner of the cage and use the "ostrich technique" of sticking their heads in the corner. They probably do this under the impression they can no longer be seen. Older birds do not do this anymore; they retreat and raise their nape and head feathers. Brave males peck at the supposed attacker.

New arrivals should at first be left completely alone. The only thing one should do is to give them food and water. Trying to win the bird's confidence too quickly would be a waste of time. The Grey Parrot must be given time to adjust to its new surroundings, because it is by nature a fearful and suspicious animal. The bird may not eat the first day, and maybe not even the second. This is no reason for alarm, particularly if the bird was eating well previously. It will eat eventually, when the room is quiet and no person is in sight. The bird should be given time to itself at least twice a day or, better yet,

Catching a Grey Parrot is best left to the seller, as it will be shy of strangers.

45

three times (about thirty minutes each time). When feeding or cleaning, it is important to talk quietly to the bird. The Grey will not understand the meaning of the words, but it will find them soothing. After many such feedings the parrot will learn to associate this talking with its feeding and in this way will more quickly lose its fear of the "grabbers," people's hands.

It would be inadvisable to let the bird out of its cage in the beginning, even if it is already tame. Even then the bird should be given at least a week to get used to its cage and the surroundings. Covering the cage at night should be done very carefully; if there is no wire frame to place over the cage, then one must expect the cloth to be bitten through.

If you already have a tame amazon or cockatoo in the room, the Grey Parrot will become acclimated more quickly, go to its food more readily, and learn by watching the other bird. In any case, it will also learn to imitate its neighbor's voice eventually; this must be taken into account. Nor are dogs the only animals that can be jealous. Completely "humanized" parrots can suddenly become quite churlish toward people after the appearance of another bird. But sometimes a wonderfully peaceful relationship, cause enough for rejoicing, can develop between the resident bird and the newcomer. This happens mainly when the two parrots are male and female; they seem to understand each other better. A second bird usually comes into consideration when the Grey must be left alone often or when breeding is desired.

For the period of adjustment and afterwards it is very important to keep the Grey Parrot occupied, for example, by hanging a rope or a short chain from the roof of the cage. Fresh branches are useful not only for amusement but are also essential for good health, since they contain minerals, among other things. One Grey Parrot owner thought of something else to keep his bird occupied:

In order to keep my Peter occupied in a healthy and amusing way, I tried using ceramic glass marbles, the kind that children play with in the street. The marbles should not be too small, so he cannot swallow them, nor should they be too large, so he can pick them up and hold them in his bill. I tossed them into the sand in his cage, after I

Small transport cages lessen the chance of the parrot injuring itself.

A wing stretch of this sort often follows sleeping or resting.

first removed the wire grid. First he played with them in the sand, then he tossed them through the bars of the cage to the floor, climbed down after them, and tossed and rolled them around the entire room. His favorite pastime, though, is when I sit on the floor with him and roll the marbles to him. He shoves them back to me with his feet and bill and then dances with glee. In this fashion, I can exercise him for a long time, and in so doing, I combine the pleasurable with the beneficial.

An example of how carefully you must proceed with acclimation is shown by the following incident: A young Grey Parrot was particularly nervous and excitable. Mice were thought to be the cause for his anxiety, so a trap was placed in the room at night. During the night there was a sudden loud clap as the trap snapped shut, with a screech from the bird and the sound of flapping wings. When the owner cautiously entered the room, the Grey was lying on the bottom of the cage, very weakly breathing its last. The bird died before morning. This shows what the result of fright may be. Even in its homeland, the Grey Parrot can become completely confused by an unex-

A veterinary examination helps to ensure that the parrot is healthy.

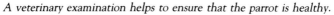

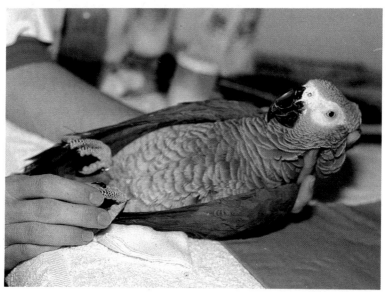

50

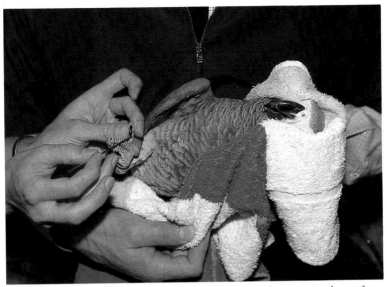

While an assistant restrains the Grey, a blood sample for testing is drawn from a clipped claw.

pected event, such as, for example, the firing of a gun. This characteristic is deeply rooted in these parrots. If this were not the case, Grey Parrots would become tame more quickly.

Often the flight feathers of Grey Parrots are more or less trimmed before they are shipped from Africa. This has both advantages and disadvantages. The advantage is that the importer can catch the birds more easily; also, they cannot fly away. As a result, they usually become tame more quickly. On the other hand, this is an unnatural condition, since the flights are a part of the bird too. The author is of the opinion that the flights of a tame bird should be allowed to grow, provided the bird cannot fly away. Pulling out the shafts forcibly with pliers is an unpleasant business. Admittedly, the feathers will grow back quickly, but the quills are often difficult to remove and sometimes a drop of blood cannot be avoided. Moreover, the bird will become afraid again. As a rule, it is more sensible to clip only one wing, so the bird can fly only a very short distance. The flights should, however, be cut only by a stranger, and in such a way that the Grey Parrot cannot see the person's hands.

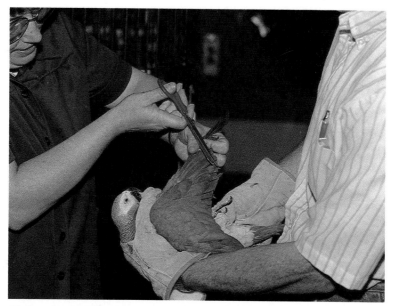

Flight is hindered by trimming the feathers of one or both wings.

On a wild bird the newly growing feathers can easily be damaged, so the feathers will be unable to unfurl normally.

For the first eight weeks or so after obtaining a bird, it should not be given a bath. The Grey Parrot will still be afraid and must be given time to get used to its new surroundings. Later, one should take lukewarm water, add a shot of rum, and then sprinkle it carefully on the bird (an old recipe). After this, the bird should be left alone, so it can preen in peace. On future occasions, the spraying should be increased; this should be done up to three times a week. The Grey Parrot should never be bathed when the room is cold or drafty; a cold or a lung infection could be the result.

Bird-keepers' reports. Since parrots are as different from one another as people are, the author considers it appropriate and instructive to include articles and letters from a number of breeders. Usually, a person has owned only one or two Grey Parrots; in my view, these experiences are insufficient to illustrate the extensive variation found among Grey Parrots. The reader will also be able to sense quickly what can be expected of these birds, both good and bad. Various opinions and experiences concerning care and acclimation follow. First we will hear from E. Prezina, who wrote in great detail about his Grey Parrots. Even though some things have changed since this account was written (the prices, for example), the observations are still enlightening and will never be out of date.

When I was staying in Hamburg for a few days twenty-four years ago, to buy some large apes for the purpose of training them, I spent my days running around the harbor, in order to be at hand when the dealers brought something suitable from the ships. On one occasion I encountered a sailor who seemed to have had more than a little to drink. He reeled from one side of the street to the other, fell down one time swearing, but managed to raise himself off the ground by twisting his body into the most unnatural positions. But throughout all this staggering to and fro, he managed to hold securely in his arms a small, round, metal cage, with bars also made of the same material rolled, like those cages that at one time were brought back from foreign countries frequently. In the cage sat two very young Grey Parrots

For trimming the thick claws of parrots, scissors with notched blades are necessary.

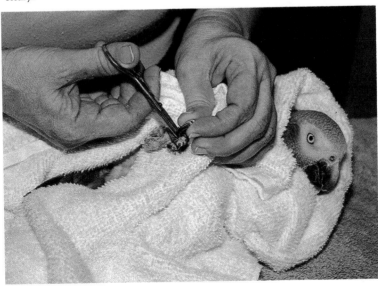

that were not yet fully feathered. The one was obviously already on its last legs and made no sound. To make up for this, the other one screeched and cried as if he had been stuck on a spike. Actually, something similar was actually the case: one of the wings of the young bird had slipped through the bars of the cage, undoubtedly during a previous fall to the ground. It had, of course, been broken, and was now stuck to the wire. The bird had good reason to screech! Being an animal lover, I naturally felt sorry for the young parrots, and so I started negotiating with the sailor to purchase them. This did not prove easy, but finally, with the considerable aid of a number of Hamburg Harbor Lions, the local beer, the deal was struck. For the sum of twenty-two marks, the two birds and their luxurious cage were mine. With the greatest difficulty I managed to turn down the sailor's invitation to help him drink up the twenty-two marks. The next morning the sick jocko was dead, but the one with the broken wing was alive, screeching to such an extent whenever I approached the cage that, had I been staying anywhere but in the area of Hamburg's harbor, I should have been thrown out, along with my parrot. Fortunately, in this area people were accustomed even to young wild parrots and their noisy outbursts.

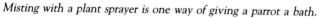

Misting with a plant sprayer is one way of giving a parrot a bath.

The danger of a bath of this kind is that the temperature of the water from the tap may change suddenly.

Now, I do not think much of feeding maize to parrots. My view is that the maize just swells up and does not give strength or staying power. In addition, parboiled maize contains too much water and spoils too easily. So I tried feeding the little animal with sunflower seeds, because he was quite emaciated, and also gave him tepid water to drink, which was accepted eagerly. The sunflower seeds were readily eaten, but were not tolerated very well. Jocko vomited them up a few times and developed—whether from the sunflower seeds or the water is impossible to say—a severe case of diarrhea. I used my old home remedy: canary seed. In my experience, canary always has an excellent, constipating effect on diarrhea in all birds. At first, the jocko did not want to approach the unfamiliar canary seed. But after a few hours, driven by hunger, he tried one, quickly finished the whole bowl, and the diarrhea soon disappeared. I now gave some sunflower seeds, which this time were tolerated quite well. I tried to think of something else I could give the emaciated bird to strengthen him. I decided on scalded milk, with which I had had astounding results with very run-down cockatoos, and gave it, three times a day at first. Since it was tolerated well, I soon gave it to the bird in his drinking bowl, always being careful to change it before it could sour. Additionally, I made sure the bird got as much sun as possible.

Given this care, the jocko recovered fully in a short time; his breast began to fill out, the feathers grew, and the wing, which I had tied in place immediately after buying the bird, healed. The wing is a bit crooked, but it has its full range of movement, and the bird is even able to fly somewhat. The appalling screeching also became less frequent as soon as the bird got to know me; if a stranger approached the cage, it still resounded in all its glory, but I could soon move near the cage without being greeted in this fashion.

As soon as the bird knew me, I attempted to tame him and to stroke his little head. The first attempts only provoked resistance with raised bill and louder screeching than before. But as soon as Jocko, which is what I named him, recognized that I was not trying to hurt him, he grew to enjoy this stroking. Once the parrot quietly allowed himself to be touched on the head and neck, I tried to get him to step onto my hand. A powerful bite was his reply when I tried to hold his legs, and Jocko screeched with all his might and flapped his wings until he broke away and plopped to the ground. I now tried to get him to step onto a short stick, and after some initial resistance the parrot finally decided to perch on it. Now he diligently practiced stepping on and off the stick, until he could do this flawlessly. After he practiced for two days, I again tried to get him to perch on my hand. At first the bird hesitated, but then he did climb on my hand without even bringing his bill into play. So I had won this game; Jocko was hand tame. Now taming proceeded very quickly; he became more trusting day by day. I soon could hold him whenever I wanted to. I could even lay him on his back in my hand, as long as I did not move too suddenly; at first this frightened him and made him screech, but he was no longer bad in this respect.

So far, except for the awful screeching in the beginning, Jocko had produced only whistles and clicking noises. But now he began mixing tones that reminded me of human speech with this natural chatter. One fine day Jocko very nicely and distinctly said the word *Lora*, the name of an amazon that was his neighbor in the next cage and which he had naturally heard many times. A few days later he surprised me with an emphatic *Cockatoo wants you now*, a remark frequently made by Marco, an ancient Salmon-crested Cockatoo, whenever something was bothering him, which is often the case. From an amazon, Jocko learned the chick-chick-my-little-chicken song—that is its first verse. Even this, unfortunately, is incomplete; he leaves out some words and adds others. In a few days I taught him to say *We stand together firm and true—hip, hip, hurrah—hip, hip,*

The Grey Parrot produces considerable feather "dust," which is best controlled by frequent bathing.

hurrah! and the first verse of "Hupf mein Mäderl" ('Hop, My Little Lass'). On his own he also learned all sorts of noises, such as clearing the throat, coughing, sneezing, and the sound of a bottle being opened. Soon he had assembled his entire repertoire, because, strangely enough, Jocko learned virtually nothing after he was two years old.

His speech is not particularly varied, and he cannot even remotely compare with the stars of his species, which have vocabularies of hundreds of words. But he has a talent that none of these have, a talent that makes him priceless to me: he speaks at any time and any place on command, whistles on request, and gives appropriate responses to a variety of questions. The amazing thing is this: there is not the slightest hint in the question that could influence the answer, as, for example, the beginning of the answer. If I ask the bird, "What is your name?" he replies, *Lora.* (The answer Jocko gives is always shown in italics.) "What sound does a cat make?" Then Jocko barks and immediately starts chuckling. I now say, "But, Jocko, you're making fun of me, do it right." After which he immediately says, *Meow!* "How does the cuckoo go?" Whereupon Jocko repeats my question word for word, and I scold him, saying, "But you shouldn't just repeat the words, you should answer the question!" Despite this, the parrot still repeats *How does the cuckoo go?* twice, which always draws laughter from the audience. To the question, What do you say to a stranger? he answers, *What's your name?* And to the question, How old are you? comes this reply: *Three years, o God, o God.* Can you count?—*One, two, three, hurray!* All these answers come as promptly as if they had been shot from a pistol. Everything is clear and understandable, in a human-sounding voice, and, even though it is not too loud, it can easily be heard even in the largest theater. Because the precision with which my parrots work in their cabaret act is in fact almost unbelievable, sometimes a member of the audience is under the impression I am really an accomplished ventriloquist. To overcome this doubt, I often perform with Jocko in the middle of the audience, and even here, surrounded by a sea of strange faces, the bird never falters.

Jocko can also whistle quite well. On request, he immediately whistles various signals, and also the melody of "Zwei dunkle Augen" ('Two Dark Eyes'). He also knows the tune to "Dort unt' im Böhmerwald" ('Down There in the Bohemian Forest'), as well as that old song from Hamburg, "Morgen kommt die Tante" ('Our Aunt Will Come Tomorrow'), which he usually improvises to some extent, giving his best rendition when he is accompanied by my truly expert

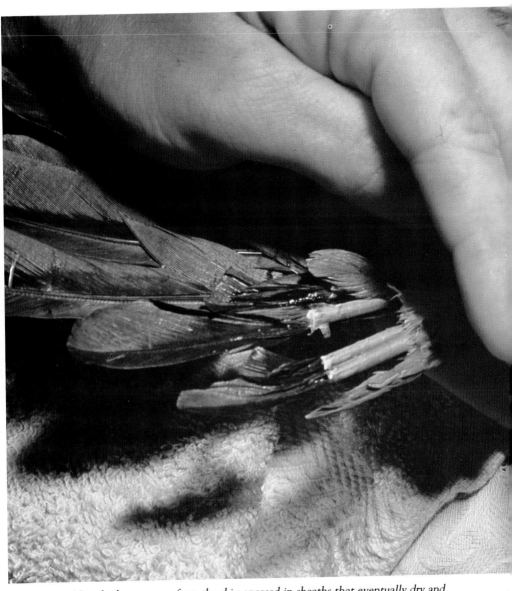

New feathers emerge from the skin encased in sheaths that eventually dry and flake away, allowing the feather to unfurl. While the feather is growing, the sheath contains blood, and it may bleed profusely if it is cut.

whistler, a stately Yellow-naped Amazon. Above all, he loves to start whistling at an inopportune moment, where it certainly does not fit in, which always draws salvos of laughter from the audience. His two-and-a-half songs—he really cannot sing the little-chicken song properly—are sung only for his own pleasure. I have not tried to train him in this, because in the amazons I possess better and louder singers.

A Grey Parrot, even though he is more intelligent than an amazon, is nevertheless infinitely more difficult to teach to talk on command. I have tried in vain for years to teach some Grey Parrots to do this; when I was successful, I found that even though the particular jocko spoke on command when we were alone, he refused to speak as soon as other people came to witness his performance or when he was brought onto the stage. It is certainly a great deal to ask of a bird: brought on stage in a dark box, with unceasing activity around him, the canvas backdrops flutter in the draft; the curtain, which has until now been hanging like a flat wall in front of the bird, is suddenly drawn up, and the semidarkness of the stage is replaced by the harsh light of the spotlight; the music plays, and hundreds of strange people are suddenly visible, making all kinds of distracting movements, lighting cigars, etc., etc. And then he is expected to calmly answer questions, without being bothered by the hubbub around him! Not every bird is suited for this, especially not a Grey Parrot. Amazons and cockatoos, which are more spirited than thoughtful and easier to arouse, become accustomed to this more readily.

I have owned Jocko for twenty-four years now. Since he survived his childhood illness, nothing of importance has happened to him. His plumage is splendid and slippery as an eel. To be sure, he is showered with lukewarm water from a watering can once a week, which he thoroughly enjoys. And twice a day I take him on my hand and walk slowly back and forth with him to make him flap and exercise his wings and, in so doing, clean the dust from his feathers, which is so abundant in this species. In my opinion, this is the best way to prevent feather plucking. My jocko never sits drowsily on a perch; he is active the entire day, climbing up and down, scraping on the floor of the cage, and making nests, since "he" is really a female. He also likes to take food when someone is friendly with him, and he never soils a transport box, even when he has to roost in the light for hours; but later he lets loose a flood of excrement, in the fashion of brooding hens. My jocko is not at all sensitive to cold. In any case, he is quite hardened to it, because the bird room is never heated in winter, and the upper casement windows stay open all day, as long as the cold is

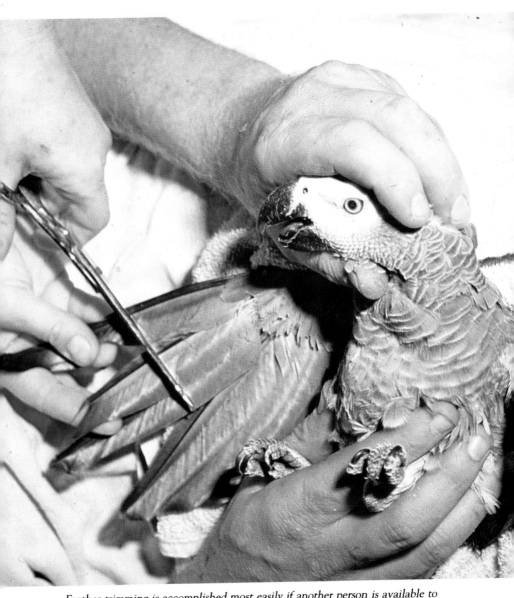

Feather trimming is accomplished most easily if another person is available to restrain the parrot.

not too severe. In this way my jocko has sat in a temperature of only 3 C. and has been in an unheated railway car, when the temperature was −28 degrees C., in a small transport case, which he could keep warm with his own body heat, or in a larger case sent express, where he was tightly packed with his colleagues.

Because of old age, a Grey Parrot had to be given away. The new owner wrote:

At first, when the bird was brought to his new home, he did not want to get to know any of the people in the house, with the exception of his master; whoever approached the cage was attacked, and this fate was shared by the writer of these lines. Only after a time, once he got used to his new home, did he remain quiet and allow us to stand in front of his cage, provided we had paid homage to him in the most flattering and gentlest tone of voice.

Another fancier fed his bird large amounts of hemp and noticed that the bird started to pluck out its feathers. Large amounts of maize make a parrot fat. Dr. Otto caused a sensation with his feeding method, because he stated that parrots should be given coffee since the birds were fond of it. Fortunately, this practice has now been abandoned.

Since my youth I have always kept and bred chickens and pigeons, and even canaries, and now I decided that I would buy a parrot. Without learning anything about the subject, I went to a bird dealer to buy a Grey Parrot, because I had heard that these birds are easily taught. Two days later I was in possession of such a bird, which, since I knew nothing about caring for parrots, on the advice of the dealer I tried to feed with hemp, maize, and white bread soaked in coffee. I filled the food bowl with hemp, occasionally gave the bird partially cooked maize, and supplied fresh water daily. He ate the hemp and maize, but he would have nothing to do with the white bread; he screeched loudly whenever I offered it to him. To quiet him, and to start him talking, I soon purchased a Puerto Rican Amazon, which was already quite tame and could say a few words. Whenever the amazon practiced its art, the screeching only became louder, so I finally separated the birds. I frequently placed them together, however, in the hope that Jocko would at least learn a word or two, but this did not seem to do any good.

This Grey Parrot belongs to the race timneh—notice the bill. It is well to bear in mind, however, that members of both races will vary in plumage coloration.

A short time later Jocko began to bite off his wing and tail feathers and pluck out others. Although I was unaware this could be a symptom of illness, I was more than a little annoyed and blamed the feeding of hemp for the problem (based on previous experience with canaries and the obesity it led to). I stopped feeding hemp entirely and instead offered, as soon as he screeched, a few walnuts. In this way also he got used to eating white bread. The plucking subsided surprisingly quickly. Soon after starting to eat white bread, Jocko started to talk. Since it had been recommended that I separate both birds if I wanted to accomplish anything, I did so, and he has become quite accomplished in repeating words and sentences.

Jocko gives kisses, offers his "paw," and enjoys sitting on my finger, using the appropriate phrase when he wants any of these. So he says, for example, *Papa, come here. Give me a kiss. Now come on, be kind to me!* When he goes back in his cage, he says, *Going home, adieu!* He is still learning all the time, sometimes very quickly; sometimes he will repeat a phrase unclearly, but then I make an effort to alter the pitch or the words. After I have repeated it a few times for him in its final form, he has it memorized. When I cover his cage with a cloth, he learns even more readily. From time to time I give him a refresher course, in which I recite everything he knows that comes to mind. The evening is best for this, for then he will repeat almost everything I say almost word for word. The Puerto Rican Amazon has also benefited from the separation, but says only single words. To be sure, I do not spend too much time with it, but devote the greater part of each day to Jocko.

Jocko disdains chewing on twigs, but he likes to play with some metal thimbles I bought for him. He also plays with shells stuffed with white bread before he eats; he does the same with his water. I would like to mention that Jocko still has gray eyes, as when I bought him, and that he screeches less and less since I started letting him out of his cage.

A teacher wrote me a long time ago about his experiences, mainly with very young, still dark-eyed Grey Parrots. His observations can be shared in their entirety, even though the need for liquids is viewed differently today.

Of all the birds I have been acquainted with until now—and the number is not small—the Grey Parrot is and remains the most beloved and important to me. I cannot lie about it, I am infatuated with this bird. I sit before my gray students for many hours, both day and night, and always appreciate their powers of observation, their acumen, and their reflectiveness. I have paid large sums for Grey Parrots, and several deaths would have discouraged me if I did not favor this species in particular. Over a hundred individuals have passed through my hands over the years; they have added to and ripened my experience, which in the beginning stood on a weak foundation. One learns something new from each bird, because each has different characteristics. Formerly, when I did not know any better, I usually bought older individuals, which could usually be aptly described as "great boast, no roast." All were sold to me with glowing recommendations: "Starting to talk," or "Already speaks some English (or Spanish)." For a time, I maintained the hope that this was truly the case, but each time their talent consisted only of screeching, which was not a pleasant sound, at least to human ears. I also had neither the skill nor the experience for taming these wild birds, which only added to my disappointment.

Next, I tried my luck with the highly praised dark-eyed Grey Parrots; but here too I had to spend a considerable amount of money to learn my lesson and become wise through experience. As great as my joy was when I brought home the young, dark-eyed jockos, it only lasted a short time. Most of them carried the seeds of death; and even though they were active and appeared to be healthy when I bought them, all but a few died after two, three, or four weeks. I was often perplexed and disconsolate, read all of the ornithological books and journals available to me, consulted several doctors, and tried many of the remedies recommended to me; yet all of my efforts were in vain. Sick and tired of the whole situation, I now tried buying young birds already acclimated, and had more luck. Even though they always had to overcome various stages of illness, I brought them through, and so I gradually became more prudent in the care and treatment of Grey Parrots. I noticed every sign of illness, assessed their condition from their droppings, dietary preferences, etc., and also followed particular preventive measures.

Now I am successful even with most of the young birds that have not been acclimated. After they are accustomed to soaked bread, I gradually give them sips of boiled and cooled water, taking the water glass away so they do not drink too much. I gradually let them drink water more freely, but only after they have a craving for it. When an inexperienced buyer gives his newly acquired jocko as much to drink as it wants, without thinking of the danger and without being warned about it by the dealer (to be sure, most dealers are honest about this), the bird will drink too much and soon suffer serious consequences.

The stomach is upset; the excrement will become thin and watery (in a healthy jocko the excrement is compact and worm shaped, and is usually bicolored: white with dark green, light green, gray, or brown). The patient will have dull eyes, lose its appetite, seem to have no more strength in its bill, sleep a great deal, and tuck its bill in his back feathers; in short, it will look quite miserable, sickly, and diseased. The bird will grow ever weaker, will no longer eat, will sit with fluffed feathers on the floor the cage, will clatter its bill frequently, and soon will be dead.

More than with all other birds, it is dangerous for parrots to be fed irregularly, that is, sometimes too much, sometimes too little. If they are allowed to go hungry and then to eat too much too quickly, they will certainly become listless and depressed, if not ill. It is extremely dangerous to give a parrot something rotten, something that has become soft or sour or stale, since they will quickly have indigestion. Giving a parrot anything from the table, such as meat, sausage, bacon, vegetables, etc., is not recommended.

The change in the color of the eyes does not take place at the same time or go through the same series of transformations in all individuals. I have always paid close attention to the change in eye color in my jockos, and have determined that after three years of age all were yellow or were becoming so.

I have also made very careful observations of the plumage. The plumage of the youngest jockos is brownish gray, and the head more white and finely frosted; the brownish gray plumage gradually becomes light gray, and then bluish gray. The bluer and more uniformly colored the jocko is, the older it is. Similarly, the red color of the tail is also determined by the age of the bird. The paler and duller red the tail, the younger the jocko is; the more beautiful and deeper red the tail, the older.

Sexing the bird by the shape, the posture, and the plumage is not dependable. I have already made many observations concerning this, but I have yet to find any certain reference points. Many bird dealers claim males have red feathers on the crissum, while females do not, but I consider the appearance of such coloration to be accidental.

Regarding the size of individual jockos, there are variations determined by care, climate, and other influences. Some very young jockos have grown after I obtained them; others did not. The smallest jockos are not always the youngest in all cases, nor are the largest jockos always the oldest. Partially grown jockos that receive poor, inadequate

Trustworthy as a pet Grey Parrot may be outside the cage, it is nevertheless wise to trim the primary feathers of at least one wing.

care in human hands are in general smaller than those that grow up in the wild with a normal, proper diet.

Whether males enjoy learning to talk more than females do is unknown, and I have not yet been able to confirm this [there is no difference, in the author's opinion]. The younger the jockos are, the greater the hope that they will learn to talk. I always seek the youngest, most dark-eyed jockos to train; adult birds caught in the wild seldom learn to talk. If young jockos are first tamed and taught to trust, then there is more hope of teaching them to talk than there is with shy, wild individuals. A young jocko that is attached and devoted to his owner learns to talk sooner than another that retreats from people and hides. For this reason, I always strive to tame my parrots first, which, of course, requires a considerable amount of experience. A tame parrot that enjoys the company of people and loves and seeks human companionship learns to talk much earlier and more readily. A tame jocko tries to get into the good graces of its master; it is attentive, listens to every word, reacts to every gesture, and pays careful attention to everything the human teacher says. To keep and increase the favor of its master, it practices every act of kindness it knows: it offers its foot and gives kisses; it stretches its head forward in order to have it scratched, and repeats everything it knows.

With a shy and untamed jocko, none of these talents are evident; it is afraid to talk, and tries to only when it is unobserved and unafraid. A shy jocko usually prefers whistling to talking, because it is apparently much easier for it to do. I have found that the surest signs that a young jocko has the talent and disposition to talk and will learn to do so are the following: the bird watches me constantly and intently; it stops short and listens attentively when it hears me speak; it ruffles its plumage, stretches up its neck, becomes excited, and wipes its bill back and forth on the bars of the cage when I approach. Also, the most talented jockos become aroused when they hear a noise during the night.

How large the memory and the comprehension of some speaking, singing, and whistling jockos can be has often been recounted in these pages. Of the jockos taught by me, I have one, for example, that repeats everything it hears; another whistles short melodies I purposely or inadvertently whistle in its presence; still another talks with such clarity, with correct stress and pronunciation even, that one is astounded. Yet another mimics almost any noise very convincingly (the meowing of a cat, barking of a dog, crowing of a rooster, the sounds of bird calls; laughing, crying, coughing, clearing the throat, sneezing). This one also knows each of my children well, and uses its vocabulary so correctly and appropriately that every visitor is delighted. Another is marked by an extraordinary tameness and devotion, fawning in every imaginable way, flying to me as soon as it hears my voice, and always calling to me in the dark whenever it hears the slightest sound from me. That talented jockos and parrots in general can be quite droll and idiosyncratic has been my experience dozens of times. When parrots fall into inexperienced hands, when they are not given appropriate care and treatment but are scorned and irritated, they can become very sad and ill tempered, talk seldom or not at all, and even become shy and distrustful again.

Many bird fanciers find "their" bird, the bird they would like to have, at a bird show. Often this is where contact with birds first takes place. "That One or None" is the title of the following story.

Since only one individual of this most talented of all birds has come into my possession so far, I have been able to observe little, compared to the fancier through whose hands dozens have passed. I was fortunate to obtain a young jocko that soon started to talk well. He has been in my possession for only twenty-one months—one of a kind, and outstanding from any point of view.

I hesitated for a long time before buying a jocko, until I had the opportunity to look and observe. Systematically I first studied the natural history of the Grey Parrot, noting all the cues to gain the necessary knowledge and confidence for care and treatment, and for evaluating the species with respect to age, condition, and talent.

When the exhibition was announced, I decided to visit it. As I had expected, this wonderful bird show, with its rare and intriguing exhibits, more than met all my expectations. Among the number of young Grey Parrots shown, two in one cage, both extremely lively, active fellows, that romped around almost continuously, like puppies, quickly caught my eye. Not too young, already tame, beginning to talk—all this was what I wanted. I would have gladly taken both, but I thought that with only one I could get better results in talking.

In the cage at home the bird at first still acted quite frantic when anybody approached; he flew with ruffled feathers at any approaching hand and at times screeched appallingly. But after barely eight days of appropriate, loving treatment and good care on my part, he changed his attitude, but only toward me (even today he still does not want to have much to do with my wife or children, even though my wife usually feeds him). I soon noticed he was fond of me in particular. Apparently, the separation from his comrade was the reason why he was so bad initially.

After the jocko had been in my possession for approximately three weeks, I was permitted to take certain liberties with him. He allowed himself—reluctantly, to be sure—to be taken from his cage and carried around on my hand. He also permitted me to stroke him and scratch his head. Later, one day when I no longer had any apprehensions, I attempted to pull out his feather stumps with flat-nosed pliers, but I had underestimated him and had to give this up after the first attempt. I had only succeeded in alienating him; he regarded me as a torturer for a long time afterward.

One morning, after he had satisfied his not inconsiderable appetite and was in a good humor, he started making gurgling, humanlike sounds, from which the word *jocko* emerged, clearer and clearer with repetition. I repeated his name and other words to him often; he practiced and studied diligently and, from this time on, made astounding progress in speaking. He said something new every day. Soon he had learned so much I could barely recall everything he said in a day. He always listens alertly and with close attention to everything I say to him. He can say single words by the following day, and any sentence clearly in two or three days. The flawless, clear, and humanlike speech, the modulation, the deceptive imitation of all voices and the correct pronunciation, along with his powers of observation, acumen,

In permitting handling such as this, a tame Grey Parrot exhibits a great confidence in its keeper.

and cleverness, are remarkable. If, for example, he is really hungry or thirsty, he will talk constantly, until he gets my attention: *Am hungry! Want something! Jocko wants something! Water! Jocko water!* or, *Please, papa, give me something; I'm hungry.* As soon as he notices that he has been understood, and he sees the preparations for feeding, he will with satisfaction say, *Sooo! Ah, how nice!*

If Jocko hears me calling to dinner the children playing in front of the house, he feels obligated to take charge of the situation. As soon as I have opened the window, he calls both children by name, and always follows with a long drawn-out whistle. If I ever scold the children, or even speak to them loudly and with authority, he immediately joins right in, talking rapidly and unintelligibly: *Gonna get hit! With a stick! Wait, wait! You, you!* He always sounds his alarm whistle whenever my children start fighting. His attachment to me is so great that a long separation from me would certainly do him no good. *Adieu, papa!* he says as soon as he notices I am preparing to go out. When I come back, he is beside himself with joy: *Good day, papa! Come to Jocko! Come on now!* He keeps repeating this until I open his cage and let him scramble to my shoulder. His plumage is splendid. When I call, he easily flies through several rooms to my extended hand.

In this story it was easy to notice the parrot's ability to mimic appropriately to the situation.

That Grey Parrots are innately mistrustful and easily frightened has already been mentioned. The following is a report in which a fright led to the death of a parrot.

That Grey Parrots are easily excited and are alarmed by the slightest of causes, so that they senselessly flutter about in the cage and sometimes injure themselves, will soon be experienced by all owners of such parrots. Anxiously concerned about this, I try to anticipate and prevent any disturbance to my Grey Parrots. If such potentially damaging disturbances unexpectedly do occur, I immediately calm my aroused darlings with gentle words and caresses to minimize and help them forget their fright. Any sudden event—a chicken, a cat, a strange dog or a brightly colored cloth; a flag, a drum, a sudden movement in the room or outside the window; a loud noise, a scream, a loud and harsh yell, or the barking of dogs, particularly at night—can be disturbing and dangerous to these sensitive jockos. A bird is rarely left unscathed by such a fright. It will at the very least probably be injured while fluttering about in the cage, and quite frequently convulsions, much more dangerous, can occur—all of which, I repeat, can lead to the death of a bird. I am able to provide new evidence here and to offer sound advice on this subject.

Last year, on September 4, at two in the morning, we had a terrible thunderstorm; flashes of lightning came one after another. Lightning struck several trees and a nearby church. The flashes of lightning and the powerful thunderclaps cost Jocko, one of my darlings, who had played with me as recently as the evening before, his life. He apparently was so frightened that he died of a stroke. To my horror, he was hanging dead over a perch in his cage when I entered the room the next morning. If he had been in our bedroom during the thunderstorm, where a light was on and he could have heard us talking, he might not have been so suddenly and severely frightened, and he probably would not have lost his life.

The following owner was successful in breaking a Grey of the habit of screeching.

The best method for curing the Grey Parrot of excessive screeching and unpleasant whistling is to cover the cage. Of course, this method requires calmness and much patience. Punishment by hitting the bird, rapping on the cage, yelling, and threatening with a stick is useless and only leads to a worsening of the situation. Covering the cage does not bring immediate success because the bird, even though he will be quiet for a few minutes, soon starts screeching again under the cloth. It is best to proceed in the following manner, which will certainly achieve the goal.

A thick, heavy, dark cloth, kept near the cage, should be placed over it, so the bird sits in complete darkness. While covering the cage, the bird should be scolded. After a few minutes, remove the cloth, praise the bird, call him by his pet names, and finally, give him a treat. If this is continued for a while, the bird will gradually come to realize the unpleasant covering is a punishment for his screeching, and he will eventually be cured of the bad habit. Progress will soon be noticeable if this training is continued. Soon the bird will stop screeching when the cloth is raised and he is scolded and threatened. To be successful, it is also important to spend as much time as possible with the bird and to teach him to talk. The more the parrot learns to say, the less racket he will make.

An Austrian who bought a Grey Parrot had this to tell:

Moko, as the chosen one is called, right from the start had a regard for my father and permitted him anything. He was conspicuously large, three to four years old, tame as a dove, and very talkative when I acquired him. He immediately learns everything he hears in the house, but he refuses to learn in an organized manner. At night, the cage stands next to my father's bed. So that Moko can always keep an eye on him, my father made a small hole in the fabric cover hanging over that side of the cage. As soon as he sees, through his hole, my father stirring early in the morning, his loud, clear voice rings out with a *Good morning, Papa!* After this he wants to be let out of his cage immediately, and then he flies to the bed where he spends some time entertaining himself by jumping and rolling on the pillows, and then sneaks under the thick covers and says, *Papa, where is your Moko? Look, look, find him*—inviting my father to play with him.

Moko wanders into the dining room for breakfast; he stays there most of the day. Only a charming and talkative Lesser Sulphur-crested Cockatoo, my mother's pet, has the same privilege and occupies the other windowsill. The rest of my feathered friends are in the next room. If Moko does not get his zwieback dunked in milk at once, in a loud voice he calls out, *Now, what's going on, Moko wants something too!* Of course, this request gets him nowhere, so he continues in a fawning tone, *Please, please, little jocko would like something too.* Whereupon he gets his morsel and gobbles it up after a *Thank you, Papa.*

He eats his sunflower seeds and hemp only at noon and in the evening, when he sees us eating. After he eats, the food bowl must be removed immediately or else everything will soon find its way to the floor; this is his only bad habit. He never screeches or whistles; only in the first few years did he have this habit, which is shared by most jockos. If my father lies down on the sofa for a while after lunch, then Moko immediately falls silent; he occasionally calls, *Pst, pst, be quiet,* if a colleague in the next room makes too much noise. He has never made friends with any of the other birds; he only wants to see Goko in the afternoon when he is alone, and then for purely egotistical reasons. Goko is a tame, powerful Salmon-crested Cockatoo that always avoids him now. This prankster, which is inordinately fond of stealing ladies' hats and gloves, waddles in from the bird room, perches on the back of the rocking chair for the amusement of his gray friend, and then gives a dreadful performance. With raised crest and spread wings he sets the chair in ever faster motion. Moko's continuous calling (*Ho-hop, ho-hop, bravo, hurrah!*) spurs him on until he frequently tips the chair over and crashes to the floor. During this entire episode Moko hangs upside-down from the roof of his cage and watches the clown. As singularly cute as this droll picture is, it can only be allowed to go on a short time, because the shrieking of the dear Salmon-crest, the original sin of his kind, becomes too loud, though otherwise he seldom shrieks.

When my father comes home in the evening, Moko recognizes him by the sound of the bell, two quick rings, and cries out, *Hurrah, master is here.* After supper Moko always sits for a while on the edge of the table next to my father, holds a little stick with his foot, lifts it up to his bill frequently, and says, *Moko too,* after which he pretends to exhale smoke. He also enjoys having a paper cone placed on his head; he then struts ceremoniously around the table while chuckling the whole time. When he is put back in his cage, he keeps talking until ten o'clock; but then he suddenly falls silent, shrugs his shoulders, and finally says, *Master, jocko wants to sleep.* Then his cage is covered, to which he responds with a *Good night,* and he is carried to the bedroom. He peeks through his peephole when my father enters, but does not talk anymore. His day is over.

A few days ago he again showed me a brilliant example of his intelligence. My mother carried him to the kitchen on her hand to shower him with lukewarm water to which a little French brandy was

In these photos one can recognize the great playfulness possible in a tame Grey Parrot.

added—one of his favorite treats. She carried him past the room next to the kitchen, where my father was occupied with the woodland birds, and Moko saw him through the half-open door. Suddenly he gave a start and cried out in an astonished voice, *Ah, it's Papa!* When he came to the kitchen and saw the maid there, he said in the same tone, *Ah, it's Anna!* In such cases one has to wonder, so to speak, whether the boundaries of intelligence are drawn in a way that leaves room for extending them. Other than these three people, he sees only me. When I arrive, there is almost no end to his caresses.

I myself have had, since Christmas, a similarly gifted specimen in my collection, which, since he is still young, does not yet have the so-called understanding of the use of single sentences, since he sometimes says *good morning* in the evening. On the other hand, in three or four days he learns everything I repeat to him frequently. I bought the bird—Aura is his name—from a local merchant, who in a year had taught him 500 words in charming, original sentences, and six verses from songs as well. Since I have owned him, his vocabulary has grown to over 700 words.

Herr L. writes on a subject other fanciers are undoubtedly aware of. Here again we find the old "fairy tale" about water deprivation and the great frailness of very young birds.

Despite the best and most attentive care, deaths occur among our feathered pets. These deaths are particularly painful for the owner of a beloved talking parrot, particularly a jocko, that perhaps has already been in his possession for a number of years, is treated with loving care, and suddenly and unexpectedly departs this life. If any of our smaller finches or canaries dies, the small pecuniary loss aside, the dead one is quickly forgotten and replaced. The situation is different, however, with a jocko. Here we are emotionally attached to the animal, and the loss of it is not much less painful than that of a faithful dog. From this point of view, the notion of the great frailty of the Grey Parrot arose, since the loss of a jocko truly pains us more than the loss of a dozen smaller birds.

"I will never buy another young jocko," a fancier once wrote me, "because I cannot stand to see the little animals die." As I stated in *Die Gefiederte Welt*, a young jocko is by no means a delicate creature if he is healthy when purchased. On the other hand, when one obtains an already sick animal from an unscrupulous dealer, or incorrectly treats and cares for an otherwise healthy bird, then one should not wonder that the bird soon goes to its grave.

That young (black-eyed) jockos are more sensitive to poor care and treatment than are certain other older birds cannot be denied. When one considers that the little animals are captured when they can barely fly, usually given completely inappropriate care, shipped here in cramped cages, and fed on a diet that is not suited to their weak, young stomachs, it is no wonder that they easily succumb to gastro-intestinal disorders. No human baby given the same treatment would be healthy. After the death of a jocko, the owner always asks what aspect of care he neglected. One morning, the apparently healthy bird lies dead in the cage. A necropsy usually provides no answers, and the fancier is left puzzled. Thus we must keep foremost in mind the unusually nervous and sensitive constitutions of most young jockos. For this reason, each young jocko should be carefully covered every night, so that any incident in the room does not disturb him. If one owns a young jocko, one must always keep two things in mind: proper care and proper attention.

I have already written a few things about proper care in this paper. Canary seed, hulled oats, paddy rice, soaked (not cooked) maize, sunflower seeds, and some peanuts alternated with walnuts should constitute the basic diet of the jocko. An ample amount of fruit should also be given. Of course, seeds should make up the bulk of the diet, but fruit should also be given every day. One should alternately offer bananas, grapes, apples, and oranges (remove the pips). The grape seeds will not harm the bird. Of course, everything must be of top quality and should not be "mushy."

I have had good results in feeding ample amounts of fruits with young jockos in particular. Some young birds consumed as much as a half a banana, a quarter of an apple, and five or six grapes a day, without any ill effects; instead, the birds were in splendid condition. Birds with large amounts of body fat should receive more apples and grapes, and undernourished animals should be given more bananas.

In addition, all birds, both young and old, should be given sufficient gnawing material in the form of fresh willow or elder twigs. Light, fresh air, a roomy cage, and daily wing exercise are also necessary to maintain good health.

I disagree with the erroneous view that jockos must be kept at high room temperatures; 18 to 20 C. is sufficient. The topic of what the Grey Parrot should be given to drink is particularly important. "Young jockos die when they are given water" or something similar can be found in many books about jockos. A young jocko that dies after being given water is a candidate for death in any case. No healthy bird given untainted water will die. A jocko is no "drinker" if given enough fruit, and it is quite sufficient to give it the drinking bowl only once in the evening. It is high time that we break with the old belief or superstition that a young jocko should be given no water. It is almost as foolish and unnatural to give a young bird strong coffee, a common practice among dealers, unfortunately. These good people are mistaken in believing that coffee stimulates the vital spirits, doing so in the hope of keeping the bird lively while it is in their possession. A sick bird can never be cured with coffee, but a healthy bird can be made very ill indeed. I have never given a jocko a drop of coffee and have managed to rear them with minimal losses. The essential point to remember is that the water given should be free of impurities. The water of our large cities is always good. If one is not sure about the quality of the water, then give the bird a mixture of peppermint, chamomile, and valerian tea. One cooks this mixture down to an essence, and then mixes a teaspoon in half a drinking bowl of boiled water.

In broad outline, these are the prescriptions for care which I have practiced for decades with excellent results.

A detailed report concerning her experiences with a Grey Parrot were sent to me by Mrs. H. Schmidt in 1976. Inexperienced Grey Parrot owners will find many interesting and informative things in these excellent observations.

One day my children decided to fulfill a long-unrealized wish of mine: to own a Grey Parrot. Following some expert advice we looked for an animal at the quarantine station of an animal dealer on the day when the authorities released the birds. In the room there were about eighty Grey Parrots, which were split up into groups of three or four in cages made of steel bars. The majority of the birds hung on the bars, many with their heads upside down, and screeched as soon as we entered the room. Only one parrot climbed along the bars from the wall to the roof and back again, among the screeching ones, without making a sound. This particular Grey Parrot was the one for me, because I did not want a screecher. Of all the birds he was by far the smallest. His plumage was gray tinged with brown, and his irises were light gray. As a result of all the scrambling around, all of his red tail feathers had been broken off; the seller later pulled out the shafts with pliers, so the feathers would grow back more quickly. His plumage looked tousled and unkempt at that time.

After we returned home with the bird, we placed the parrot cage over the opened transport cage and waited. It was not long before our Grey, apparently driven by curiosity, moved into his new accommodations. We had already removed the round plastic perch from the cage and had replaced it with a forked branch from a cherry tree. He apparently felt quite comfortable on this perch and soon began to gnaw on it. He likes to gnaw and remove the bark from the twigs of fruit trees or willows primarily. After the move to his new cage, our Grey resumed his customary wanderings across the bars of the cage walls and roof. If we approached too near the cage, he fluttered in fright to the floor of the cage but did not stay there willingly. In order to make his acclimation easier, we placed the cage up high, so that he could always look down on us. In this way he quickly became calm and ever more confiding. During the day we placed his cage on a small table at a window that looks down on a busy street. In the beginning, he reacted with curiosity to the passers-by standing in front of the small garden in front of the house. He was afraid of the cars driving by, which was indicated by his increased climbing activity. He gradually became calmer, and we now began to accustom him to us. We sometimes took away his food bowl for two to three hours at a time and offered him sunflower seeds in our fingers through the bars of the cage. With much love and patience, he had progressed so far in five to six weeks that we could on such occasions stroke his feathers or his little feet with our fingers. While doing so, we noticed that he was particularly nervous and timid when we wore a white blouse or shirt; we also found that he clearly disliked men. After about six to eight weeks, we opened the door of the cage for the first time, and he climbed out very quickly. He was very awkward on the polished bars of the cage, so we built a wooden frame that could be placed on top of the cage. This wooden frame is now his favorite place to spend the day. He does not like wooden trays with attached climbing trees; he likes flat frames best. These days he either strolls on this wooden frame or hangs outside his cage on the bars, usually with his head down. He tries to make mischief from this vantage point—he either tries to bite his own wings, legs, and feet or tries to nip our fingers. He also strolls back and forth along the windowsill, talking or screeching, and raps his bill so firmly on the window pane that one can hear it from a considerable distance. His taps with the upper mandible express many things. He also playfully taps on the finger that is scratching him and tries to feed it with food from his crop. He taps his bill on anything he is examining when he does not know what it is, and he also taps his food and water bowls.

When he is frightened or tired, he goes back in his cage, which signifies safety to him. He never likes being stroked, scratched, or held when in his cage. We respect it as his domain, totally a place he knows he can always retreat to. But he also sleeps on his "roof garden" (the wooden frame), and today—after a year and a half—one can carry him around on it. In the evenings he allows *head scratch*, as he

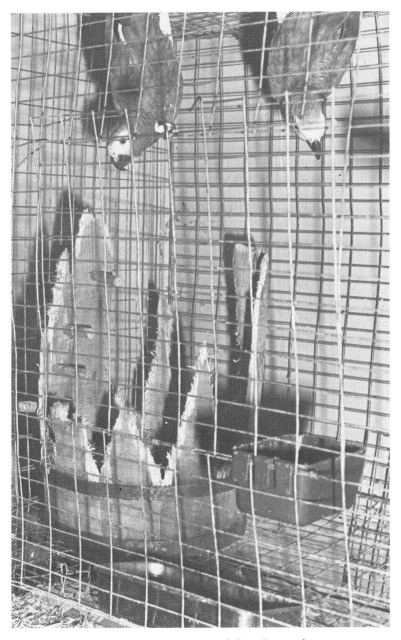

The urge to breed makes the propensity of Grey Parrots for gnawing even more marked: the nail keg had been fitted for nesting.

himself calls it, which he enjoys immensely. Circumstances permitting, he lays his head all the way back or to the side, and no places, not even under his wings, are left unscratched.

His timidity means that we must be especially careful, for he flies loose headlong. One time he flew from the balcony to a tree, even though we had trimmed his wings. With the aid of the "roof garden" and the cage we placed there, he allowed himself to be captured. We therefore clip his wings again immediately after each molt. We are still afraid to clip just one wing, because he can still fly so well. He is still very reluctant to go down onto the floor. He climbs down the side of his cage to the table, and even climbs down the legs of the table until he can reach the floor with his bill, but no farther. At one time he ignored anything that had fallen to the floor of his cage. Now he fishes up this or that—seeds, fruit, or toys—without going onto the floor. His diet consists of sunflower seeds, fruit, potatoes, vegetables, and lettuce. When he sees us eating, he hangs on his cage and stretches his neck as close to our plates as he can manage, always from the most advantageous position. If we do not react, he begs continuously, making a mournful, pleading sound. He has learned to distinguish between what he likes to eat and what he does not. In the latter case he gives the dining table scant attention. But when we are having eggs, for instance, he climbs to his watch post and does not move until he has received his portion of egg yolk (he does not like egg white) in his food bowl in the cage. The seed bowl, from which he eats only in the evening, must be removed from the cage during the day, because he refuses to rest until it is lying on the floor, since he has long since learned how to unfasten it. He also likes to play with the cage door, opening and closing it at will unless it is latched. He particularly enjoys gnawing on fir cones, from which he extracts the seeds. He removes the scales until only the stalk remains. He is given only mineral water to drink. He likes to put pieces of orange into the water, and then drinks it after a while; he also enjoys drinking pure orange juice.

Because the bird became hand tame so fast (in about two to three months), it seems that it took very much longer (about eleven months) before he spoke his first words, despite the fact that he had already learned to whistle a few short melodies. He first imitated his name, Filou, and followed this with *boy,* which soon expanded to *boy-o-boy, chatterbox,* and the like. He now commands a vocabulary of about thirty-five words, ten to fifteen of which he rarely says anymore. He reserves the use of certain words for specific situations. So,

Pet Grey Parrots are able to occupy some of their time playing by themselves, provided the owner furnishes suitable playthings.

for example, after waking in the morning, if he thinks uncovering his cage is taking too long, he calls, *So, come on already,* or he says, *Good morning, Filou.* When he sees me with the shopping bag, *Bye, darling,* he calls. With the same word (*bye*) he once greeted a visitor he did not much like. In response to the question, How is my little dear, he answers with a drawn-out *good.* If one wants to hear the answer again, the second time the *good* is shorter, and the third time he only whistles. When he wants to play with us, he usually lures us with the call *look, look,* which he learned while playing on a shelf, where the hand disappeared time and again. He knows quite well to associate searching with the word. When playing, he always distinguishes between his playmates. With me or my oldest daughter he knows he will get a firm smack if he bites too hard. With my youngest daughter and my husband he boldly goes right on. When he manages to nip himself a little too hard while playing, he scolds, *Ouch, be gentle, Filou,* which is what he hears from us. Yet he can be gentle as a caress, if he wants to.

The Grey likes to sit on the shoulder and be carried around, during which he shows a particular interest in glasses. When he is on my husband's shoulder, he is so high spirited he immediately pinches him on the ear. In the beginning, he always bit holes in our clothing, particularly when we went down the stairs. This was certainly caused by insecurity, because now he has gotten out of this bad habit.

81

When I was teaching him to talk, I always repeated the same words to him in the evening. He learned very few of these words. In contrast to this, he says words that he has heard in our conversations. Above all, my husband's deeper voice appeals to him; he coughs and laughs like my husband and uses some of his words, even though my husband has fearfully avoided him for over a year. His favorite toy is a yellow plastic spoon; he loses interest in metal spoons and keys after a short time. He takes the plastic spoon and scratches under his bill or hits himself on the head with it. If he hits too hard, he takes himself to task by saying, *Ouch, be gentle, you, you.* In the course of almost two years, from an unusually fearful animal he has developed into a jovial, in no way timid, sociable bird.

The tapping of certain species of parrots on the perches or on the walls of the cage was also observed by the author inhis Eclectus and Rüppell's parrots; another fancier noted the same behavior in his Blue-naped Parrots. In these cases, however, courtship behavior was involved.

The fascination with plastic objects can also be confirmed. So, for example, plastic clothespins are the only objects my Rüppell's Parrots play with daily, even in a large outdoor flight. They even retrieve these from the floor, which they otherwise avoid. If one has the opportunity to rear nestlings, they readily accept a plastic spoon for hand feeding, but not metal spoons. A stand or climbing tree placed atop the cage is extremely important for already tame Grey Parrots. Here they can spend their time, with a sense of freedom and the opportunity to move about.

Closely trimming the flights of one wing prevents the bird from flying in a straight line; at best it will be able to fly in an arc.

7.   Diet

The diet of the Grey Parrot has already been discussed in the various articles and contributions in this book. About a hundred years ago, peculiar notions concerning diet were prevalent and contributed to the high mortality rate among parrots at that time. Today the situation is completely different, and there can no longer be any doubt about the correct diet. The difficulty lies in convincing the Grey Parrot to eat the correct foods! As with other large parrots, the food preferences of Grey Parrots are so strongly ingrained that it is often a great test of patience to convince the bird to accept a wider variety of foods. In practical terms, this means the bird should take foods as diverse as possible to keep the body and plumage healthy. The parrot cannot be forced to accept the food, and only great patience and repeated offerings can lead to the desired goal.

Those species of parrots that spend their lives in trees are very reluctant to go down to the ground; they are often so stubborn they would rather starve to death than climb down. The author has had parrots that immediately accepted foods offered to them on twigs and branches, but the very same food on the ground was left untouched. It is therefore recommended, if the food bowls are not situated high up in the cage, to place temporary food bowls in the upper part of the cage at first, until the Grey Parrot learns to go down. Introducing an apple should be done in the same way. It can drive a person to desperation when a piece of apple that has been wedged between the bars of the cage is torn out and thrown to the floor, where the bird immediately loses interest in it. It is best to drive a nail in the end of a high perch, and to stick the apple half on this. Other fruits, such as cherries and rowan and hawthorne berries, should be fastened with a clothespin to the bars of the cage near a perch. Chickweed and dandelion can also be offered in the same way. Other fruits such as sweet pears and melons, and vegetables such as cucumbers and maize ears, can also be stuck on a nail. It goes without saying that all food offered should be as fine in quality as possible.

Unfortunately, these days it is not always possible to detect whether foods have been processed or sprayed. The shelf life of fruit is usually extended by treatment with certain chemicals, and almost everything has been sprayed with insecticides beforehand. For this reason, it is recommended to at least wash everything thoroughly and even to peel certain fruits, such as apples, though most of the vitamins are found directly beneath the skin. Feeding lettuce bought in stores is very risky and should be avoided. During the winter a supply can be grown in pots, since the birds should not be given too much at any one time anyway. A day's portion should at most be as large as the surface of a tea cup, and should be given three times a week.

Providing the Grey Parrot with the proper diet is extremely important; above all, the diet must be as varied as possible. From my own experiences with large parrots I am well aware how difficult this can be. The birds can be so stubborn they sometimes drive their owner to despair. One means well and offers the birds the nicest things, but they are totally ignored. Many breeders therefore give up the attempt and offer only those foods they know the birds will accept. Amazingly enough, many Grey Parrots thrive for years under such circumstances. One much less frequently hears of negative events, since who wants to report that his Grey Parrot has been fed a one-sided diet and now has died suddenly? Necropsies are not often performed on dead birds so far, so the cause of death usually remains unknown.

Like people, Grey Parrots also require in their diet certain substances that are essential to health. Among others, these include carbohydrates, proteins, fats, minerals, and vitamins. The nitrogenous portion of the diet, or raw protein, is essential for good health. Some species of parrots require more protein,

84

others less. While the Grey Parrot requires a certain amount of raw protein, an excess can be damaging to the bird's health. A further difficulty is that individual birds utilize the protein differently. There have been Grey Parrots which were given ample amounts of cooked fish, meat, and poultry—regularly, not occasionally—and nevertheless remained in good health. It is the author's opinion that meat, fish, or poultry should never be given raw, but should always be cooked. Even though in England fish is sometimes fed to parrots, this should be avoided because of the smell and the fish bones. Cooked chicken or veal (1 tablespoon) or even a bone can be offered once a week. Highly seasoned food should not be given, because an excess of these substances entails the danger of feather plucking or cannibalism.

An English fancier took great pains in his breeding attempts (in which case the raw-protein requirement is greater) and had the following idea: He took neck bones of lamb and roasted them until all the fat had been cooked out. These were stored in small pieces in the freezer. They were taken out from time to time and, after reheating them in the oven, given to the Grey Parrots. The birds could easily hold the pieces with their feet and accepted them greedily. Another fancier I am aquainted with owns valuable cockatoos. Not only for nutrition's sake, but also to keep the birds occupied, were cooked bones fastened to the branches in the flight. My Eclectus Parrots, which have managed to rear thirteen young, ignore bones and such altogether, but they readily take cubes of cheese or pieces of cooked chicken eggs. The Hawk-headed Parrots ate mealworms but then became very ill. They swallowed them whole, and the chitinous armor of the larvae is dangerous. My Swift Parrots also eat mealworms, but they squeeze them out and let the chitinous armor fall to the floor. If they are given too many, they start to pluck the feathers from their youngsters. Once the larvae are withheld, they stop.

In Australia we observed Galahs remove the maggots of blowflies from their nests and feed them to their young until they feathered in. After this, they no longer showed an interest in the numerous maggots still in their nest. One can therefore conclude that the need is different at different times. The author has been able to confirm time and again during his twenty years of parrot keeping that the requirement for particular substances can be strong at some times and less strong at others, while at other times there may be no need for them at all.

A young Eclectus Parrot, which was no longer being fed by its parents, was given a supplement of fresh ant pupae. It soon developed symptoms of lameness in its legs, and it took a number of weeks before the bird's condition improved. Everyone knows that fresh ant pupae are the best food for the majority of softbills, but the digestive enzymes of birds can be very different. Similar cases have been described many times. If one thumbs through the century of issues of *Die Gefiederte Welt*, one can find well-meant advice from fanciers who own one parrot species or another and who believe in good faith that their recipe can be recommended for all other species of parrots as well. One should always keep to the safe, middle course when it cames to diet.

All kinds of nuts are a good food, but one must keep in mind that all are high in fat. For example, the walnut contains approximately 35–50%, the peanut 30–55%, and the palm nut 60% or more oil! It is best to offer nuts to the parrot after they have been cracked; then the parrot will be kept occupied removing the contents from the shell. Unfortunately, certain kinds of nuts spoil very easily. These must definitely be avoided, because they usually become rancid and can then cause gastro-intestinal disturbances. This problem usually occurs only with peanuts, because these are preferably offered in the shell. The parrots enjoy crushing the shells and extracting the kernel. One can also roast the peanuts; since the shell becomes very crunchy, these are taken even more readily. In my experience, peanuts that do not taste or smell good are usually barely touched or not touched at all. Unfortunately, it occasionally comes to pass that such nuts are eaten, and the bird becomes ill. Therefore, it is safer to shell the peanuts first. There are some nuts, however, that look edible even when they are rancid; the peanut always looks good whether in the shell or a kernel; only a trial will reveal a bad taste. So-called feed peanuts, even when their shells are uniform and unbroken, should not be purchased. In my opinion, these nuts—and also spray millet, for example—should be carefully examined beforehand. It is therefore recommended to buy them only in small quantities; otherwise one takes a loss and is annoyed when they have to be thrown out. Birds are always alleged to have a relatively poor sense of smell. But if this is true, then how can one explain the fact that parrot species refuse to approach and in fact completely avoid certain apples and other fruits they otherwise like? The only reasonable conclusion is that parrots do have a well-developed sense of smell.

Maize is usually accepted readily, particularly in a fresh and, if possible, milky state. Ears of maize of this sort can be obtained only in the autumn. It is best to speak with a farmer ahead of time and to arrange to buy about 50 pounds (depending on your needs) after the harvest. The green husks should be removed and the ears stored in a freezer. In this way it is possible to have a supply of fresh maize the year round. To minimize waste, each ear can be cut into two or three pieces. This means about two ears per week will be enough for one bird. More should not be given, because this leads to an accumulation of body fat. Approximately 100 ears will suffice one parrot for an entire year. Freezing can, of course, also be used to ensure a supply of other fresh foods, provided there is enough room in the freezer.

The fruits that come into consideration are cherries, apples, pears, peaches, bananas, apricots, and grapes (the last must be washed especially well). Only sweet fruits are accepted by the birds. As the pits of cherries, peaches, and plums contain hydrocyanic acid, it is not advisable to allow the Grey Parrots to crack these open. Apples, which quickly turn brown after they are cut, are not well liked. Above all, they must be juicy, and not overripe and mealy. In my experience, the varieties Golden Delicious, Ingrid Marie, and Granny Smith are favored. Often bananas are eaten only by younger Grey Parrots. Figs and dates, which must first be softened, are also eaten.

Berries are also good to feed. The following may be considered: red currants, strawberries, blueberries, cranberries, haw-

Composition of Seeds Fed to Parrots		
Seed	*Raw Protein*	*Raw Fat*
Sunflower	13.4%	27.6%
Hemp	21.0%	31.6%
Maize	10.6%	4.4%
Wheat	12.3%	1.9%
Canary	17.5%	5.5%
Oats	10.7%	5.1%
Spray millet	13.5%	3.8%

thorne berries, rowan berries, and those of *Cotoneaster* and *Pyracantha* (firethorn). The latter two usually have thorns on the small twigs, which are best removed. In rose-hips (the fruits of the wild or cultivated briar rose) we find yet another commendable addition to the diet.

Green peas in their pods are also liked particularly. Young birds with dark eyes should not be given too many of them, because they can act as a laxative. Other half-ripened food, such as oats or wheat, are also very important for maintaining good health. Sometimes weeds such as plantain, chickweed, and dandelion are also taken. In the spring, the birds should be given twigs with leaf buds, particularly from willow, linden, poplar, birch, elder, conifers, and fruit trees. All of these twigs contain, among other things, minerals that birds require. The bark is not only gnawed, but eaten as well. Conifer twigs are particularly important for the growth of the plumage.

Young Grey Parrots, in particular, readily accept biscuits or stale white bread and zwieback, which should be softened and squeezed out before feeding.

The major portion of the diet should consist of cereal grains and other seeds. It is important to know the main constituents of each kind, so the diet can be adjusted in one direction or the other. The most commonly offered seeds are listed in the accompanying table.

Hemp contains the most raw protein and raw fat. It should only be given sparingly, but it is also not advisable to give it in large quantities for other reasons. Its hull is believed to contain poisonous substances. Many bird fanciers have noted its disadvantages. The author has owned parakeets that have tumbled to the floor after eating large quantities. Hemp can also lead to feather plucking, eggs can be broken, and nestlings have even been torn apart by their parents.

The seed portion of the diet should consist of approximately 60% sunflower seeds, and the other 40% can be made up varying proportions of canary seed, millet spray, wheat, oats, paddy rice, and maize. Hemp should be given in the daily quantity of about ten seeds per bird. Pine or fir cones and their twigs contain resin, which has a favorable effect on the growth of the plumage.

The Grey Parrot will eat his favorite food first, and therefore one should not immediately refill the bowl, or else the bird will never eat any other kind of seed. It is much better to have several food bowls: one for sunflower seeds and hemp, another for wheat, oats, canary seed, and millet, and, if possible, a third for maize. The latter should be given in softened form if it is not fresh. It is very healthy to give sprouted sunflower seeds twice a week. The same can be done with spray millet, but the seeds should have barely germinated, because if the sprouts are too long, the birds will not eat them.

Minerals are also important for cage and aviary birds. Parrots kept in cages suffer particularly often from deficiencies of chlorine, manganese, sulphur, calcium, phosphorous, magnesium, and iodine. The trace elements are obtained from vegetable matter in the diet. By providing supplements of provitamin D, the bones and plumage will be kept in good condition. Fresh river sand should be placed on the floor of the cage every day, or at the least every other day. Mineral and iodine blocks and the like can also be hung in the cage. Crushed seashells or egg shells from healthy hens can also be offered. A thick piece of turf placed in the cage will be thoroughly worked over after the initial shyness is past, and will also provide essential minerals.

Acclimated Grey Parrots can be given ordinary tap water without hesitation. It is better to give newly imported birds boiled water. The intake of water is largely dependent on the kinds of food consumed. If the parrot is given large quantities of fruit, the water requirement will decrease; if more seeds are given, the requirement will increase. A pinch of glucose can occasionally be given, provided the droppings are normal.

Vitamins. Vitamins play a very important role in nutrition. A deficiency in these substances can lead to illness and disease. In my experience, there are great differences among the various parrot species as to whether they like, tolerate, or avoid taking vitamin supplements, particularly when these give off a strong odor, as is always the case with multivitamins. One can attempt to fool the bird by sprinkling a few drops on their favorite food or in their drinking water. The most important vitamins are A, D_3, E_1, B-complex, and K. These supplements become more important the more one-sided the diet is. If the diet is multifarious, less attention need be paid to supplements. In the winter months, when the birds do not get sufficient sun, approximately three drops should be given three times a week; in the warmer months this amount can be reduced. An excess is not recommended, because the birds then molt more frequently and not at the normal time.

Bird-keepers' reports. No final conclusions concerning the diet of birds should be drawn from the experiences reported in articles, whether old or new. Instead, they should merely show what used to be believed and was experienced and how much the various experiences differ. What one fancier swears by is contradicted by another. Young, black-eyed birds in particular are at first difficult to accustom to a diet. What follows deals with this subject.

In the beginning I gave him rice softened in milk. He greedily drank the milk but did not want to have much to do with the rice; he pulled apart white bread more than he ate it and always wanted to drink more. I did not feel this was beneficial, so I gave him less and less water at longer intervals. From the beginning he had a fairly definite case of diarrhea, but I soon cured this by giving him carbonate of magnesia mixed with his water. How I should go about feeding him was not yet clear to me, because he did not like anything I could discover in reading about the feeding of such birds, or anything similar, with the exception of hemp, which he had been fed before I bought him. But I had developed a mistrust of hemp, which arose from my conversations with my friend Sachs, a building contractor in Altenkirchen, who is a considerable ornithologist and always warned me against feeding birds too much hemp. You too, Doctor [Karl Russ— *Ed.*], are no supporter of feeding hemp, as I discovered in your *Handbuch Für Vogelliebhaber.* Well-baked zwieback finally appealed to him, but since he always spilled so much while feeding, he wasted astonishing amounts. I always gave him a little hemp on the side. Later, maize was recommended to me on occasion. So I bought some maize, set it in front of him, and let him screech in disapproval for a couple of days, until he became used to it and started eating it with pleasure. I used the same method with buckwheat, and now he is given maize and buckwheat almost exclusively and is doing quite well. He quickly became quite tame with me, and he recognized the place where I stored the zwieback after the first few days, and then as soon as I entered the room and approached its storage place, he immediately came down from his perch and emphasized his presence by squeezing his head through the bars of the cage.

Elsewhere this is said:

I seized the opportunity to buy a very young gray-eyed jocko, which someone had brought with two other Grey Parrots from Algiers. The seller told me the bird had been fed almost exclusively with hemp and canary seed so far, but that he also liked to gnaw on bones, particulary from cutlets. I wish to make clear the fact that it is easy to be misled by unscrupulous dealers in this regard, so the newly purchased bird, when he is forced to quickly become accustomed to an unfamiliar diet, frequently dies or at best "stagnates" for a while. I soon found out this was true in my situation. My jocko was extremely wild, gnawed on everything, bit through even the wire bars of his cage, screeched pitiably at the slightest approach, and—the most unfortunate aspect of the situation—did not eat the slightest bit of any of the food he was supposed to be accustomed to. I tried everything, fearing for the life of this beautiful animal, as one day after another passed by with the same lack of success. Only after a few days had passed did it occur to me that most parrots are fed maize while they are being shipped. When I gave him some, he accepted it greedily, so now I had one less thing to worry about. Maize still makes up the main part of his diet; he refuses to eat any other seeds, such as hemp, oats, rice, and canary seed. On the other hand, he loves all kinds of berries, such as strawberries, elderberries, and grapes, and all kinds of fruit. He eats fresh fruit, according to the season, as well as dried and soaked. He now feels quite well and comfortable. In addition, year in and year out, he is given buds and twigs from fruit trees and hazel and elder bushes, among others, which he contentedly gnaws. Against my wishes, he was also accustomed to boiled and roasted meat. But since the result of this, namely, the unfortunate feather plucking, did not disappear, he has not been allowed to have any for a long time.

The following lines should certainly not be taken to heart, because to allow any kind of animal to take food from your mouth is unhygienic.

The author has had bad experiences with feeding ant eggs to Eclectus Parrots, for example. The birds developed lameness in their legs, which subsided only after a number of weeks. There can be no doubt that the fresh ant pupae were the cause of the lameness. Mealworms are also always damaging if given in large amounts; however, this is only true when the whole larvae are swallowed and not when only their contents are chewed out. Withholding water is also foolish, and was the subject of heated arguments in earlier times. Offering meat is appropriate only very conditionally, because an excess can lead to feather plucking. The droppings became watery because of the inappropriate diet. If really necessary, one can give cooked chicken or veal in small amounts. But there are always some exceptions to these rules, and certain animals can survive, at least for a time, on an unhealthy diet.

The regimen I employ in part with my Grey Parrots consists of the following: In the morning when I eat buttered bread while I'm drinking my coffee, I give each bird a mouthful of the bread which I have thoroughly chewed. The most confiding (females) take the bread from my mouth, and the others take it from my hand. As a result, the birds quickly become tame and confiding. At noon each of them are given two large or three small cracked walnuts; in addition, they get whatever happens to be on the table, such as eggs, dumplings, stewed plums, raisins, carrots, potatoes, meat, and bones—but only one, or at most two, of these items a day. In the evening I give them good, juicy pears, apples, grapes, and the like. If I don't have these, then I again give them a mouthful of buttered bread (homemade). When the weather is very warm, they are given as much to drink as they want; when it's cooler, every second or third day; when it's cold, every six to eight days—but they always get water that has been standing in the room for an hour. Milk as well and even a mixture of half wine and half water is also given and readily taken. Eating meat has not led to any feather plucking at all; on the contrary, I have only seen this vice when the birds were kept in small cages. Ant eggs and mealworms are always welcome to them. If the excretion becomes watery, then I feed them more nuts, and soon everything is back in order.

In the above the result of an improper diet may be recognized; one should not choose such an easy way out!

It is very satisfying when one is able to rear a young, black-eyed Grey Parrot despite the great risks involved. When this is successful, the birds will be unusually tame and usually also very good mimics. From letters and articles it is possible to see how fanciers of an earlier time fared with these birds. Getting the birds accustomed to maize ears is recommended if the birds will be introduced to other kinds of food later. Importation of nestlings with downy plumage no longer happens these days.

I found the highest incidence of mortality in those young Grey Parrots on which the plumage was still very soft and downy, that is, those birds that were not full grown and were taken from their nests. On the other hand, I noticed that gray-eyed jockos with firm feathers responded very well to correct care and showed good progress. These birds should be treated as follows. One should first make the effort to obtain the birds during the time when young, juicy ears of maize can be found, which is possible in our region from the second week of July until the beginning of November. The birds should be given young, juicy ears of maize the whole day and a little hemp in the evening. In the morning, they can also be given a little piece of roll, which has been soaked in milk and then squeezed out. When fed in this way, a jocko will often not drink any water at all for as long as two weeks, since the juicy maize contains a sufficient amount. As long as young maize is available, it should be fed exclusively; at other times of year the bird should in the daytime be given dried kernels that have been cooked until they are quite soft, and again some hemp in the evening. Until a young jocko has been completely acclimated, which can never be assumed prior to at least five months, it should neither be sprayed nor given water to bathe in. As was previously mentioned, an early death in the first weeks or days is the almost certain fate of young jockos in downy plumage.

Diet was still controversial around 1900. Many famous bird keepers considered sunflower seeds, for example, to be damaging to the birds' health. Today, they are fed to the majority of species of parrots as a matter of course. A physician wrote the following on this subject:

On the subject of sunflowers, I have fed them exclusively to parrots for over four months without the slightest sign of ill effects. Why should sunflowers be dangerous? Since fat is easy to digest when sufficient potassium is available in the diet and since sunflowers contain little potassium, it seemed obvious to feed the birds as much fruit as possible. As a result, my parrots are given and feed on cherries, gooseberries, red currants, raspberries, apricots, and as much melon as possible, and this diet suits them very well. They have now completed, at the end of July, the second, autumn molt with little apparent difficulty. From time to time they also get raw carrots when there is a shortage of fruit; in winter they always get roast chestnuts. It is also difficult to see why the previously mentioned provisions should be damaging, since the parrot is in the first place a vegetarian, which is confirmed by examining its digestive system.

The author has already warned against feeding large quantities of hemp, because the seed hulls are supposed to contain poisonous substances. There also appears to be several kinds of hemp, since fanciers have had successes as well as failures in rearing parrots when hemp is included in the diet. Hemp is supposed to be most dangerous in its unripened (green) state.

The following lines are reasonable and agree almost exactly with the opinions of the author concerning diet. Healthy birds will also have a normal need for water. This bird keeper also expresses his opinion on feather plucking. It is certain that plucking can have many causes, and can be caused by illness, as well as being simply a habit.

The main part of my birds' diet consists of canary seed, hulled oats, paddy rice, little or almost no hemp, sunflower, nuts (hazelnuts and walnuts only), and one or two peanuts a day. I also feed them fruit: apples, bananas, oranges. I also give them fresh willow and elder twigs for gnawing, when they are available. When feeding nuts, pay close attention to their quality. Fresh walnuts are taken most readily; old, oily nuts can lead to gastric disturbances and intestinal inflammations. Strangely enough, not all birds will eat maize. Maize should never be fed in large quantities. The hard kernels should be softened in cold water for twelve to sixteen hours. One should be careful with fresh ears of maize. It is not tolerated by all jockos and, because of its milk content, occasionally causes diarrhea. Heavy feeding with hemp should never be attempted. Hemp can cause convulsions and can initiate the first attempts at plucking by the bird. If a bird does start to pluck its feathers, then in most cases it cannot be cured of this illness. I dispute the claim that this deplorable plucking by jockos (this habit is less common in amazons) is caused by incorrect care, because properly cared for birds also pluck with obvious delight. In any case, I have observed that all plucking jockos were unusually intelligent birds.

Depending on the time of year, I give my jockos fresh buds from fruit trees, and above all, fresh peas (sweet peas) in the pod. With this feeding the jocko will stay healthy and active, as long as the other aspects of care meet the needs of the bird.

In my experience, feeding too much hemp is always particularly damaging to the jocko, while feeding it sparingly does not seem to produce any ill effects. The diet must, as was pointed out above, be as diversified as possible; then small amounts of hemp will not cause any damage. Tea and oatmeal gruel should be fed to birds that are not feeling well. Milk is completely unnecessary and even damaging in large quantities, since it can cause diarrhea in many birds. Water should only be given three times a day, and then the bowl should be removed. Many birds otherwise develop into "drinkers." After all, birds drink seldom or little in the wild. Excessive drinking causes diarrhea, particularly when the bird eats a lot of fruit. Mild cases of diarrhea should be controlled by feeding oatmeal gruel and ample amounts of oranges; severe intestinal disorders require the removal of seeds from the diet and substituting rice cooked until soft.

Be cautious with showering and especially with bathing because of the danger of catching cold. In a warm room or in the warm summer months one can thoroughly wet the bird with lukewarm water if one exercises caution, but always make sure a constant, warm temperature is maintained in the room. The assumption that, since the jocko is a child of the "hot part of the globe," it requires a high room temperature, is ridiculous. Whoever places his jocko near a warm stove will

95

have to expect that it will one day go into convulsions, an illness jockos are susceptible to. A normal room temperature of 18 C. is quite sufficient for the birds; my birds have shown no signs of discomfort even at a temperature of 15 C.

If one's bird does not have a large cage, then one must make sure the bird can exercise its wings sufficiently outside the cage. The bird can either do this on its own atop the cage, or by being raised and lowered on the owner's finger.

An owner of a Grey Parrot once told me his bird had lived for thirty years, eating sunflower and hemp almost exclusively. That is certainly a very long time, but Grey Parrots can live to an age of 100 years, and it is known that some parrots have maintained a good appearance even when given an abnormal diet. Another jocko owner responded on this topic as follows:

It is certainly not rare that an animal (and not only a jocko), will live to a very old age, despite the fact that it is fed a completely improper diet. I was familiar with jockos during the war that were given the same diet as people, because seeds were not available at the time, and still looked splendid. Exceptions make the rule, and one jocko surviving on a wrong diet does not give us the right to feed all the rest of the birds incorrectly. Such cases at most give us the right to claim that the jocko is a tough and resistant bird. Many other animals will quickly die if given an incorrect diet.

According to my experiences, feeding hemp is unquestionably damaging to jockos, particularly young ones. Even the more robust amazon parrots should not be fed much hemp. I once observed such a "hemp bird" in a fancier's collection. It was quiet, slept most of the time, and was only interested in its midday meal; it seemed to live to eat. These animals are usually obese, because they climb very little, and their plumage is unkempt, which is the first symptom of an excess of hemp in the diet. It is best not to feed a jocko any hemp at all. In feeding Grey Parrots there is such a large menu to choose from that it is completely unnecessary to feed them hemp.

I must urgently warn against purchasing prepared "parrot food" in stores and feeding it to your birds. Each fancier must always mix the food himself, because only then is it possible to know what the birds are getting. The prepared food in most cases contains hemp, peanuts, cembra-pine nuts, and some hard maize, and is therefore a completely unusable mixture.

Many species of large parrots, like the Grey, relish nibbling on cheeses of the harder kinds—and these foods are nutritionally beneficial.

Now the fancier probably wants to know why hemp is damaging, that is, what damaging substance does hemp contain? Above all, hemp is an unnatural food, because no hemp grows in Africa. In my experience, the high oil content of hemp seems to have a damaging effect on the longevity of young birds. Hemp birds always seem to be weaker than jockos raised on other diets. For this reason, I have always removed hemp from the diet of all new birds within two weeks.

Interesting information about hemp can also be found in the many volumes of *Die Gefiederte Welt*. In one of the issues, Herr Lauer of Freiburg reports on a starling that developed a severe intestinal disorder and had convulsive attacks after being fed hemp, which quickly disappeared after hemp was removed from the diet. Herr Lauer states: "The fact is clear that the illness began after feeding hemp and disappeared as soon as the feeding was discontinued." The question he asked at the end of the article, "Is hemp damaging?" was answered by Herr A. Adlersparre: "Yes, and particularly when it is not of the best quality. Completely ripe," Adlersparre adds, "and when grown as far north as possible, it can have little damaging effect, except in isolated cases." Herr Lauer continues:

The poisonous substances (which are presumed to occur in hemp) may be completely absent or present only in small traces in Scandinavian hemp. Hemp contains (Adlersparre agrees) poisonous components, including a narcotic (hashish), and should only be fed in small quantities after carefully checking its quality (Adlersparre).

Based on my own experiences, I recommend that hemp should be completely removed from the diet of all jockos. What is the point of offering a food with which one runs the risk of causing damage, when there are so many acceptable kinds of food available for feeding jockos? No fancier is in the position to determine if his hemp has a "northern" origin, and only a small percentage of fanciers are able to ascertain whether the hemp is better or poorer in quality. Old, stored hemp has an extremely deadly effect on jockos, particularly when the oil seeps out with the slightest pressure. In my experience, hemp causes epileptic fits, gout of the feet, feather plucking, and frequently causes chronic head colds in amazons. For these reasons, I again counsel all jocko owners, particularly the owners of young birds: Do not give the jocko hemp.

8.

Taming and Mimicking

Taming. Not everyone who has the will also possesses the empathetic capacity necessary for taming parrots. In addition, an individual Grey Parrot will sometimes have feelings of sympathy or antipathy toward its owner which are difficult to get to the root of. The taming potential of a bird is tied to this fact. A person can expend a great deal of effort, but nevertheless, the Grey Parrot could still be attracted more to another person. In many cases a bird is willing to tolerate one or more people, but the bird places its full trust in one particular person only. We do not know what determines this—the voice? the appearance? the hands? Even today the theory that male parrots are attracted more to women, while female parrots are attracted more to men, is still accepted by most fanciers. It has been proven, however, that this is not the case, though of course it can be true in individual cases. A male bird fancier reared a female parrot and later also fed it daily. Despite this, the bird gave its full trust only to his wife. One speaks therefore of "men's birds" and "women's birds." In Grey Parrots in particular this can be quickly noticed by seeing whether a bird more readily approaches a man or a woman.

In 1944, Prof. B. Grzimek studied this "crosswise rule" in parrots. The author is able to cite verbatim his article from the *Zeitschrift für Tierpsychologie* (6/1949).

Few hypotheses have found such a wide currency and have so often led to self-deception as the "crosswise rule," which, as far as I know, was proposed by Th. Zell. According to this theory, female animals are supposed to attach themselves more to men and male animals to women and girls.

A parrot puts its beak to many uses: very likely this Grey is testing the finger to discover whether it is sturdy enough to climb onto.

In an earlier publication I was able to prove in passing that this did not apply to a female wolf, despite the claims of her owner. With birds, to which the crosswise rule has been preferentially applied, the hypothesis seems unlikely from the start, based on the following considerations. From the observations of Heinroth and others, it has been recognized that in species of birds in which the two sexes have identical plumage, conspecifics recognize the sex of one another primarily by behavior. Stuffed or dead specimens can from either sex elicit instinctive behaviors, whether those meant for males or those for females. Bird breeders, particularly pigeon breeders, claim they can certainly speak of two birds as male and female because they act like a pair when they are kept by themselves. But these could just as easily be two females, less often two males, of which one, in the absence of a partner of the opposite sex, behaves in a sexually perverse way. More information concerning so-called ambivalence in certain fishes and birds is reported by K. Lorenz. The same Common Raven can behave in all particulars like a male and at another time completely like a female, depending on whether the conspecific it is attracted to has a higher or lower social position than it does.

Animals kept isolated from other members of their own species undoubtedly view the trusted human as a substitute for an absent sexual partner. So why should such birds be better able to distinguish between the sexes of people than of their own species? They cannot have been born with the instinctive knowledge of the sexual characteristics and behavior of people. Also, how can they during their lives possibly acquire the ability to distinguish between them? The proposition, at best vague, that they can sense some factor independent of species, such as the hormones and vitamins that all vertebrates have in common, a kind of olfactory "sexual fluid," has little to recommend it in this case, since it is known that the sense of smell is very poorly developed in birds. And if this "fluid" can fail even within a species, how can it be expected to make the sex of a person clear to a bird?

In any case, it must be noted that a bird which is mistaken about sex while living with conspecifics generally does not have a partner of the opposite sex to choose. Yet it is also true that singly kept birds, when they have contact with a number of men and women, sometimes choose one of them to be a "bosom buddy."

While making a study of right- and left-handedness in horses, parrots, and apes, I had at my disposal 131 completed questionnaires from owners of large parrots. The question asking whether the sex was known was answered by a surprising number of owners solely on the basis of the crosswise rule, such as: "He is a male, since he lets only my wife scratch him."

The owners of 13 parrots confirmed that their birds had laid eggs in captivity. These amounted to 7 Grey Parrots (of a total of 51), 5 amazons (of a total of 72), and 1 macaw (out of 4). If one assumes half of the 127 parrots were females, then 20% had laid eggs while kept singly. Thus I am able to assume that large parrots, when they are kept under natural, social conditions in flights, would breed just as often as Budgerigars and lovebirds do when kept under similar conditions. Concerning Grey Parrot #51, the owner wrote: "It announced the presence of the egg by scratching in the sand." Grey Parrot #31 "laid in the early morning hours while sitting on her cage tray. The pains lasted about twenty minutes, during which the bird winced while pressing, until the egg fell out after a final push. She continued to sit on it. After an hour I was able to remove it; she then went to a perch, making clicking noises, and started eating, which she did very actively." Grey Parrot #85 "laid an egg every two years, which was very diligently incubated."

I was thus in the fortunate position of having information on 13 large parrots, the sex of which was known while they were still alive. For this reason I again wrote to the owners and asked them about the

Species No.	Years Owned	Number of Eggs Laid	Favorite Person	Second Favorite Person	Handedness	Assessment Man's Bird	Woman's Bird	Neutral
Grey Parrots								
31	1	3	♂	–	R	1	–	–
51	18	3	♀♀[1]	–	L	–	1	–
71	31	46	♂	♂	R	1	–	–
75	31	3[2]	♂	–	L	1	–	–
85	29	?[3]	♂	♀	L	–	–	1
102	8	?[4]	♂	–	R	1	–	–
111	14	2	♂	♀	L	–	–	1
Amazons								
13	12	1[5]	♀	–	R	–	1	–
89	34	?[6]	♀	♂	L	–	–	1
94	31	3	♂♂[7]	–	L	1	–	–
116	20	1	♀	[8]	L	–	–	1
100	16	?[9]	♀	[10]	R	–	1	–
Macaws								
10	1	1	♀	–	L	–	1	–
						5	4	4

OWNERS' COMMENTS: [1] Aversion to men, confiding with women. [2] Many. [3] One every two years. [4] Many. [5] In 50 years. [6] Many. [7] Hates every female creature, confiding with men. [8] Hates the mother. [9] Many. [10] Hates men except for one of my sons.

behavior of these birds toward people of both sexes. The results can be seen in the accompanying table.

In the responses to the questions, the Favorite Person is designated as that person in whom the parrot places the greatest amount of its trust, while other people are simply tolerated, or even bitten maliciously, depending on circumstances. When another person is also trusted, this is marked in the Second Favorite Person column. It rarely happens that a large parrot which is kept in a household will tolerate familiarity from just any stranger; this is more likely to happen in a zoo, where many large parrots (particularly cockatoos) apparently enjoy being scratched by anyone who can do it with some skill.

The evaluation (the last three columns) assumes, of course, that sufficiently numerous observations are available. Not every owner will have determined how many strangers have been allowed, after suffi-

Probably wild-caught, this mature Grey Parrot at least tolerates the attentions of pet-shop owner Barbara Patterson, yet its posture suggests that it may not be a "woman's bird."

cient effort, to become familiar with the parrot. Not even all members of the household will have made an earnest attempt, because some people do not particularly enjoy being bitten. Amazon #116 had a female for a favorite person but hated the housewife. As a result of this inconsistent behavior toward the female sex, she was designated as neutral. Amazon #100 is counted with the women's birds, even though she trusts one of the sons of the household. On closer examination, these inconsistencies show that this kind of analysis has already run into difficulties. Additional difficulties were also encountered, of which only one very important one will be mentioned. Behavior toward the same person can change considerably over a period of time. In the absence of the favorite person—this has also been observed in monkeys (O. Heinroth)—another will take his or her place; the need for companionship must be satisfied.

My Grey Parrot Agatha, for example, allows me alone to pick her up in my hand, touch her under the wings, and she "kisses" only me on the mouth or climbs on only my shoulders. She viciously bites everyone else. But if I am away for a long period of time, then my wife can do the same after a while. But as soon as I again enter the room, she starts to bite or ignore her. I had always considered this to be a peculiarity of my Agatha, but learned from my questionnaires that this is a characteristic feature of many large parrots. Even in those animals for which sex was not certain (since they had not laid eggs), the favorite person and the second favorite person were frequently of different sexes, that is, the parrot gives its affection to the wife, and after a long separation transfers this affection not to a daughter but to the husband. In all cases the sudden change of attitude toward the substitute favorite person was immediately reversed at the return of the principal favorite person.

(Note from the editor of Die Gefiederte Welt: The same is true of my Grey Parrot, for which I am the favorite person. He has always bitten my wife. Two female domestics, who made the effort to get on his good side, were rewarded with some measure of trust but were never allowed to get too familiar. My daughter, who frequently sprays him with water to his great regret, was never allowed to get close to him. But one time when I was away for three weeks, she was able to successfully continue with my attempts to teach him to count from the first day on; but he never climbed on her hand, though she was able to carry him around on a perch or the handle of a cooking spoon. She was finally allowed to scratch him all over, just like me. But when she proudly tried to show me these successes immediately after my re-

Toward a man (Mr. Patterson), the Grey Parrot seems more confiding.

turn, he bit her viciously. Once, when we all took a trip together, we left him with a family who were friends of ours. There, in the new place, from the first day on he trusted the master of the house just as much as he did me (during our first encounter he had immediately climbed on my hand and even allowed himself to be scratched all over). He was reserved toward the mistress and servants in that household too, and remained so. When the man visited us about six months later, the parrot was reticent toward him in my presence—I stood about 4 meters away—if not hostile. With the bird's first owners, who had him for many years and from whom I obtained him, it was the husband who was the favorite person. The bird always bit his wife, even though she loved him, fed him, and taught him to talk. Finally, a young man, who spent four weeks in my house, was able very quickly to enjoy all my rights during a time when I was seldom home and finally was away for two weeks. On first viewing, anyone would think my Grey Parrot is a typical man's bird, but we are quite justified in calling him neutral, as was the case with Amazon #116. In the same way that my daughter was able to succeed, I think that any woman who has some skill in the matter and is persistent, could win the favor of even the most notorious man's bird, provided the favorite man did not spoil everything by interfering.)

But even if we take the summary at face value, the 13 female parrots are by no means all men's birds. If a parrot seems to prefer men or women, this is certainly no clue to its sex. The number of well-defined men's birds and women's birds among parrots is apparently also much less than is generally believed, so the widely held belief is completely contrary to what an unbiased examination on a broader basis discloses.

Even so, it can hardly be disputed that many Grey Parrots, for which the first favorite person was, for example, a man, continue throughout their lives and even after a change in ownership to continue to more easily become attached to men than to women. But this, consistent with the findings of my study, has nothing to do with the person's sex as such. What this is actually based on could perhaps be more clearly understood by a broadly based experiment employing disguises, for example. Perhaps the bird is noticing the differences in clothing between men and women, the differences in voices, or who knows what else. In the same way, there are some parrots that dislike all children and others that dote on them. The sex of the children is immaterial here, but early experiences with particular children may be decisive, with the result that all people of similar appearance (small

Thus far, there is no satisfactory explanation for such plumage anomalies as this Grey Parrot, apparently a timneh, shows.

ones, in this case) would be given the same friendly or hostile treatment as the first.

A fancier reported there was a pronounced woman's bird in his family, one that permitted only the lady of the house to handle it. The bird, however, laid three eggs, then four weeks later another two eggs. This female Grey Parrot regurgitated food for the woman. Here again is proof that who the favorite person is, is determined without regard to sex.

Older Grey Parrots may beg for food from their favorites with drooping wings. This was observed in four-year-old birds. Apparently, only sexually mature animals do this. The bird sees in its favorite, whether the person is a man or a woman, an object for its sexual inclinations; in such situations it also does not matter whether the Grey Parrot is male or female. From long experience in keeping birds, we also know that occasionally even two males will feed each other if no female is available. In certain situations female parrots also feed males. My female Golden-shouldered Parrot (*Psephotus chrysopterygius dissimilis*) continually fed the male for some days after the young had left the nest. It is also possible to observe sexually aroused female parrots trying to copulate with the male, which almost leads one to the conclusion that a mistake has been made in sexing them.

Thus we come to the conclusion that, with Grey Parrots, sex does not play a role in the matters we have been considering. On the other hand, the author believes female birds are naturally more reserved and distrustful than males. It is possible that taming a female bird will take somewhat longer than taming a male. In general, it appears that parrots are more confiding toward women and children. This could of course simply be true because they have more patience and also spend more time, and have more time to spend, with the birds. Whether the bird's sense of smell is really that poor, as was implied in the previous article, must be evaluated in the context of the reports and experiences of others. For example, Dr. Johann Schwartzkopff reports that "the olfactory nerve is formed from the processes of the olfactory cells, the so-called 'primary' sensory cells. The processes extend to the olfactory bulb, where approximately twenty of them join each 'mitral cell.' Through this 'switchboard,' which has a ratio opposite to mammals with good senses of smell, a loss in the ability to make fine distinctions in smells must be effected; possibly the sensitivity to smell, slight in itself, may be increased. In some parrots, the olfactory bulb is barely discernible." (Berndt and Meise, 1959, *Die Naturgeschichte der Vögel.*) Rensch states that parrots have 300–400 taste buds in their bills.

Based on my observations, I have been able to determine that many species of parrots refused to touch fruit or water containing vitamins, even though they made no attempt to taste them. Sometimes apples and oranges are also left untouched. One could conclude from this that the sense of smell must be present in some form.

It was already mentioned that the Grey Parrot should be given a place of its own, if possible, and should be given a permanent stand that is no more than head high. Feed the bird quietly and slowly, show no sign of haste, talk to the bird, and take your time. Do not experiment, and do not allow the parrot out of its cage until you really have the feeling the bird will not

The nominate form,
P. e. erithacus,
has bright red
tail feathers and
a black bill.

flutter wildly against the window anymore. It will take quite a while to reach this point, and any use of force or impatience can set the whole process back by several months. One should never tease a Grey Parrot, or offer the bird a finger and then quickly pull it back (a favorite game with children!), or else one will soon have a "biter" on his hands.

A single bird will of course become trusting much faster than two animals. The two will continue to keep each other frightened, and one can easily start a panic in the other. Only after many weeks or even months, when the parrot stays completely calm while being fed and the frightened, screeching voice is no longer heard, can an attempt be made to offer it treats through the bars of the cage. It is sometimes better not to start out with the hand, but to use a flat piece of wood instead.

Only when this experiment is successful should the hand be used. But even now the hand should be held so that the head of the bird must move toward the treat; the hand should not move farther into the cage. Some animals get used to this quickly, others take longer. These attempts should first be tried in the early evening or after dusk, because the bird is more approachable at this time of day. The next step is to try to stroke the bird's feathers lightly with a finger. If it allows this, then one is well on the way to taming the bird. At this point, it is a matter of sensing when the time is ripe to open the cage door, so the Grey Parrot can come out of its cage and, if possible, climb to a stand or a branch placed atop the cage. Some Grey Parrots simply refuse to leave their "homes," because they feel comfortable and safe there. With animals of this sort, a round stick (such as a broom handle) about 1 meter long often helps; through the door of the cage one slowly places the stick under the belly of the parrot. Usually it climbs on, and then one must slowly and deftly take the stick out of the cage and transfer the Grey to the branch. If the parrot will be left completely unsupervised, it is better to put it back in its cage. The first time, if the bird is not yet very tame, the stick method should be used, so the animal does not have to be held in the hands.

Another step is completed when the bird allows itself to be scratched outside the cage as well. Most birds do not like to

Enclosures for Grey Parrots are best made of materials that will withstand gnawing. Perches, however, should invite gnawing, as they are the easiest furnishings to replace.

have their backs scratched; it is better to try the side of the head. It usually is not long before the Grey Parrot climbs on a finger held against its belly. If this is successful, any owner should be pleased, because now everything will be much easier, even if the bird still refuses to go back in its cage on its own. With Grey Parrots that allow themselves to be stroked while they are sitting on a finger, the goal of taming has been achieved. The author must again point out that the Grey Parrot is by nature distrustful, and this should never be forgotten. Even a tame Grey Parrot can behave foolishly when confronted by something strange, perhaps flying to a tree in the garden out of fright.

The practice of fastening one foot of the parrot to a perch with a chain is fortunately almost a thing of the past. The ring of the chain can gradually press into the leg and leave a permanent groove. Taming by means of force is also an unpleasant matter, which is not recommended under any circumstances. In earlier times birds were grabbed with thick gloves and forced to sit on the hand. After a shorter or longer period of time the

A Grey Parrot will step onto a stick more readily than a hand because it is already accustomed to perches, which are similar.

At first, a large parrot likely perceives human flesh—whether a finger or an arm—to be unsafe to perch upon.

bird finally gave up the struggle and allowed itself to be stroked with the other hand. This process could take several days or even a week. In some cases the bird even died of a heart attack. It was also difficult to find gloves that could withstand such a powerful bite.

Mimicking. Exceptions make the rule, but in most cases it is true that a tame Grey Parrot mimics more readily and sooner than a shy one. When considering the subject of mimickry, it is important to keep in mind that not only pleasing noises but others as well will be imitated. So if we, for example, let an amazon hear a terrible racket continuously, then we can be sure our friend will learn this sound and repeat it. Therefore, it is in the interest of the owner to keep the parrot isolated from unpleasant noises or sounds as much as possible.

The belief, still widely held, that the bird understands the meaning of its words should finally be cleared up in the following discussion. The parrot learns the words and other things and can use these again in their appropriate situation. It remembers in which situations the particular words were used. If I invariably pick up a beer glass and say "Cheers!" then our Grey will say *Cheers!* whenever I pick up a beer glass. If I had always picked up a hat instead and said "Cheers!" then the Grey Parrot would learn to associate *cheers* with picking up the hat. Sometimes there can be almost unbelievable coincidences, so one in some instances is inclined to believe that the bird understands the meaning of the words. But this is certainly not the case.

There are Greys that learn quickly, well, and easily, and are true geniuses at mimickry. On the other hand, there are also birds that need a long time to learn words, learn few words over the years, and quickly forget them again. Whoever buys a Grey Parrot must understand that not every bird can be a genius. If one is prepared to accept this, then the disappointment will not be so great.

Children learn more quickly than adults, and young Grey Parrots mimic sooner, faster, and more than old birds. But here too, as with people, there can be exceptions, because even very young animals have different learning abilities. In all books of this kind, one can only deal with averages, not with exceptions. This is true not only for mimicking, but also for tameness and diet, among other things. I have mentioned this point in my other books as well.

S. Lichtenstaedt of Berlin has owned sixteen black- and gray-eyed (hence very young) Grey Parrots. Two of these became outstanding talkers, and all the rest were birds of average ability.

One cannot tell by just looking whether a bird has mimicking ability. It is a matter of luck, and only the dealer can possibly give an indication that this or that bird has already spoken a few words. In this case, one must depend on the honesty of the seller. It must also be understood that as a result of the transfer from the seller to the new owner, the bird may not say anything for the first few days or even weeks. In fact, he will probably not even eat anything for the first day or two. A Budgerigar behaves completely differently, because a change in sur-

The only race, or subspecies, of the Grey Parrot recognized today is P. e. tim-neh. *Its upper mandible is flesh colored, and its tail is rust color to dark gray.*

roundings does not affect it very much. In this respect it is possible to recognize a certain degree of intelligence in the large parrots. A finch or a softbill will soon go to its food, because it is upset less by a change in surroundings.

If it is possible to obtain Grey Parrots that are already very tame, then they will of course adjust to their new surroundings much faster. There are extreme cases, for example, in which a jocko began to talk after almost twenty years and then even became a kind of genius at talking, learning more than 200 words in three languages.

Even as late as 1930 it was still argued whether the Grey Parrot could understand the meaning of its words or not. An excerpt from F. von Lucanus follows.

The talking of the large parrots is known to be not only a purely external, phonetic imitation of human speech; the birds also associate the learned words with definite impressions which they were exposed to while being taught. So a properly instructed parrot will learn to greet its master with a *good morning* in the morning, or will learn to say the words *please, please* when it is shown a treat. This is of course not a question of a real understanding of the word or of reflection; the word is nothing more for the bird than a noise which it imitates and which it associates with a certain situation or event. I was able to teach a Grey Parrot to say *adieu* whenever I left the room. After a while, the bird began saying his *adieu* while I was still sitting at the writing desk, but was on the point of standing up and leaving the room. I had a habit, before I left, of taking hold of the handle of a drawer in the desk to make sure it was locked. The bird evidently associated grasping the handle of the drawer with leaving and therefore called out *adieu*. The behavior of the bird gives a clear indication of his considerable attentiveness, because it shows how much attention he paid to everything I did. On the other hand, it also shows that the jocko had absolutely no understanding of the meaning of the words, and that he did not have the ability to discriminate between an incidental event, which completely coincidentally preceded the act of leaving, and the main event, the actual leaving the room. He also could not abstract. Lacking insightful thinking, saying *adieu* is only an external association without meaning and understanding. Like most Grey Parrots, this bird also had the habit of being quiet in the presence of strangers. If the visitor happened to stay too long, then Jocko would suddenly call out, *Adieu!*, which gave the impression he wanted to influence the stranger to leave. The mental capacity of the bird is not suited for purposeful reflection of this kind, because after numerous attempts with my well-trained parrots, I have always been able to ascertain that the parrot does not try to make itself understood to its master by using words and gestures purposefully. For example, a parrot will say *please* before its empty food bowl even when there is no one in the room who could satisfy this desire. For this reason, my jocko's practice of saying *adieu* in the presence of a stranger cannot be taken as a purposeful declaration of desire. This incident can be better explained in the following manner: As the presence of the stranger made the bird ill at ease, he desired his removal. By association, the word *adieu* was tied to the act of leaving. We can see then that the desire for an event to take place, with which an association is already bound, can produce this incident. Certainly this involves a

Some Grey Parrots enjoy soft fruits, while others do not.

process more complicated than simple association, but no intellectual reflection is required.

The larger parrots have an exceptionally good ability to discriminate. I owned a Grey Parrot that was a pronounced lover of women. If a woman came in the room, the bird immediately became very lively and talked and whistled. If a man appeared, he remained quiet and with raised nape feathers sat angrily in the cage. This bird could always tell immediately whether a woman or a man had entered the room, without needing to hear the stranger speak. The sound of the voice was therefore not used to make the distinction; the outward appearance was not used either, because jocko was never fooled by disguises.

The exceptional memory of parrots is characterized by the following observation. Among the many birds I have kept, I once owned a very tame Hoopoe, which was called by the pet name Hoopy. My Grey Parrot quickly learned this word and always applied it to the Hoopoe. The Hoopoe died after a few months, so the word *Hoopy* was no longer spoken by us; the parrot did not use it anymore and seemed to have lost it from his vocabulary. Two years later I again obtained a Hoopoe. As soon as the parrot spotted him, he called out, *Hoopy!* He had therefore retained the word in his memory for those two years and even recognized a Hoopoe again. Since I had owned many different kinds of birds in the meantime and had occasionally allowed them to fly around the room, it follows that the parrot could quite clearly distinguish between the Hoopoe and the other birds, since he had never called any of them *Hoopy*. For the brain of a bird, which is significantly less advanced than those of mammals, this is a significant and noteworthy achievement, which nevertheless does not go beyond the realm of association. Association is the simplest mental function, for which intellectual thought is not required. Association consists of the purely external connecting of two events in such a way that the reappearance of one event automatically produces the other. In this case, the sight of the Hoopoe and the word *Hoopy* constitute the association. An association is of course also a thought process, but thought of a very primitive kind, for which no intellectual reflection or logical reasoning is necessary.

S. Lichtenstaedt of Berlin for twelve years owned a Grey Parrot that could correctly sing three complete songs, which is quite unusual. This bird could mimic about 200 words and was incredibly devoted. This female laid approximately twenty-five

Singly kept parrots are happier if their cage is situated where they can actively observe and participate in the life of the household.

eggs during this time, without a male. The presence of other birds near her master was not tolerated.

About another bird that was also a skillful mimic the following is reported:

The little animal snapped up everything that was spoken in the room, imitated a telephone conversation as soon as the instrument rang, and called in a loud and ringing voice through the house, *Attention, attention, attention, Berlin!*, which he had heard on my radio. *This is Berlin*, he says in a metallic tone of voice. He imitates a phonograph record superbly; he can imitate a man's voice, a woman's voice, and even the scratching of the needle true as life. If I scratch his little head, then he always says, *That's nice, so nice*, which I had often repeated to him previously in the same situation. If one talks to him, then he frequently tilts his head to the side and interrupts the conversation with a droll *So, so.*

I would like to mention a few more unusual experiences. Volker Wode of Hildesheim recalls the following about a Grey Parrot:

Around the middle of 1957 we took him along with us to the sea for the first time. He spent the night with us in our tent, and since it was very cold, he suddenly started hopping around on my sleeping bag. When he reached the head of the sleeping bag, he was satisfied. He climbed and wormed his way into the sleeping bag with me, as I had a fairly warm hot-water bottle. He wriggled down to my knees, where he spent the rest of the night, without being particularly concerned with my tossing and turning. He seemed to have enough air to breathe, and he was very quiet during the night.

After we owned him for nine months, he was always allowed to fly about in our house. He followed us around, and he always seemed to follow me in particular. I was his favorite, and my wife was suitable only when I was not at home. At night he slept on the roof of his cage. There we placed a tunnellike creation of sand and cement, on which Koko whetted his bill and claws, an activity he took great pleasure in.

There are also Grey Parrots that are mainly able to whistle and imitate all kinds of noises. Others more easily learn words, and some can learn to do both. Naturally, foreign words can

120

In many parrot-training programs, hand taming is undertaken after the parrot becomes accustomed to stepping onto a stick.

also be learned; others can sing one or two songs. The pitch also varies.

A Grey Parrot named Lora Eston performs on television and was at the Hansa Theater in Hamburg. It can even play question-and-answer. This bird has an unusually deep voice, so it can therefore be assumed that a man taught the bird how to talk. The following conversation is performed on stage:

Frau Eston holds the bird and asks, "Now tell me Lora, did you behave today?" The parrot: *Yes!* "Lora, do you understand a question in French?" A sentence is spoken in French, and the bird answers, *Oui!* "Lora, are you really paying attention?" Parrot: *Yes.* "You're not angry?" Parrot: *Yes!* "What, you are angry?" Bird: *No!* "Can I depend on you?" Grey Parrot: *Yes!* "Then please tell me your name, Lora, nice and loud. What's your name?" The bird, quite clearly: *Lora Eston!* "Yes, Lora, do you know my name too? What's my name?" Answer: *Annelie!* "So, now don't play, and be nice! What are you? You're my . . . ?" Lora answers: *Little parrot!* "Now Lora, I want a nice little kiss. Will you give me one?" Answer: *Yes!* Then the bird makes a loud popping noise, as if a cork is being pulled from a bottle. "The little kiss even smacked!" Parrot: *Yes!* "Well, what do you say now?" The bird answers: *That was great!* "But Lora, can you whistle too?" Answer: *Yes!* "Then show us! Please, Lora, whistle!" The Grey Parrot loudly and clearly whistles the melody to "Du bist verrückt, mein Kind!" ('You're cuckoo, kiddo!'). "Now that's rude, you're being naughty!" Answer: *No!* "Yes, you are naughty!" Parrot: *No!* "Now please, Lora, tell the audience nice and loud what you are!—you don't want to?" Parrot: *No!* "But you will say it now?" Parrot: *Yes!* "Now, Lora, you are . . . ?" Answer: *Fresh!* "That's right! Lora, are you paying attention now?" Bird: *Yes!* "Tell me how you wake me up in the morning! Think, Lora, what do you say to me in the morning?" The parrot says: *Good morning, get up!* "Now pay attention, what sound does my alarm clock make?" Parrot: *Trtrtrtrtrtrtrtrtrtrtr!* "That was very nice! Again, please, what sound does my alarm make?" *Trtrtrtrtrtrtrtr!* "Now, Lora, what do you say when someone knocks?" Parrot: *Come in!* "Come in, that's right! Do you

A stick is handy for, say, retrieving the parrot from a high perch and for returning it to its cage.

That Grey Parrots talk so volubly is testimony to their natural curiosity and sociability.

Between November 1975 and February 1976, the German television program "Großen Preis" ('Grand Prize') aired four shows featuring parrots. The Grey Parrot "star" was Lora Eston, shown here with host Wim Thoelke and contestant Eckart Zimmerman.

know how a dog barks?" Parrot: *Yes!* "Really?" Bird: *Yes!* "Lora, pay attention, how does a dog bark? Lora, did you forget?" Parrot: *Yes!* "No, Lora, I don't believe that! Think—I won't give you any hints!" Parrot: *Yes!* "No, I won't!" Parrot: *No!* "Please think for yourself!" Bird: *Yes!* "Now, please, how does a dog bark?" One hears from the Grey Parrot a deep *Bow, wow, wow!* "Will you do that again?" Parrot: *Yes!* "How does a dog bark?" Parrot: *Bow, wow, wow, wow!* "But Lora, that was a big dog!" Answer: *Yes!* "Do you know how an itsy bitsy dog barks, Lora?" Answer: *Yes!* "Now, please, how does a little tiny dog bark?" The Grey Parrot, now in a high-pitched voice: *Bo-wow!* "Good, Lora, but you can count too, isn't that right?" Bird: *Yes!* "Then, please, pay attention and count to three! Pay attention! Count nicely, Lora!" Bird: *One, two, three!* "Well done. Now show the audience how well you can laugh! You

Eye color is the best indicator of whether a Grey Parrot is an adult. A mature bird—that is, one with straw yellow irises—will probably be less facile at learning than a youngster.

can do that, can't you?" Bird: *Yes!* "Now laugh, Lora!" Parrot: *Hahahahahahaha!* "Please do it once more now!" *Hahahahahahaha!* "That was good. Now you must pay very close attention, because we're going to do something completely different! You do love sports, don't you?" Bird: *Yes!* "Do you know the 'Sportpalast-Walzer' ('Sports Palace Waltz')?" Parrot: *Yes!* "Lora, can you whistle it?" The parrot answers with *Yes!* "Then pay very close attention, Lora. Pay attention! Whistle the 'Sportpalast-Waltzer!' " Now the melody follows, along with *pscht-pscht-pscht*. Frau Eston says, "That was nice, and now whistle it along with the music!" Bird: *Yes!* "And you'll pay attention to your parts?" Parrot: *Yes!* "Well, Lora, I'm looking forward to it!" Frau Eston now says to pay attention, the orchestra starts playing, and the Grey Parrot adds its *pscht–pscht-pscht-pscht–pscht* at the appropriate moment, which it has to repeat four times. At the end, to the delight of the audience, one *pscht* too many could be heard.

This performance was for me the most phenomenal I have ever heard from a Grey Parrot. The execution was unbelievable. Despite my request for a meeting with Frau Eston, this was not possible because of lack of time. How much I would have liked to furnish the readers with a life history of this amazing parrot!

At the end of 1975, Willy Mexiko did a show with his many tame parrots on television and also in many cities. Anyone who saw them must have been impressed with the fabulous condition of the parrots. Grey Parrots were also included in this exhibition. No parrot fancier should miss the opportunity to see such performances.

In 1953, the German Zoological Society published a very interesting piece by Prof. Otto zur Strassen, in which he replies to an article by the famed scientist from the Max Planck Institute, Dr. Konrad Lorenz. In his article "Zweckdienliches Sprechen beim Graupapageien" ('Expedient Speech in Grey Parrots'), zur Strassen writes the following:

Konrad Lorenz—in the charming, funny, and nevertheless scientifically serious book, in which the principal heroine is the little goose

Willy Mexico with two tame Greys, one of each race: the differences in bill and body coloration are evident. Audiences in many countries have enjoyed the parts these and other tame parrots have played in Willy Mexico's perform-ances as a magician.

Martina (1951)—categorically states that "even the best talking birds" (which are, of course, the large parrots) "strangely enough, never learn to connect the simplest purpose with their knowledge." This is an emphatic judgement to which the scientific community has to sub-scribe, more or less. Lorenz sets an upper limit that makes the speak-ing ability of parrots very meager. Without doubt, this was urgently needed; from time immemorial the astounding talking ability of par-rots, and the Grey Parrot in particular, had always presented the dan-ger of greatly overestimating their "mental abilities." But the question of whether the limit given by Lorenz is not in fact much too low still remains.

Why did Lorenz consider the facts of the case given by him to be "remarkable?" Now, on the one hand, the speech of parrots, even in his opinion, is not always idle chatter, but is often "the expression of definite and almost meaningful thinking processes." On the other hand, parrots, he writes, are capable of "making various movements designed to attain an objective the bird desires, without learning anything else; that is, such movements that have the explicit goal of influencing the human keeper to act in a specific way." Why, then, do they never make use of their speech, which is after all a kind of movement too, to convince their keeper to act in a certain way? This certainly does sound dubious. But the entire enigmatic complexion of such a position can be understood only when one is able to survey the speech of parrots over its rise to Lorenz's boundary. This ascent can be separated into four stages.

In the simplest case, the "speaking" of parrots is nothing more than plain mimickry. They have the ability to learn sounds, noises, and human words and sentences; and, with the aid of the syrinx, tongue, and bill, to reproduce them with wonderful accuracy. They amuse themselves in this way for hours; they prattle mindlessly and mix everything up.

The second stage is that of association. The mimicking of sounds is connected with visual or acoustical impressions of the situation in which the pertinent sound was heard, in such a way that the repetition of the situation will act as a "releaser" of the reproduction of the imprinted sound. In other words, mimicry is a signal of the repetition of the situation. Any respectable Grey Parrot has learned to say *come in* when someone knocks at the door—but that is nothing. A young one I raised, when asked the question, Jocko, what are you?, learned to answer, *I am a Grey Parrot*. And to the question, What is your name? he replied, *Psittacus erithacus*. This produced a very comical effect, because he pronounced the *Ps* with an open bill, which is for us is an impossibility. When he was discharging his feces, he groaned, *Push, push*, which had been repeated to him without thought in the same situation; and when he was finished he said, *Sooo!*

The third stage is considerably more advanced. Parrots, like all intelligent creatures, possess the gift of abstraction, that is, the ability to recognize what is fundamental and mutual about a "class" of similar things or processes, so as to form a "concept" for the class, to fix this in mind, and to employ it associatively. Such an abstract, generalized impression of class often appears in the speech of parrots, in that a sound signal that was heard during a previous encounter with an instance of the class in question is associated with it. In this way an amazon parrot mentioned by Grzimek (1951), based on apparently re-

130

Greys, like other parrots, can learn to associate sights and sounds with situations. With proper training, the raised finger here could initiate a specific behavior.

liable personal communication, called all youngsters, both large and small, boys and girls, even though he was able to designate them singly as Gregor, which was the name of the first child he met. My jocko understood the concept of fluidity and announced the presence of a liquid, whether it was water, tea, soup, or something else, with a splashing noise that he apparently knew from the washbasin. The same Grey Parrot (like another that belonged to my sister also did, independently of him) designated everything that was made of glass, even a bottle of ink, with the sharp ringing sound that is produced when one strikes a glass container with a hard object. And parrots are capable of making even finer abstractions with appropriate verbal designations. A jocko owned by Fr. von Lucanus (1923) frequently said a short *So!* in human fashion whenever any task was completed in his presence, such as closing the cage door, placing a lamp on a table, or lighting a cigar.

By far the most significant stage for us is the fourth, the stage of anticipation. In the previously mentioned stages, the things or events that were designated with their particular or generally conceptualized sound signal were always at hand when the signal was given: a glass, a child, a spoken word, and so forth. Their visual or acoustical stimulus prompted the release of the associated verbal signal. But now the content of parrot speech ascends from the perceived to the "imagined," from the present to the future.

It has long been known—and Grzimek (1951) mentions a number of credible cases—that parrots which are good talkers have the ability to produce the sound signal, which is used to designate an event, thing, or class, ahead of time, when the external object in question is not yet present but is expected to appear soon. The parrot Lora said *adieu* when von Lucanus left the room; but often it also said it when he picked up his hat, put on his coat, or locked the desk drawer. It therefore anticipated the expected departure and announced it with the associated sound signal.

When we came home late in the evening, my wife occasionally took a liqueur bottle from a small cabinet, the door of which had squeaked at one time, and poured out two glasses. Jocko described this whole process using a series of appropriate sound signals, but before they actually took place. Before my wife went to the small cabinet he squeaked, then gave an accurate rendition of clinking glass; next, the sound of a cork being pulled out, and finally the rising *glug glug glug glug glug,* which he always used to announce the pouring of a liquid from a bottle. It appeared as if he invited us to do this, as if he wanted

Out in the garden, this Grey Parrot prefers to perch in an apple tree.

133

us to complete the event he had signalled, and used his speaking ability to bring this about.

But we have absolutely no right to make such an interpretation, which would of course pass far beyond the limit proposed by Lorenz. Why should it be of any interest to the jocko whether or not we drank any liqueur, since he did not get any? And why was it any concern of Lora that von Lucanus should leave the room? On the contrary, that was certainly not desired by the bird. The production of these verbal signals still possesses the character of "intentless playfulness," as Lorenz calls it, and still lies below Lorenz's boundary.

What we can claim and must claim with certainty is that there exists in the brain of the bird an ordered series of images of situations (the "affective-group series" of zur Strassen, 1908) which have been developed from previous experience. Each of these images, or only some of them, are connected with a sound signal, and the whole series is set into action as soon as the initial one is released. The bird reacts to one of these purely internally-recalled stimulus states, often only the last one of the series, with the sound signal appropriate to it, just as it would to the external, sensed series. In this way, the considerable extension of the basic neural mechanism of parrot speech here proposed (which is indubitably actual as well) leads directly to Lorenz's boundary itself. A tiny fifth step would have to pass beyond it. It would require only the replacement of "anticipated" with "desired": the anticipation of a situation from a series that in past experience had proved beneficial and useful. But this in itself is by no means something new. The ability to learn "various movements" that would influence the human keeper to perform a specific act, something desired by the bird, is, according to Lorenz, within the capabilities of parrots! Shall they never then be capable of using the product of their organized vocalizations in place of the "movements" associated with the desired goal situation? This would be not only "remarkable" but, almost absurd. Nevertheless, Lorenz believes he must accept it. He is not personally familiar with any cases involving expedient parrot speech. And apparently he does not recognize what was reported on this subject in the older literature as being sufficiently substantiated— and he is certainly justified in taking this position in most cases. (Among these reports are the wonderful stories which could formerly be read in Brehm but which have been removed from the fourth edition.) For this reason, when I attempt to prove the opposing view in the following, I will depend exclusively on observations of my own Grey Parrots, over which I have had control from their youth onward.

In my opinion, expedient speech occurs, for example, when Jocko, who learned early to say *zwieback* when he was given a piece of zwieback (buttered on both sides), and in later years unfailingly warbled and repeated the word *zwieback* as soon as he saw the well-liked treat, even from far away, during which he hopped excitedly from foot to foot and pressed against the bars of the cage. But if some fruit was lying on the table, he never begged by saying *Zwieback,* but with *Orange, please,* instead.

I must admit that in the cases just mentioned the object toward which the desired process was directed (the zwieback, the fruit) was always in view. But at times the situation was not so simple. When our Jocko was alone in the room and bored, or thought it was now time to set the table, then he would loudly call out, *Come in!*—without of course having heard a knock—until someone came. Frequently, however, he knocked first himself, which he accomplished in two distinct ways: with his vocal apparatus or by knocking on his perch with his bill. Before Jocko had learned the particular requests for fruit and zwieback, he had been taught to say *please, please* when he wanted a treat; and continued to do this when the table was set, but only when neither fruit nor zwieback could be seen. But on one occasion he used this nonspecific need signal for a very specific goal. I quote from the notebook concerning Jocko kept by my wife: "March 23, 1928. This evening, long after dinner, he answered everything I said to him with only a persistent *please, please.* When I finally went to him, I saw that his tea dish was empty and that he apparently was very thirsty. When I gave him some tea, he drank greedily. Afterwards, he said all kinds of things." In short, I must believe that the boundary into expedient parrot speech has actually been crossed.

Now, purely from the point of view of animal psychology, there is not too much difference if parrot speech is nearly or is actually meaningful, that is, expedient. In another light, however, the ecologicophyletic, this question has a fundamental significance. Lorenz was quite aware of the uncertainty that arises in this context. But he stands perplexed, apart from it, on this side of his boundary. He writes: "The extremely complicated apparatus of syrinx and brain that makes mimicking and the association of thoughts possible does not seem to us to have any understandable function to further perpetuate the species. One asks in vain why it is there." In these lines one senses all the anguish of a scientist searching for clarity and parsimony, who at a decisive point hits a barrier which he believes impossible to overcome. The existing complicated mechanisms are under-

135

With Grey Parrots, ruffled
neck feathers basically
purport to intimidate.

stood only in a parsimonious—that is, mechanistic—way: if they are useful. Otherwise, the disturbing alternative of vitalism, of goal-seeking development, enters in!

We get a completely different picture from the other side of the boundary. If the speech of parrots in its fifth and highest stage is expedient—that is, is useful—then in one blow it becomes likely on principle that the neural mechanisms and such necessary for its execution have been produced in the struggle for existence. Of course, the relationship to people or to human speech, for that matter, does not play the slightest role in this matter. A species-specific utility must come into play within the species, in the lives of pairs or in the flock as a community. And this must be true not only of the fifth stage, which, from the point of view of people, is the only expedient one, but also of the four stages that precede it, which appear to us to be intentless playing, a kind of "wasted motion," even though they are physiologically and phylogenetically preliminary to the fifth stage. Parrots, and especially the Grey Parrot, must possess a highly developed and multifarious acoustical communication system that, at least in part, is not only instinctive but is also based on mimicking, association, abstraction, and anticipation of "desired" goals—all of which is made possible by a complex mechanism, the presence of which is shown us only by the speech accomplishments of parrots in captivity. If this is too much for someone to come to terms with, then let him instead look for answers in vitalism and goal seeking. There is no other choice.

One has, of course, so far heard nothing of such conversations between free-living Greys and other parrots. They appear only to screech and shriek at each other, and little can be made of this. But consider how little their behavior in the wild has actually been studied! It was not so long ago that we heard only croaking and quacking from the corvids, ducks, and geese too, until K. Lorenz came and learned to understand and speak their language, as with the goose Martina.

From these and other experiences and observations it is now possible to assert that Grey Parrots, and possibly other large parrots, possess not only the ability of mimicking by association (connecting conceptual contents) but also that of anticipation (gift of foresight).

Nonverbal mimicking. Frau Ragotzi, who is known to many bird fanciers, writes as follows:

138

Otto zur Strassen points out that the mimicking ability of the Grey Parrot must have an adaptive significance. In this content, it is interesting that the two subspecies do not seem to exhibit differences in learning ability. These Greys belong to the timneh *subspecies.*

When I was a school girl, I had the opportunity to observe the behavior of a Grey Parrot over many years. He not only imitated the voices of the individual family members with incredible clarity, but also imitated movements. For example, he imitated the sweet-toothed cook, who swallowed liquids with her neck stretched in the air. *Tastes good, tastes good,* he would say, when he had brought his stretched neck back to its normal position.

The author has personally seen numerous Grey Parrots that rocked their upper bodies back and forth in time to music, just as their owner was doing in front of the cage.

In this same category belongs the practice of placing the hand to the hat, military fashion, when departing. The result of this was that the Grey Parrot later lifted his foot to his head, nodded slightly, and then said either *good morning* or *adieu.* The author maintains that there is no better proof that parrots can also to a limited extent perform imitative movements.

Another Grey Parrot knocks on the bars of his cage and then says, *Come in!* The bird must have seen someone knocking at some time, because this is a repetition of a sound in conjunction with a movement.

Bird-keepers' reports. Publications usually stimulate new discussions and arguments among fanciers, so that a large number of reports soon appear in response to the initial one. But they can also be absent for years. This was the case in *Die Gefiederte Welt* between 1962 and 1972. During these ten years only two articles about Grey Parrots appeared. Even in 1962 a fancier complained that there was almost no literature on parrots. In the mean time, much has changed, but even so, there has been no monograph on the Grey Parrot since 1909.

This chapter was conceived primarily as a forum for many Grey Parrot owners, to make clear on a broader basis just what kinds of experiences it is possible to have with these parrots. In this way, the knowledge and experiences of a large number of Grey Parrot fanciers from a period of time covering approximately 100 years will be presented to the reader. It is possible to sometimes think that this or that bird keeper has exaggerated, but even if this were so, there are still many others who

An adult specimen
of the nominate
subspecies, P. erithacus
erithacus.

have experienced something similar. For now, we will concentrate on mimicking:

My wife bought a young jocko in July. This bird was even given to us on a trail basis, and thus we noted that she was teachable and could already whistle and talk a little. When we arrived home in Kiel, the lovely bird easily became accustomed to her new home and surroundings. As soon as she felt comfortable in her cage, the next morning she started to cluck like a hen, and as soon as she saw the breakfast on the table, she called, *Bake, bake cake*, and *Give, give parrot.* Then she said, *Come, Lora, come—scratch my little head—one, two, three, hurrah!* When someone knocked, she let loose with a hearty *Come in!* We were certainly surprised that the bird seemed to have an understanding of everything she said. We spent a lot of time with her, and she learned the following expressions in a very short time, sometimes in one day: *Major, what are you doing? Do you have money, you old Swede?* If we answered with a no, then she called out, so quickly that she sometimes got tongue-tied, *That doesn't suit me.* She quickly learned to distinguish between the dogs, calling them by their right names, as soon as they came near her. She loves to play tricks on them, so she speedily learned to employ the pertinent phrase: *Karo* (or *Penny*), *sit up!* While saying this, she stamped her foot and nodded her head [another nonverbal imitation—*Author*]. At times, to the great pleasure of Rosa—that is what we call her—the little dog obeys her commands. A barber, who came to our house every day and who took a great interest in the parrot, always knocked on the door, and the bird always cried, *Come in!* The barber then walked up to the cage, made a deep bow, and saluted with his hand. In a very short time, the clever animal had learned to do this: she lifted a foot up to her head and made a deep bow while she was saying *good morning.* As soon as Rosa noticed that the barber was done cutting hair, she again made a deep bow and said, *Adieu.* She does this with almost every person when she notices they want to leave the room. Even when we go out late in the evening for entertainment and the jocko is already sitting dreamily, a tender *adieu* follows us out the door.

This owner also provides another report [about a different bird—*Ed.*]:

In the beginning he used to speak only when he could see no one in the room; but after a short time, he chattered without taking any

Parrot "kisses," founded no doubt in courtship feeding, demonstrate the bird's devotion to its owner.

notice of his surroundings, laughed along with us in the heartiest tone, and today only the slightest stimulus is needed to set him off. If someone whistles softly for the dogs, he immediately calls out, *Karo, where is Karo?* and follows with a whistle of his own. His whistling shows the highest artistic skill; he whistles the most diverse melodies in the correct rhythm. He mimics the barking of a dog and the meowing of a cat so well that visiting strangers search for the source of these sounds everywhere but in the parrot's cage. At the ringing of the dinner bell, he continually cries out, *Katti,* ever more loudly, until the summoned one appears. In the same way, he answers any knocking on the door with the call *Come in,* but only rarely is he fooled when someone tries to wheedle a reply out of him by knocking on something in the room.

When a bottle is being uncorked in his presence, long before the cork pops out of the bottle, he sounds such an accurate *sook* that the person uncorking the bottle moves his head to the side to avoid being hit by the cork, which actually pops out somewhat later. He frequently mentions his own name during his conversations, particularly at the start. He might say: *Little Jockie, good Jockie, give me your little head, let me scratch your little head, you good, good Jockie;* this is said in the softest, tenderest tone, just as if he were a person who took great pleasure in self-flattery.

In a powerful masculine voice his call rings out: *Wake, the prince makes haste!*—and after this the mandatory drumming: *Tra, ta, tata, tra, ta, tata!,* which he either vocalizes or sounds by tapping on the cage with his bill. *One, two, three, boy,* he sometimes shouts in a soft, at other times gruff, tone of voice, which he learned by eavesdropping.

If he makes a mistake while counting or if he says a word unclearly, then he practices until it can be heard clearly and correctly. In the most varying tones, first pleading, finally scolding, three to four times he repeats, *Johann Schnaps, Johann Schnaps!,* until finally he supplies the reply *Yes, yes, yes, yes,* himself, if he does not first hear it from another source.

When the green parrot kept near him annoys him with his screeching or if it is too noisy around him, he immediately uses the silencing call *Pst! Wait, wait, you!* If this has no effect, then he repeats it more emphatically. He quickly made friends with Frau Kastner, even though he did not like her at first, and often called to her in the most loving tone of voice: *Marie, good woman—where is the good, good woman?* If she then appeared outside his enclosure, or

144

In general, Grey Parrots are considered to be less steady in temperament than amazons, such as the Double Yellow-head.

only answered him, then he would add *Pussi, pussi* to his usual sentence. After ten at night he falls deep in conversation with himself, which usually ends with the wish *Good night, good night, Jockie.* And when his cage is covered by Frau Kastner, he repeats *pussi* a few times in thanks from under the cover.

His devotion to his master is placed above everything else. Herr Kastner is favored above all others; he can stick his hand in the cage and his fingers are only carefully chewed and licked. When the cage door is opened, Jocko immediately flies to his hand, climbs to his shoulder, and manages to crawl between his coat and chest and, as soon as he has a firm perch, pushes his head in the armpit, where he gladly stays as long as possible.

To the question, For what price would you sell me your Jocko?, I should answer: What your house is to you, Jocko is to me. Let each of us keep what is ours.

In the next lines many imitated phrases are recounted as examples.

Accordingly, I will allow myself to describe to you the quite considerable but apparently still incomplete enumeration of the phrases my jocko knows, which the reader is already to some extent acquainted with. This bird has since added a considerable number of new phrases to the ones I told you about previously, so that he will still have exceeded almost all others of his species in this regard, even if I myself have forgotten some of what he knows.

Here are some of the individual names he knows: *Mama, Papa, Grandmama, Grandpapa, Bertha, Gustel, Rose, Marie, Heinrich, Jocko, Jockie, Rappo,* and *Kitschel* in place of kitten. He frequently combines complete phrases in the most comical ways. I now wish to list at least the most important of these: *Sorrow, oh what sorrow, we must fast tomorrow. Hansemann has trousers on! One, two, three, hurrah! Adieu, Papa, come back soon! What do you want? What's your name? You shouldn't peep like that!* (Unfortunately, he once heard a door squeak, and makes that sound from time to time.) *Please, please, Papa, a plum! Give me a kiss! Do you want a drink of water? Now drink some water! Will you be good? Go to your room! I'm coming with the stick! Stupid fellow! You're a foolish fellow! Come out of that cage! Come here, Papa, come to your Jockie!* He also says *come in* when some one knocks on the door. If I had mentioned even a fraction of his frequently comical combinations, then the list would be who knows how long. So, for example: *Mama, tell me, what does Papa want? Grandmama, will you be good now? I'm right behind you with the stick! Jocko, please call Kitschel!* He laughs, coughs, clears his throat, barks, squeals like a dog that's been stepped on, and even makes the sound of clapping hands. Shortly after hearing any noise, whether pleasant or not, he tries to mimic it, so that we cannot be too careful in keeping him from hearing unpleasant noises. Since he is still young (he is, after all, only three years old), his vocabulary is certainly not yet complete, and he will certainly learn to say much more. At the moment, even while I am writing, he is saying *Rappo come here! Now drink some water, you stupid fellow, you!*

His most appealing quality is his almost unbelievable tenderness toward me; his affection is so great that he sometimes tries to feed me from his crop. Unfortunately, I do not appreciate his acts of affection, since he pulls my hair, chews on my ears, etc. Since he does not have

146

A tame Grey Parrot playing with a piece of rawhide. The unusual position is
learned, of course, since parrots naturally spend all their time on their feet.

the slightest idea that this hurts, he is frequently careless, at least when it comes to pulling my hair. In my hand, he allows me to scratch him like a glove, without showing any signs of resistance. On the command Play dead!, he lies on his back in the palm of my hand for quite a long time. I now can close, assured that I have not told too much, but too little.

In another report, the bird did not start talking much until eight months had passed. What the following Grey Parrot is capable of is astounding.

The process of taming proceeded very slowly at first. He refused to give up his blood-curdling shrieking despite all our cajoling, until I finally set him down on the railing of a lawn chair. Here he had no support and could not move forwards or backwards, and after a few days he had progressed so far that he perched on the hand placed in front of him, allowed himself to be carried around, and even allowed himself to be stroked and scratched on the head. The shrieking also ceased. I mention all these particulars at this time, because often most of the mistakes are already made during the taming process, since few possess the patience and perseverance to tame and rear any bird, much less a Grey Parrot. With some people, the bird is expected to be able to imitate everything on the first day. If not, then they immediately conclude that the fellow is a dolt, capable of nothing but screeching. It is without a doubt more convenient to buy an already tame parrot, but how much it will learn to speak is another question.

My Jocko proves how little one can afford to lose patience. I had to wait for eight months before he said his first word, *Jocko.* However, my wife, who has more time to spend with him, and I were richly rewarded for our effort, because then something new came almost every day. Today, four years later, he knows so much that it would be impossible for me to mention everything he says in a day. There is almost no phrase used in daily conversation he does not know, and he has learned everything well, particularly in respect to the correct use of words. My wife engages in a kind of dialogue with him almost the entire day. To mention just one of the many things he is capable of, he greets all the people and animals in the house by their correct names: *Darling Marie—are you there? That's wonderful! Where's my Emily? O my darling, wonderful Emily! Nero, go over there! Marquise, your master is coming!* (These are the names of two dogs.) *Yes, yes, Marquise, you can come along!* To the two cats he says, *Peter! Ivanoff! March on out, you pack of rats!*, or *Petie, pst! pst!* He whis-

The Grey Parrot listens attentively while its master whistles.

The extent to which a Grey Parrot will become tame varies among individuals.

tles and calls both dogs and cats with equal skill. If my Blackcap or Blackbird make their *tak-tak* calls, then there immediately follows *Pst! Wait, Blackcap!* or *Wait, Witch* (this is the name of the Blackbird), *be quiet! Wait, I'm coming! Wait, you're gonna get it!* And he never mixes up their names, for he knows quite well which bird he is calling. He also recognizes his *Hanserle* ('canary'), his *Rotkehle* ('European Robin'), and his *Papageile* ('Budgerigar'), and calls to them.

He frequently repeats the following verse four to six times, one after another, without making any mistakes:

> *With the arrow, and the bow,*
> *Over mountain, hill, and dale,*
> *Comes the marksman we all know,*
> *Early in the light yet pale.*

And this too:

> *A girl who's filled with love,*
> *Papageno wants to see,*
> *Yes, such a gentle dove,*
> *Would be truly bliss for me!*

If he makes no mistakes, he then praises himself: *So, my darling, good Paperle, my bijou! That's right! Sing one more time!* Then he sings it again. But if he does make a mistake, he laughs and says, *That's not right! Stupid fellow!* He of course knows how to use greetings too: *God be with you! Adieu, farewell! Good morning! Good night, sleep well!* He calls out greetings even to strangers. But it is really remarkable when he sees that my wife or I want to go out, and he says, *Adieu, darling Marie! Farewell! Give me a kiss!*, or *Adieu, Papa! Farewell! Come back soon!* When he sees us coming, though we are still far away, he calls out, *God be with you! Is that really you? How are you?* If he notices that the coffee is being served, he promptly says, *Do you have coffee cake? Should I get you some cake?* Besides all this, he also plays hide-and-seek, saying, *Look, look, there, there,* and knocks on his cage and calls, *Come in.*

I could mention a great deal more, such as how he counts to eight while doing his gymnastics, gnawing on wood, or bathing. The last, bathing, is a passion of his. He will not keep still but continually begs, *Want a bath? Paperle wants a bath,* until he has been thoroughly scrubbed with a toothbrush, after which, as a rule, he voluntarily takes another bath in his drinking dish.

While most Greys will eventually perch on a hand, few will be prepared to lie on their backs.

What follows is an exceptionally detailed article about taming and mimicking. The bird's owner observed even the smallest details, omitting virtually nothing that is important on these topics. Time and again, bird keepers prove how much Grey Parrots can differ from one another. The way a bird develops is certainly determined to a great extent by the owner. But the development of an exceptional animal also requires luck, since Grey Parrots do not all have the same amount of talent.

There are jockos that can very easily learn to imitate all kinds of noises, tones, and sounds; that can quickly learn to whistle the most beautiful melodies; and that can accurately learn to imitate laughing, crying, coughing, clearing the throat, sneezing, barking, crowing, and other things of this sort; but which cannot seem to learn human speech, and barely have the ability, after years of trying, to learn to say a few words, even when they can say these with the greatest of clarity and accuracy. I once owned such a jocko, who could immediately mimic everything he heard with surprising accuracy, but could not learn a single word, even after months of trying. The only word he knew was one taught him by his previous owner. So he could say only a single word: *Lora*. On the other hand, he could accurately imitate a scale run on a piano or the splashing of water as when washing. He did not change, even though I expended a considerable amount of effort over a period of three months, trying to teach him a new word. The bird must have been over three years old.

Any newly imported jocko—even if he acts quite wild in the beginning—sooner or later, even if only after many months, will become ever more confiding and loving toward his master, given proper, considerate treatment. Soon he will even demand to be given attention; he will indicate this by climbing on the cage wire and turning his head this way and that to try to catch the master's attention whenever he enters the room. One can clearly see that he would like a caress but does not yet have the courage to stand still for one. Once the situation has progressed to this point, one can risk an attempt to touch the bill or even the head of the animal with a finger. After this, the next step is to stroke his head a little with one or two fingers, during which one should continually speak soothing words, particularly those that he can already say. I have also made the observation that jockos that have reached this stage in the taming process are more confiding in the evening and allow themselves then to be petted even more readily than during the day, so that it is frequently possible to scratch around

*Allowing a parrot
outside its cage helps it
to accept people
into its living space.*

on his head, and even to take the head completely in the hand, without meeting with any resistance. All of these attempts should only be done through the cage wire (in a parrot cage, there should always be ample room between the bars to allow the entry of the hand flat or at least to permit a few fingers to comfortably fit in). One should never stick the whole arm into the cage through the door to reach for the bird. Once he has become accustomed to being touched through the bars of the cage for some time, one can then, when it is particularly quiet in the room, attempt to open the door of the cage and let him move around outside. It is usual for the bird to be quite distrustful at first, and it often takes several hours until he decides to leave the cage and climb to its roof, which in properly built cages should be flat. Before long, he will go in and out, and will wait with impatience for the moment when the cage door is opened. Outside the cage the bird should be touched in the same way as inside. Later, one should train the parrot to climb on the fingers of several different people; in this way, the parrot will become gentle and confiding to the highest degree. Similarly, the jocko should be given instruction and spoken to even when strangers are in the room. In this way, the jocko will talk not only when left alone but will also exhibit his accomplishments in front of strangers.

It is also advisable to spray a Grey Parrot with tepid water from time to time. During the winter this should be done carefully, in a well-heated room. Spraying should not be attempted until the Grey Parrot has been in one's care for at least six months. One should never leave him for long periods of time without something to occupy his attention; the parrot should frequently be given small pieces of soft wood to chew on, or else he will direct his considerable passion for gnawing toward his own plumage. The jocko should be introduced to this occupation during the first days after his arrival. Finally, it is never advisable to keep several jockos in the same or in adjacent rooms, because their mutual calling will draw their attention away from other, more important purposes, and they will never lose their natural tendency to shriek and screech.

One should begin instruction as soon as possible. A talented bird hardly needs instruction; he learns, as it were, everything on his own. In the beginning, one should stand in front of the parrot's cage and speak any simple word clearly, particularly in the mornings and evenings; but always make sure the student behaves calmly in the cage and directs his attention toward his teacher during this time. If the bird is restless in any way, then it is advisable not to try to teach him, for the effort would be wasted. It is striking how much variation there is in the amount of time it takes for a jocko to begin to repeat his first word; a short period of time should by no means be construed as any indication that the bird is especially talented. There are Grey Parrots that required a very long time—yes, even months, to the dismay of their teacher—before they began to repeat their first words, but then they learned ever more quickly. Such birds often learn in the shortest time what they hear only once or twice. These birds, which at first are thought to be talentless, develop into very teachable students, once they have learned their first word after a considerable amount of time and effort. On the other hand, it is usually axiomatic that a jocko that quickly, often after three days of instruction or even sooner, begins to say his first words, is a very talented animal and will later be able to perform real marvels.

Apart from the varying abilities of individual birds, other factors appear to be involved as well, such as the bird's well-being, the care it receives, the degree of tameness, and the method of instruction, as well as certain external conditions that often escape us but do affect the bird. Sometimes too, once the first period of instruction has been completed and the jocko has said his first words, then the distinct fact remains that, instead of now learning quickly, he still requires many weeks until he learns a new word. Thus in the education of such a bird, there will be a point which may require a shorter or longer time to reach, at which he will again attempt to repeat what he hears. Another point in his education will be defined by the limit of his retentive capacity. A jocko may be unable to recite every item he once learned, even though he frequently hears it repeated. He also may say something already learned, especially if he has not heard it for a long time and he has a special predilection to constantly repeat the newest things. In this respect, there also are otherwise very teachable jockos that remember a very small repertoire of words and sentences at any one time, because they forget what they had learned just as quickly as they learn something new. But there are also birds that have a large repertoire of words and sentences at any given time and also retain what they have learned for a very long time; and since they learn quickly, they must as a result have a very extensive amount of knowledge.

In addition to the speed of learning and the extent of his retentive capacity, the greater or lesser degree of clarity of a jocko's speech is also an important consideration. The jocko is clearly superior to all other talking parrots in that he can most accurately and deceptively

Above: A Grey Parrot of the timneh race. **Facing page, above:** *Grey Parrots relish gnawing on wood, fresh or decaying. Spruce and fir twigs are important for maintaining good feather condition. This bird belongs to the nominate race.* **Below:** *A king jocko, a variant which is extremely rare. Besides the belly, this bird also has reddish feathers on its back.*

mimic human speech—and not only human speech in general, for he can also accurately mimic the speech of individuals.

In this regard, there are birds that can speak with a greater or lesser degree of clarity, that can mimic clearly and cleanly, and also those that have nasal, screeching, or hoarse vocal apparatus. On the other hand, speaking requires extensive practice, and every jocko expresses his first words so unclearly that they are recognizable only if one knows ahead of time what the bird is supposed to be saying. But the more he practices a word, the clearer it will sound, until he can finally say it so that anyone can easily understand what is being said, if the bird has an otherwise good apparatus. The further a jocko progresses in his learning, the more quickly the initially unclear sounds will be formed into clear speech, until he will eventually be able to speak a word clearly after only a few attempts. But one also finds birds that retain a hoarse, nasal tone even after long practice, just as there are, to a lesser extent, birds that can speak some words clearly but others not so well. Always take special care to speak the last syllables of words distinctly and forcefully.

At this point I must mention a peculiarity of some parrots. It is quite common for an otherwise very teachable jocko not to be able to learn a word or sentence that is repeated to him every day, yet in the meantime he mimics words and sentences he has heard accidentally and that we have no intention of teaching him. On the other hand, the jocko seems to retain certain words in his memory extremely well, which he practices and repeats with passion. He will always say *good morning* in the morning if one has spoken these words to him only at that time of day. Similarly, he will call out *adieu* at departures, whenever he sees his master with hat and walking stick, if *adieu* has always been repeated to him in this situation. This ability of the jocko to employ words and sentences appropriate to the time and situation elevates the value of the animal immeasurably and truly makes him a participant and conversational companion. One should always make the effort to teach a jocko to speak only in the first or third, and never in the second, person. Never say, "Do you want coffee, Jocko?," but "Jocko wants coffee," which makes an effect when the coffee is presented.

Besides the ability to mimic the human voice and speech, the jocko also possesses the ability to accurately mimic all kinds of noises, sounds, and tones, even those that have a metallic sound; he mimics the meowing of a cat just as well as the sound of a doorbell, the creaking of a door just as well as the rasping of a saw, the splashing of water just as well as coughing, sneezing, and laughing. For this reason one must always be careful not to expose a talented jocko to any vulgar words, because the bird is quite capable of saying something undesirable with great pleasure at any time and at any opportunity. Otherwise, one has no end of trouble in trying to break the habit, because there is no way of making the bird understand that he should not say something.

Once the iris of a Grey Parrot has reached its mature color, then there is little possibility of determining the bird's age. Only in very old birds are the feet very rough. Birds that are not kept singly mimic little or not at all.

The owner of the next bird needed a lot of patience to teach his parrot over 200 words in three years.

Right in the beginning I will mention the important fact that old and completely yellow-eyed birds, and not only young gray-eyed birds, can often accomplish every good and pleasant thing that can be expected from a jocko, if they are handled and cared for correctly. In this regard, I would like to share a particularly instructive and interesting case with you. Herr Neubauer of Radautz bought an old, yellow-eyed jocko from the owner of a traveling menagerie in Czernowitz. The age of the bird was given as fifteen years. Moreover, the bird was very wild. Neubauer gave him the company of an amazon parrot that could already speak a few words. Both parrots were soon so used to each other that they formed an inseparable pair. After a year, the Grey Parrot still could not speak a single word. Then the amazon had an accident and died shortly thereafter. Jocko was inconsolable for a time. Only after nine months did he start to repeat a few words, but he did so very seldom. After three years stay with Herr Neubauer, he finally began to diligently practice speaking, and today he speaks over 200 words, some in sentences, some alone, and in three languages even: German, Polish, and French. I had the opportunity to see the bird and was impressed with his tameness and teachability. But he perches only on the finger of his owner, because he is the person who spends by far the most time with him. This old parrot became a good companion after all, even if it did take a long time.

Older birds always need much more time than younger ones before they get used to a new situation. This is the reason why so many parrot fanciers try to purchase young birds. But, just as it is possible to find some old birds that eventually prove to be very talented and

159

Reared by hand, young Greys become accustomed to the animals of the household as well as to the people.

teachable, one also finds some younger parrots that are completely unteachable and incapable of ever accomplishing anything significant. Accordingly, every Grey Parrot is born with a certain amount of talent, and a talented bird will always satisfy his owner, even if he has straw yellow eyes when he is purchased; an untalented bird, on the other hand, will always be a bungler, even if he had dark eyes when he was first given instruction.

As was just mentioned, eye color is used to estimate the age of a jocko. A very young bird has dark ash gray eyes. But this color appears to be a lighter ash gray whenever the pupils are dilated, which always occurs when the amount of light is reduced—when, for example, the bird is moved from a window to a dark corner of the room or when he becomes irritated, in which case the bird dilates his pupils and then contracts them at will, an ability I have so far observed only in parrots. After six months the eyes become dove gray, and here too they are lighter when the pupils are dilated than when they are contracted. After a year they appear to be grayish yellow, particularly when the pupils are contracted; when they are dilated they look pale yellow.

This eye color is retained for about a year, until they take on their final straw yellow color at an age of about two to three years. A jocko with grayish yellow eyes is therefore still a young bird and is the most highly recommended because it no longer has such a delicate and sensitive nature as a very young, dark-eyed jocko.

It is always the young jockos that occupy the minds of fanciers:

On January 2, I obtained a jocko with ash gray eyes from Rotterdam. The bird was quite lively and completely healthy. With the greatest of ease he learned to whistle signals after a few days and mimicked all kinds of noises, particularly the creaking of a door and the splashing of water. But it was not possible to teach him a single word. Only after three months did he finally learn the word *jocko*. Though the bird was always very active during the day and hardly kept his beak still, he did not expend much effort in learning new words. A phrase like *give me a kiss* was said to him for many weeks without his making the slightest attempt to practice it. After I had repeated these four words to him continuously for almost two months, he finally began practicing them, but not in the way a talented bird usually does, by first practicing the word *give*, then *give me*, then *give me a,* and finally the complete *give me a kiss;* but instead by first making a screech that had the rhythm and stress of *give me a kiss,* but in which the words were finally formed slowly over a long period of time. For this reason he found it much easier to learn the sharply stressed words of a higher female voice than of a deeper male voice, which had no particular stress. Birds that are not especially talented try to comprehend a whole sentence as a noise of some kind, and the more accented the syllables in the sentence are, the easier this is for them to do. Thus even an untalented jocko will learn a name spoken by a high female voice more quickly, because the word will be given a sharply defined accent. For this same reason, an untalented bird will include a high percentage of names in its vocabulary. In contrast, the talented parrot always learns syllable-by-syllable and word-by-word; it is not necessary to make comprehension of the word easier by giving it unusual stress.

Some friends of mine had a Grey that could whistle for the poodle just like his master. He could do it so clearly that the poodle was fooled the first time he tried it. If someone as much as picked up a wine bottle, they were immediately greeted with the sound of a popping cork. Whoever picked up the phone did not only hear the turning of the dial and the *tut-tut* signal, but also *Hello, Oldenburg here; how are you?* and so on. This wonderful bird managed to get out of his cage without supervision one day, strolled over to some flowers in the window, and sampled the bulb of a plant that was poisonous. The bird became ill and had to suffer for months, because his liver was damaged—a tragic end.

The following passage in many respects reminded me of this Grey Parrot. This contribution also shows how close the friendship with other animals can be.

If the dog went out the gate and into the street while the bird was sitting in the garden, then he whistled to him or yelled, *Leo, will you come here!* He of course praised himself in no small measure; he was a brave little parrot, a good little parrot, but from time to time also a bad little parrot. If he was locked in and wanted to get out, he called to my wife, *Woman, good woman.* If he was not heard, then he called again louder: *Good woman; good, good woman;* or *Gustel, come now.* He would also creep into his box and say, *Look-look.*

His speech sounded deceptively human. Even I was sometimes fooled when he called me by my name, Theodor; I would answer, thinking it had been my wife. If he was spoken to in an interrogative tone, he would say, *Hm?*

His best friends were Peter, a Long-billed Corella that was a funny and extremely trusting fellow, and also Leo, a St Bernard, and Maunz, a half-breed Angora cat. He lived in a cage with Peter, ate from the same bowl, flew with him and the doves, burrowed with him in holes in the garden, and carried around small stones, just as he did. If Peter misbehaved or screeched, which was not too uncommon, Paperl whistled once piercingly, as I do, or said, *Peter, be good,* or he himself screeched and then whistled.

He often teased the dog and the cat, pulled their hair and nipped, but never in such a way that they took offense; on the other hand, he allowed himself to be licked, particularly by Leo, until he was quite damp. One of his greatest pleasures was bathing in wet grass. If it rained in the summer, he could not be kept in the room. While cooking was going on, he and Peter were always in the kitchen with my wife. For this purpose I had had a low stand built; this consisted of a board with a raised edge, in the middle of which was placed the food bowl.

In the evening at dinner the two parrots sat on their little stand on the table and ate. The cat sat next to them, and the dog laid his head on the table and waited, like the cat, for scraps. It was also quite comical when Paperl whistled after the chickens like my wife, and then would not be quiet until he was given a little piece of bread. He sat with this either on the window ledge or on the fence and dropped crumbs to the ground. The chickens running after the bread crumbs seemed to give him considerable pleasure. He could whistle quite well—no complete pieces, but a little from everything, which he put together at his own discretion.

The house is dead since he passed away, almost haunted, I might say. When his friend became sick, Peter did not eat for several days and became completely unbearable. This bird is as faithful as a dog. He also relishes, as was already mentioned above, his freedom, which last summer he exercised to the extent that he flew with farmers out to the fields. After that, I cut some of his feathers to prevent him from flying too far. Otherwise, he is very obedient, at least in regard to screeching. If this becomes annoying, then I only have to threaten him; he immediately shuts up. We also have a Blue-fronted Amazon, of which I do not have much to tell.

My wife does not ever want to have another Grey Parrot. She claims there are no others like her Paperl, and she is also afraid of the pain of another accident. I think that she will change her mind after a while, though.

In the following sentences the ability to discriminate between two different rings is recounted, and quite rightly it is noted that no thinking is employed.

When the doorbell rang and the maid soon after came into the room, one of my jockos asked, *Who's there?*, or *Who's outside?* He never did so when the telephone rang. He could therefore clearly distinguish between the two bells, and he never made a mistake. Naturally, he learned the questions from us and knew quite well that the maid was asked these questions only after the doorbell rang. This is a sign of high intelligence, but not a sign of reflective thinking.

The Grey Parrot in the following description must have been a genius of mimicking.

Our Jocko, whom I alone feed (we have had him for a number of years), is nice only to my husband; I am a matter of minor importance. He is a splendid talker, and above all he learns while playing. If we ring, he says, *Lina.* If he sees someone reaching for hat and gloves, then he says, *Adieu.* If the doorbell rings, he barks. When we pick up our little dog, he yelps just like the dog, since we sometimes squeeze him. No matter how late we come home at night, he always greets us. A few days ago he developed the bad habit of throwing his bowl to the floor; as soon as it is there, he yells, *Intolerable!* He has heard me say this a number of times. When we sit down at the table for lunch, he calls, *Little Jocko is hungry. Yes, the golden jocko is hungry!* He says: *Good morning, Papa. Good day, my little Jocko. Good evening. Good night, sleep well. Are you my little golden jocko?—yes, you are! Come, scratch my head. Give me a kiss. One, two, three, hurrah! Doctor Nixdorf.* He calls all of us by name. For quite a while he has been able to sing these words with great charm: *But I really only kissed you on your shoulder;* and *One, two, three, on the bench with me.* This singing can make you split your sides with laughter. A dealer heard him once, and thought he was an unusually talented bird. His vocabulary is certainly very large. For the last few days I have been taking care of my sister's green parrot, which she bought at the last exhibition. But what a difference. He sleeps, sits still, and eats. Once in a while during the day he says, *Lora, Lora,* but that is all. But in the meantime, our little jocko has learned *Where is our dear Lora, little Lora?* His only failing is that he is not completely tame. I can scratch his head, and when he comes out of his cage I can hold him, but only with some effort. On the other hand, he loves my husband, gives him kisses, and is gentle with him. He mimics almost everything: barks, cries, laughs, and even the chirping of the canary.

The next good mimic started to say his first word very timidly after only three months. After another three months the next words came, and then the talking escalated.

Finally, after three months, we heard one morning, from under the cover, a quiet *jocko, jocko.* He spoke the word as clearly as a person. For a long time he spoke only this single word. After another three months had passed, to our not inconsiderable joy we heard him say, *Jocko comes from Africa; Good morning, Papa, good Papa, come in;* and much more, at first indistinctly, but then with increasing clarity. Now the parrot speaks very many words and has learned some that were not intentionally spoken to him; to our delight, he usually uses these in the appropriate situation. When my husband walks into the living room in the morning, he calls out to our maid, *Auguste, is the coffee ready? Then bring it right in!* Our maid, who has to listen to his speech practice, which he undertakes in the morning under the cover, as she is cleaning the room, is apparently not edified by this performance and yells at him, "Oh, boloney, boloney!" Recently my husband had new aquaintances over and, as the men argued over current politics, Jocko called out his *Oh, boloney, boloney!* in between.

In the evening, Jocko has permission to pay us a short visit at table. He enjoys making use of this opportunity, for he takes a big swig from my husband's glass and tosses, as if to express his thanks, a piece of sugar from the sugar bowl into the glass, and finally retreats back to his cage with a shelled walnut, which he takes from the bag by himself. Jocko puts on a funny performance if a small mirror is placed on the table as soon as he arrives. He bows low in front of the mirror and says, *Scratch my head,* then holds his head out to the supposed comrade. When he notices that his flattery is getting him nowhere, then he tries again by striking with his bill. He calls Nero, our St. Bernard, by name, mimicking the voice of my husband so convincingly that the dog immediately obeys the order.

We had a Blue-fronted Amazon, but, despite the fact that she spoke a great deal, we had to get rid of her on account of her continual screeching. When Lora was scolded for this bad habit, Jocko supported me and yelled, *Do you have to screech? Wait, wait, should I cover you?* If he now gets a little noisy, I have only to say, "But, Jocko," and he answers right away, *Do you have to screech? Wait, wait!*

Shortly before 1900, Dr. Karl Russ reported on two Grey Parrots that enjoyed mimicking. No one would suppose that Dr. Russ, who is so well known in ornithological circles, had exaggerated. At this time, not many people were aware of the great mimicking ability of Grey Parrots.

The honored reader will perhaps wonder why a subject that has already been discussed in this place is being taken up again. Nevertheless, I believe that, on the one hand, this report concerning a very talented speaking bird will be of interest to every nature lover; on the other hand, I have a special motive for making such instances known. Observations about talking birds that have lately been made known

165

to me and other bird fanciers prove that this ability of birds is underestimated in many circles. At the last *Ornis* exhibition a newspaper reporter asked me, "Can you tell me, just between the two of us, can a bird really speak clearly? I have never heard one that could!" I have to admit that this left me speechless at first.

Even more questionable to me is the opinion of a famous zoologist whom I heard many years ago. This man of learning spoke before an auditorium full of people and discussed in a very ironical tone, among other topics, the Grey Parrot and its ability to mimic human speech. He claimed that such a bird could actually learn to speak very little, that it could sometimes employ what it had learned in the appropriate situation and sometimes not, and that it would sometimes learn what the owner wanted to hear and sometimes what the owner did not want to hear. In closing, he mentioned that he had once owned a Grey Parrot himself and had found that its vocabulary would never exceed a certain number of words—thirty, for example; if it learned more, then the bird would forget some of the words it had learned before.

But what do the majority of fanciers, and highly experienced parrot fanciers in particular, have to say on this subject? Have we not had before us over the years dozens of examples of parrots that already knew over one hundred words and continually added to this total? Often a bird has surprised its owner by saying words and sentences that it has not used for a long time, which is proof that it has not forgotten them. Additionally, talented parrots that already know a large number of sentences frequently can also whistle a number of songs and even sing them with words. In light of this, how can it be claimed that the memory of the bird is limited? This is just another example of what happens when the learned fraternity intentionally ignores the successes and practical experience of bird fanciers. Precisely for this reason, is it desirable to publish reports of talented parrots now and again. In the following, I wish to report on two such birds.

Dr. Heck, director of the Berlin Zoological Gardens, was so kind as to notify my father that Frau Councilor A. Buschius of that city owned two exquisite Grey Parrots, and the lady generously agreed to record the vocabularies of both birds and to give me the opportunity to hear them in person.

The first bird, named Jocko, can say the following: *Jocko wants to sleep—do we both want to sleep? Papa's going away, Jocko's staying home—adieu, dear Papa. Papa's going to sleep, Jocko too, good night, sleep well. Whose jocko are you?—I am Papa's good little Jocko—yes!*

Did you already say good morning?—Good morning! Jocko wants bread and butter. Jocko is hungry! Are you hungry? Come in! That's my beak—that's my little paw. Do you want down, you old Oswald? Rosa make coffee! What does the dog say?—*Uff, uff, uff!* Jocko, what's your name?—*One, two, hurrah! One, two, three, Jocko, parrot.* Now, how do the hounds bay?—*Wu-wu-wu-wu-wu!* Jocko sing!—*Tararaboomdeay, tararaboomdeay, tararaboom-boom-boom.* Jocko, do the wood auctioneer—and he does. Jocko, whistle in Italian—he whistles a sad melody. *Jocko wants something. Papa's going away, Jocko too! Papa? Papa's little Jocko, yes! Jocko, call the pigeons*—then he whistles like you do when you are calling pigeons. *Do we want to hit Jocko?—no! There he is, hahahahahahahaha! You old Oswald. In Friedenau, Anna, Marie, etc. Jocko, warble for me.*

The other parrot, named Little Jocko, says: *Little Jocko, say for me good morning! Little Jocko, say for me good evening! Are you my Little Jocko? Not true, my Little Jocko. One, two, three, hurrah! Oh so nice, how nice. Give me a kiss;* then he makes a loud kissing sound and says, *That would be nice. Little Jocko, do you have to yell so loud? Whistle loud! Little Jocko, call Leo for me. Leo, come here; Scherri, come here! Go outside, will you get down?—go outside, will you get down? You old fool. Jocko, what's your name? My darling, don't yell like that. You old fool. That's my beak, give me your paw, that's my paw. Little Jocko, who's there?* He whistles like the wood auctioneer. If you say, "Little Jocko, warble for me," then he warbles very nicely. *Do we want to hit Jocko? Give me a little kiss. So go ahead. Auguste!* If I call a messenger, he says, *Madam?* How does the pack go?—*Wu-wu-wu-wu-wu. Do you have to do that? Now, my Little Jocko? Now, a little kiss. You, you, you, you. Jocko, what's wrong. Little Jocko, call the pigeons for me;* then he whistles for the pigeons just like the other parrot. *One, two, three, Jocko, parrot. So, Little Jocko? Now, now, now, give me your hand. Forward march, will it be soon? Are you going to say that? Do we want to hit Jocko—No.* He laughs exactly as I do.

Any unbiased person will have to admit that examples of such talent are worthy of consideration and that by examining such reports even the learned fraternity could for once seriously address the question of how far the speaking talent of birds really goes.

An enthusiastic animal and bird fancier, who for many years did not want to have anything to do with parrots because she had been bitten twice by different parrots under unfortunate circumstances, later tried it again with a Grey Parrot. This bird gave her nothing but pleasure, because she chose her to be her favorite person. What follows is an excerpt from her report.

Lora knows not only the dogs, but also the birds by name. If, for example, the shama makes too much noise when a conversation is in progress, then the parrot immediately calls out, *Shama! Really, Shama!,* just as I do in this situation. But it is even more charming when I reach for the mealworm container. Since Lora knows from experience that the usually free-flying flycatcher will receive a portion on this occasion, she feels obligated to notify the little bird ahead of time. So as soon as she sees a mealworm or a fly in my hand, she turns her little head in all directions, and calls out in a clear voice, *Neppi, Neppi!* (a contraction for the apparently more difficult name Schneppi).

The parrot learns easily and effortlessly on her own and indeed can often learn a word spoken unusually loudly after hearing it only once, and can even do this with words that are not easy to say, such as *Kathrin, Fadentisch, aufgeplatzt,* and many others. But she is unwilling to learn words that are deliberately spoken to her. The only things that Lora has learned systematically are the questions asking what sounds the dog and the cat make and their appropriate answers, and the question, How big is the good Lora?, which she answers by raising up on her toes, spreading her wings, stretching her neck, and saying in the most admirable tone, *So-o-o big!*

On the other hand, for over a year I have said, "Good night, Mama" to her before she goes to sleep, but she has not learned it yet. But from time to time, when any stranger opens the door, she says, *Good night.* She also says *Good night* when they leave.

It is certainly a shame that I do not have the ability to whistle tunes for the bird, because she has such an interest in and such an ear for music that she sits as if bewitched and flaps her wings in pleasure when she hears a pleasant song; she immediately tries to whistle or sing any melody she hears, and usually it is only the last tones that she cannot repeat right away. She mimics all of the songs of birds that she hears; she can imitate the song of the thrush and the swallow with ease, and she does it so deceptively true to nature that one can only detect the difference of her coarser voice when one is standing right next to her.

One can sometimes find Grey Parrots that have red feathers in unusual places. For more than a hundred years these have been called king jockos, or king parrots. These unusual birds were much sought after at one time; they were even treated as a separate species. Fanciers have always paid high prices for these birds. The red coloration is also found in other species, such as the Plum-headed Parakeet and the Peach-faced Lovebird. These Grey Parrots have not been modified in any way; the red coloration does not disappear after the molt. Even today such parrots are found on the market, though very seldom. The red feathers can show up on the back, on the underparts, or on the wings. The king parrot mentioned in the following report must have been an excellent mimic despite his unusual coloration. This article first appeared many years ago, and it accords with the current wave of nostalgia.

For the last year or so I have owned a very talented king jocko that in all respects is an original of her species, an animal that is one in a thousand. This bird, which is a so-called king bird, has, besides her red tail, other red feathers on her body, particularly on the thighs, belly, and back. It will therefore be of interest if I mention something of the life of this king jocko. In the first place, I would like to note that the animal can distinguish clearly between a large number of people and animals; she knows the grandfather, the father, the mother, and the children (Babette, Frieda, Pepita, Auguste, Lorita, Lucia, Karl, Willi); Lehmann the mailman, the policeman, Karo and Hektor the St. Bernards, Fricka the dachshund, Musch-musch the cat, and many other individuals.

If anybody comes into the room early in the morning, the conversation starts immediately, in that she greets the person with *Good morning Lora, did you sleep well?*, or *Lora, get up!* At this point she knocks with her bill on the cage and calls out, *Come in; good morning, Herr Lehmann,* or *Good morning, Grandfather.* Somewhat later, when someone perhaps leaves the room, she says, *Adieu, Herr Lehmann.* In between she whistles various melodies and sounds, or talks to herself, until the coffee is carried in; she immediately greets the maid by saying, *Good morning, Susanne. Lora wants coffee too, Lora wants to eat.* Obviously, she is not given any coffee, but milk instead, or a roll cooked in milk and then squeezed out. While this is being handed to her she says, *Good appetite,* which she also says when one or more people sit down at the table. Meanwhile, the mother and one child have come in to eat breakfast; she immediately says, *Mother, mother, Willi is here; come and eat. Lora wants coffee; come eat.* There is now more activity outside in the street; the milkman drives by, the oil man, the beer man, and these give her the opportunity to mimic the various whistles of these drivers with surprising accuracy; she even sounds the distress whistle of the Hamburg policemen (a very high-pitched trill), particularly when it is very noisy outside, and she adds, *Quiet, quiet there,* in the deepest bass. Breakfast is now over and the table is cleared; she now calls out, *Did it taste good, did it taste good?* She calls the children by name as they enter the room: *Lucia, Frieda, Babette, Karl.* The big St. Bernard has also slipped into the room with the children, something he is not supposed to do; now a sharp whistle is heard, and the bird commands, *Karo lie down, Karo lie down now.* But if the little dachshund comes into the room by mistake, which seldom happens, she only calls out, *Fricka.* She also says this when she sits out on the terrace and she sees the dog running in the garden.

The morning has now advanced; the civic guard has marched out on maneuvers. In the distance can be heard martial music, the sounds of commands, and the regular footsteps of the soldiers. The bird greets this approaching noise with *One, two, three, hurrah! Left-right, left-right, left-right! Company halt! Present—arms!* Or also, *Second battery, halt!* If she happens to be outside her cage at the time, then she immediately flies to the windowsill, runs busily back and forth, and, if she happens to slip, then she says, *Now, Lora, don't fall.* Drawn by the military spectacle, Karl has also come to the window; the bird says to him, *Come my child, come now, scratch my little head.* Karl scratches her head; but since this is too boring for him, he soon stops, whereupon Lora says, *Scratch some more, come and scratch a little more.* Because she tolerates little girls quite well, she goes to the window as soon as she sees one, lets out a sharp whistle and calls out loudly, *Come, Anne, come in,* meanwhile nodding her head, flapping her wings, stamping her feet, and playing the fool in general. One has to laugh over this comical behavior, praise her, and perhaps say to her, "Quite right, Lora," whereupon she says, *Bravo!* Since a large crowd assembles during such a military presentation (or at any other opportunity), a policeman soon appears to disperse the crowd. As soon as Lora spots the policeman, she imitates the high, shrill whistle, pecks hard on the window pane, and calls out, *Now, if you're not quiet, then I'll come up,* or *Now, just wait you, rascal, till I come up.*

170

A policeman may have once said something like this to her.

Now the bird will feel compelled to return to her cage. This always happens after one of the children offers her a shoulder, which she climbs on, saying, *Good, you're a nice fellow. Lora, come to Lora; come, give a kiss.* The girl offers her lips, Lora gives her a kiss with a smacking sound, and then says, *Nice fellow.* Suddenly the shrill doorbell rings; it is time for the postman to make his second round. Lora says, *Good day.* The postman really does appear, and Lora calls from a distance, *Good day, Herr Lehmann; good day, Herr Lehmann.* Father quickly opens the letters, reads them through, and mumbles something incomprehensible through his teeth, which prompts Lora to say, *Well, what nonsense are you saying now?* Everybody laughs, of course, and Lora laughs along and says, *Lora is good, Lora is a nice fellow* (she also says this when the other parrots screech; she of course never screeches). Now the maid looks in the room, partly out of curiosity, partly to ask a question concerning lunch; since the maid is now wearing a soiled apron (caused by peeling potatoes), Lora says to her, *You swine.* The maid blushes and is embarrased, and slips as fast as possible back to the kitchen; Lora calls after her, *That was just as well.* To get some exercise and to while away some time, Lora climbs down from the cage, walks for a while back and forth around the room, goes over to a cabinet, looks under it and says, *Look-look, I'm a good Lora. Now, where is Lora, where is good Lora?'* Now and then she points her bill at something and says, *Look, look.* If it happens that someone in her vicinity has something to do, she says, *So, what are you doing?,* or *Get away from there.*

Finally, it is noon and time for lunch, a time Lora recognizes from the clapping of plates and jingling of tableware, and which is her favorite time of day. Now Lora calls everybody to the table; for example: *Willi, come in. Babett, Babett, Lora wants to eat.* To grandfather, whose room is close by, and who likes to eat cake, she says, *Grandfather, do you have cake? Wait a little bit, the cake isn't done yet. Mother, Mother, Papa, Lora wants something too, a roll.* The maid now carries the soup in; while doing so, she happens to spill some; Lora says, *My, what an awful mess.* If the soup is very hot, so that it is steaming when it is brought in, then she says, *Pooh, hot!* The youngest of the children has come late to lunch, after the soup has already been eaten; Lora says, *Well, if you want something, then come.* Since it happens to be a holiday, Karl is told to bring some bottles of wine from the cellar. As soon as Karl walks into the room with the bottles, Lora goes *clink, clink,* and mimics the sound of a cork being pulled; soon after, she makes the splashing sound of the wine being poured and adds, *Lora can't eat.* She says the same thing when someone offers her something she is not supposed to eat. She also says, *My Lora, you can't eat that; Lora is full, I ate already;* or *I can't eat.* Walnuts and apples are special treats for Lora; she of course is given plenty of these, and she makes her desire for them known by clicking her tongue. After lunch, everybody generally rests for a while; even the parrots take a little nap. Lora does not take a long one, and soon she starts to tease the neighboring jocko through the bars of the cage; however, the other jocko bites her roughly on the bill, which prompts Lora to say to him, *That was mean,* or *You're a blockhead. Babett, Babett, where are you hiding? Let me out!*

A Grey Parrot left alone in a room and out of its cage can do some very stupid things; one has to reckon with that. It is always better to put the bird back in its cage before leaving the room—more on this topic in the following report.

I do not think it is a disgrace to do something stupid, particularly when it is done with good intentions, but I find it reprehensible to repeat a known blunder, and even worse to repeat it a third time. My Peter should have helped me see the error of my ways when he demolished all my knick-knacks one day. On another occasion he tore my laboriously completed list, which was lying on the desk, into shreds; when I returned I thought it had just snowed. And the third time— horror of horrors—he polished off a pair of juicy pears that were lying on the corner of the desk—and how! My hair still stands on end whenever I think back to the scene that greeted me when I walked into the room. Within a meter's radius everything, and I do mean everything, was covered with the signs of his misdeed. Let us not talk about it—it was too horrible! I immediately pronounced his sentence: "Back to the cage!" And "poor" Peter was punished by spending the next few days in the hated confinement in his cage.

I have since supplied him with a handy perch, on which he spends the entire day when he is not alone. But if I leave the room for any length of time, then the command Go in the cage! compels him to go back to his cage as fast as greased lightning. He chatters and whistles the whole day and watches everything that goes on around him. When I lure my tame, sweet-singing European Robin, named Rudi, back to his cage in the evening, then Peter supports me right away, and whistles and calls out, *Go in the cage, go in the cage! Come, come, come here!* On one occasion Rudi landed on a picture frame;

172

then big Peter stretched out as far as possible, called to the Robin as tenderly as he could, *Give me a little kiss!*, and then mimicked the sound of kissing. But Rudi did not allow himself to be dazzled; he did not want to have anything to do with Peter.

Even if he is not yet as accomplished as the famous king jocko of Dr. Otto, I still think that what is not, can still come to pass. He is, after all, a king jocko too; on the lower part of his nape he has a few beautiful red feathers, and on his left wing he has one feather with a red spot; he also has a white claw in addition to seven black ones. He can already speak Latin too; he can say, *What's your name?—Psittacus erithacus!* What do you think of that!

My parrot never ceases to astound me with all he can accomplish with his thick tongue. At one time I was of the opinion that the speech of parrots is only a completely mechanical chattering. I have long since changed my opinion completely: a bird of reasonable intelligence connects the idea of what he says with the word or sentence that he speaks. I by no means claim that my Peter is an unusually talented bird, but I do believe that how such a creature will turn out depends very much on who takes care of him and how he is taken care of. It is the same with children, dogs, and cats: they are a reflection of the person who raised them.

And now to proceed from the general to the specific: It is quite obvious that my jocko enjoys learning very much; he listens so attentively that he would take the words right out of my mouth if he could. He comes as close to me as he possibly can, and often enough he has reached for my teeth when I brought my face too close to him. Time after time, it gives me great pleasure to observe how the little fellow tries in his own fashion to make speaking easier. One of the first words he had to learn was *bitte* ('please'); first he said *batte,* then *bette,* and finally *bitte.* The long vowel *a* is easier for him to say than the short *i.* When he was learning to count *eins, zwei, drei,* he also found the *zw* sound of *zwei* to be very uncomfortable, so he substituted a short whistle at first: *eins,* whistle, *drei.* He frequently shortens whole sentences and short phrases, which he knows how to say in complete form, by compressing them into two or three words, such as by changing *Good morning, Doctor* to *Good motor.*

It is completely astounding to me that he can mimic the rapid stirring of a toothbrush in a water glass. One can become quite dizzy at the racing tempo. If one tries sometime to imitate this sound with his own tongue, he will see what a clever trick it is! He can also distinguish dialects; he can say something in the purest, dialectfree High

German and then again in the broad dialect of his nurse.

The number of communications about genuine geniuses among Grey Parrots are increasing all the time, and everyone thinks his is the most intelligent bird. One can see from the following good observations just how shy the Grey Parrot can be at first. This bird was even afraid of a swing, although later he could not do without it.

I bought a Grey Parrot in Hamburg five and a half years ago. Anyone who has ever seen and heard him in his element will agree with me that they have never seen a more "intelligent" animal. When I obtained the bird, he could not speak a word. In other respects as well, his "intelligence" then left a great deal to be desired. When, for example, he was moved from the transport cage to his brand-new cage, he acted like a complete fool. He was afraid of everything and everybody, but above all he was afraid of the swing. He crouched on the floor of the cage and, without moving, stared up at the violent thing that just hung there and then swung back and forth every time he made a sudden movement. I actually had to tie the swing in a corner for eight days, and then gradually loosened it, before Koko finally got used to it. Now he cannot sleep anywhere but on his beloved swing, and how he plays with it! He performs gymnastics first this way and then that; he hangs from both feet and pushes it back and forth; and sometimes, when he gets a hard knock on his bill, he says, *Stupid fellow!*

I would like to mention at the outset that a great deal depends on how a parrot is treated, as is amply shown by Koko's behavior as described above and in what follows. I and those around me have spent a lot of time with Koko, and therefore he has learned a great deal. I know other owners who spend much less time with their parrots; the results are correspondingly modest. My Koko is also unusually fond of learning; he never gets tired, even when we practice for hours. When I speak to him, he comes closer and closer to me and seems to want to take the sounds, whether they are spoken, whistled, or sung, directly from my mouth. If I happen to pause during the instruction, then he pokes me with his bill or even bites, as if he wanted to say, "Just get on with the lesson!" How often have I already said that I wished that all teachers could be blessed with such an attentive and eager-to-learn student as my Koko always is!

174

The first word that he learned to say was *Koko,* his name; and he learned this in the most varied stresses and shadings; it is certainly no exaggeration to claim that Koko can say his name in at least twenty distinct ways; sometimes in a high, sometimes in an intermediate, sometimes in a deep pitch; in the soprano of my cousin, in my baritone; sometimes tenderly, sometimes angrily, sometimes interrogatively, sometimes timidly, sometimes reproachfully, sometimes arrogantly; sometimes he chants it, sometimes he only repeats it, sometimes it is shortened, sometimes drawn out—in short, in all possible forms of expression. It is quite comical when he encounters anything new and unknown, whether it is a thing or a person. He carefully goes up to it—we regularly allow him to stroll around on the table after lunch and in the evening after dinner, and this is the time, as a rule, when he displays the most comical side of his character—and before he touches the strange object or person with his bill (this is an essential part of his examination), he says in a quiet, somewhat timid tone of voice, *Koko!* When he bows while he is saying this, one has the impression that he is formally introducing himself to the stranger!

For humor's sake, I have taught him a few questions and phrases that can be used in the greatest number of situations in normal conversation, and Koko has at times been able to cause quite a sensation when using them. If, for example, a conversation is being conducted in his vicinity, he unexpectedly adds a *So?* to the conversation, or *You don't say;* or *I'm sure;* or *What? Oh, how nice;* or *What do you mean?,* or *Do you understand?* Usually he triggers a general outburst of laughter. It often sounds as if Koko has really understood the conversation and that he wants to express his agreement or doubts.

Just as we do, he also knows all the animals around him quite well: the dog, the White-rumped Shama, the European Nightingale. To the nightingale he calls out, *Philomela, are you ill? Poor knave!* To the shama, hanging over his cage, he looks up and calls out, *Where is Shama? Shama, come! There, Shama! Smack!* He says the last word when the shama is given a mealworm and she swallows it. He commands the dog exactly as he has heard his master do it: *Quiet, Othello! Go to the corner!* In any case, Othello has been fooled by Koko's command two or three times, when he crept very sadly with his tail between his legs to the corner, naturally to our great amusement. As a rule, he can easily distinguish the voice and whistle of his master from the clever imitations of Koko. He does not like Koko at all, out of jealousy naturally, because Koko gets much of the attention

A Grey Parrot can befriend other house pets. The author was acquainted with a jocko that liked to ride on a dog's back.

that Othello would rather have exclusively for himself. For this reason he usually barks at Koko with unfeigned hostility. But Koko does not react to this enmity in any way; he stays aloof from all the dog's barking. Sometimes he mocks Othello's yapping, but sometimes he also peers down at Othello from the edge of the table, calls him quite tenderly by his name, and throws him a treat from the table, which Othello naturally does not disdain, being true to his dog's nature.

If I wanted to write down everything else Koko can say, then I could easily fill several more pages. For this reason I will only list a few at random: *How does the dog bark?—Bow-wow-wow-wow. How does the rooster crow?—Cockadoodledoo. How does the clock go?—Tick-tock, tick-tock, tick-tock* (he repeats all three of these questions one after another, but he never makes mistakes, and never confuses the questions, such as, for example, How does the clock crow?). *Who's there?—Postman. Good day, Minister* (he never says this without making a low bow). If someone knocks, he frequently, but not always, answers with a *Come in. March straight home!* (when he is supposed to go back in his cage). *Will you please be quiet! Thank you, leave me alone.* He also coughs, sneezes, and best of all, laughs. His laughing must be heard to be believed!

Are there also sentences, words, or letters that Koko cannot say?—or should I say, that he does not want to say? One feels unwillingly compelled to give an affirmative answer to the this question when one considers that he does not even try to say some words and phrases, and very easy ones at that, even after hearing them spoken to him for years. This applies, for example, to *good night*, which he has heard just about every evening for the last five and a half years but never once repeated. The word *patience* is also not in his vocabulary, even though he hears it frequently, very frequently, when he impetuously demands his *"coffee,"* that is, his piece of bread. With other words, ability may be more to the point than willingness, as, for example, with this verse: *Koko comes from Africa, Shama from the Himalaya.* He cannot say the word *Africa* perfectly to this day; at first, he only said *A,* then *A—a;* now *Africa* can be heard, but one can tell that it takes an effort on his part. In the same way, he has trouble with the word *Himalaya;* he either says *Humalaya* or, omitting the first syllable, *malaya.* One of the funniest sentences that Koko was supposed to learn is *Hullo, hullo, what a racket.* This was always repeated to him during any unexpected noise; he learned it relatively easily, and he can even say the word *racket* very well. But the part he never says and always leaves out are the words *what a;* so his version sounds like this: *Hullo, hullo, racket!* As a rule, he uses this phrase only in appropriate situations, but never with more success than during a thunderstorm, when after a particulary loud thunderclap his voice can be heard calling, *Hullo, hullo, racket!*

Koko can also speak French with perfect pronunciation, even the nasal sound: *Monsieur, que voulez-vous? Bonjour, Monsieur, comment ça va-t-il?* For some inexplicable reason he always leaves the *t-il* out, and is satisfied with the still understandable question, *Comment ça va?* Can't he say this *t-il,* or does he simply not want to? This is a complete mystery to me.

I have spent so much time discussing Koko's speaking ability that I can only touch on his singing and whistling. He has an outstanding talent for whistling. If he had a better teacher in this, then he would without a doubt have learned to whistle much more and certainly much better than he does. Although I am musically inclined to some degree, I am a failure at whistling. But, even so, I have been careful always to whistle a particular melody in the same key, and so Koko whistles "Alle Vögel sind schon da" ('All the Birds are Already Here') in C major; "Bin i net a lust'ger Schweizerbub" ('Am I not a Jolly Swiss Lad'), "Alles neu macht der Mai" ('Everything is New in May'), and a little melody from *Il Trovatore* in D major; and in A major "Steh nur auf, steh nur auf, du lust'ger Schweizerbub" ('Stand Up,

177

Stand Up, You Jolly Swiss Lad'). In addition, he also knows the chromatic scale and a few scraps of melodies. In the summer, when he sits outside in the garden when the weather is nice, the boys in the neighborhood whistle all kinds of sounds for him until he can repeat them with complete accuracy.

As good as Koko is at talking and whistling, he is almost a total failure at singing, despite his good—indeed, his best—intentions. He really wants to learn to sing so much, and expends the most superhuman effort in this regard. And it is not just that he is unbelievably alert when I sing to him, or that he never tires; he torments himself with attempts at mimicking as well. *Koko, sing! Sing, Koko!* he encourages himself energetically, and then he tries again: *Cuckoo, cuckoo, calls . . . the wood.* He has not progressed any farther than this in five years; he only learns the occasional word of the occasional scrap of a song: *Let . . . sing . . . dancing . . . ring . . . Spring . . . Spring . . . soon, soon.* This is enough to make one laugh; but perhaps crying would be more appropriate, because of all the wasted effort, both mine and Koko's. Nevertheless, I will try it one more time with another, even easier, little song. But in the event that this fails too, then I will have finally to admit that "Apollo, the sweet wellspring of song," has denied my Koko.

In the year 1911 people did not yet agree whether a parrot could understand what it said. In these lines the conviction that the bird "uses words according to the situation" will be apparent. The bird remembers the corresponding situation and connects it with what is said.

Does the bird speak instinctively, or does it know what it is saying? With reference to the article asking whether the parrot understands what it says, by E. von Müller, I will share several pertinent observations.

A Grey Parrot has been in my uncle's possession for more than thirty years. Jocko is unique, and not only because he can say more than three hundred words. The most amazing thing is that he does not use the words arbitrarily but only in the appropriate situation. I wish to mention only a few examples from his large vocabulary. If someone opens the piano, then, before anyone can sound a note, he gives the tuning-fork A. His master is over eighty years old and therefore usually wears a dressing gown and slippers around the house. When he wants to go out and puts on his shoes, Jocko asks, *Where is my coat?* If one goes out the door, he calls, *Adieu, come again soon.* When the lights are turned on in the evening and his cage is covered, he says, *Good night, sleep well.* But I have definitely noticed that he says the latter only in the evening, never when he is covered during the day. At lunch he calls out until someone gives him something: *Jocko is hungry.*

My uncle is a great animal lover and once owned a dog, named Schokkel, and a cat. The parrot never got the dog and the cat confused; he never called to the cat when he saw the dog and wanted to tease him. If someone knocks on the door, then Jocko calls out, *Come in.* But if someone knocks on the table and he sees it, he says nothing. When someone walks into the room first thing in the morning, they are greeted with *Good morning, did you sleep well?* He never says this at any other time of day. From the examples and explanations given, one can see that the parrot always uses the words and sentences in their correct place. In my opinion, this is more than instinct; and if this is more than instinct, then the parrot also knows what he is saying. It would be very interesting to me if other fanciers would use this space to write something on this topic.

The following is another pleasant little incident; even a Little Corella that could also mimic many things is involved.

It was early in the morning, and everything was still quiet, when the low, muffled voices of several men sounded a chorus outside the door of my house. I was deeply moved by this unexpected attention and listened closely. The birds were also completely silent and stared with wide eyes at the door. Suddenly, Hellmut the jocko said, *Hullo, hullo, what a racket!* And Tessi the cockatoo seconded this, saying, *Goodness gracious, what kind of an awful mess is this?* They both talk a lot, and these are by no means the only phrases they know.

Peter, my other Grey Parrot, yelled *Huhuh!* whenever anything unpleasant had happened, for example, when he left his "calling card" where it did not belong. He yelled until I came to clean up the mess. But he carried this even farther; when he yelled *huhuh,* I came to him; so now he started to yell *huhuh* even when he had not delivered a little blotch. If he succeeded in luring me to his cage, then he quickly climbed down and held out his little head to be stroked, in order to keep me at his cage for a while.

Another little story: I had a very large bouquet of flowers in a vase standing in the room. That morning I thought to myself, You must take this out when you let Peter out of his cage. But I forgot to do this after all, and the result was as expected. I had gone into the adjoining room for a short time, then heard the horrifying clattering, splashing, and frightened fluttering. Upon quickly returning to the site of the deed, a colorful chaos of stems, shards, and puddles of water greeted me. Peter stared at the damage down below from a corner of his cage; I started to scold him, but the words stuck in my mouth because I started laughing so hard when the rascal called out, *Bravo, da capo!*

The following thoughts from a jocko owner deal with teaching the bird to mimic in "human" fashion as much as possible, so that the bird responds to a situation in a "human" way too.

Several months ago I was visited by a foreign fancier who was greatly astonished by the conversation I had with my Grey Parrot. He had believed exclusively in the mechanical repetition of learned words and phrases and, after hearing our conversation, had to think that the bird certainly spoke "humanly," that is, reflectively. I replied to him that I also believed in mechanical repetition, just as he did. The most important requirement is that one's bird is highly intelligent. The greatest difficulty lies not in the training, but mainly in bringing the bird to the point where he will also show his speaking talents in the presence of other listeners. The difficulty in training a parrot to display his talents in the presence of strange people is well known to almost every parrot owner. As a rule, the more intelligent and talented a bird is, the shyer he will be in the presence of strangers. But how much an intelligent bird can accomplish in apparently human speech is nothing short of incredible.

I wish to now briefly tell the friendly reader how I teach my birds to speak "humanly." If one already owns a highly intelligent jocko, then it will not prove difficult after some consideration to also raise the bird to be a "feathered person." Above all, one must stop using the old teaching methods, namely, the senseless repetition of more or less inappropriate words. *One, two, three, hurrah; look-look, Lora; Lorita, give me a kiss* (particularly when the bird then gives his little master a firm bite); or saying *Jocko is hungry,* when his food bowl is full—these things do not speak well of the "little master's" teaching ability.

Please note one thing: a bird will always use words that are associated with a certain situation whenever that same situation recurs. This is the whole secret of teaching the bird to speak like a person. For example: my jocko calls, *Come to me,* whenever I approach him. I immediately walk up to his cage. If I stand next to him, he says, *Come, scratch my head.* He immediately holds his little head out to me and says during or shortly after the scratching, *That's nice, oh, ah!*

A second illustration. I approach his cage with a little piece of apple. He says right away, *That sure tastes good! Ah, that tastes good.* He is given the apple; he then says, *Thank you.*

Or I walk up to his cage in the morning. He immediately says, *Good morning, my lad, did you sleep well? Good morning.* If my wife walks in, he immediately says in a high, female voice, *Good morning, my little Jocko.* Here we can already see an error in his training that, unfortunately, we have been unable to cure. He should of course not be allowed to say *my little Jocko,* because then he is greeting himself. Unfortunately, my wife had unwittingly greeted him with these words a few times upon entering the room, and he repeats them in the same way. When I leave, I say to him, "Adieu, my lad," and he instantly replies with the same words. He also says them if I put my hat on. It would have been incorrect to have said to him, "Adieu, my little jocko." When I turn out the light in the room in the evening, he always says, *Good night, my lad, sleep well.* But if I turn out the light in the afternoon in the winter, he never uses these words; therefore, the bird can clearly distinguish the time of day.

But the most astounding thing about this bird is the way he on his own learns expressions that fit appropriate situations and uses them when that same situation occurs again. If the telephone rings, he says, *Hello, who's there?* If the doorbell rings and the maid comes in, he asks, *Who's there?* If my wife calls her dog, he immediately says, *Jumbo, go to the little woman, go.* How is it possible that a bird can use a correct expression? Very simple. Let me give one example. First I walk up to the bird's cage and say to him, "Come here." Then I say to him, "Come, scratch my head," and I immediately begin this action that he finds so pleasant. While I am scratching his head, I repeat to him, "That's nice, oh, ah," at least ten times. Before long, he says to me, *Come here.* I go to him, and he soon continues with the next sentence, *Come, scratch my head.* And then while I am scratching his head, he repeats the words he learned in that situation. Of course, an observer will get the impression that the bird speaks with understanding, while he is actually only connecting the corresponding action and words. But even this seemingly simple connection indicates such a high degree of intelligence that one can almost talk of "human" speech.

181

In the second example the same method is still used. I raise a little piece of apple, walk to his cage, and say to him, "That sure tastes good," four to five times a day. I of course then give him the apple. If he has grasped the words, then when I again approach him with a piece of apple, he will say the words as soon as he spots the apple, which will give an observer the impression that he knows that the apple tastes good.

He must, of course, hear those words that he is supposed to say in the morning only when one enters the room in the morning. The same applies to the evening. How firmly words learned in this way are kept in the bird's memory is shown by the following example. About a year ago, one of my jockos died of convulsions, which he had suffered from for a number of years. When an attack ended, I would always stroke the poor little animal and would speak soothing words to him. Only two hours before his death, after he had only partially recovered from an attack, I stroked him, and he said in a quiet voice, *My little darling, my poor fellow.* Thus the words always used in this situation had been imprinted firmly in his memory.

I believe that a dedicated fancier will not find it difficult to teach his bird to speak in a human way by using the principles given here. The most important requirement is that he owns an intelligent bird.

A jocko is not a screecher by nature. If he does screech, this is an indication that the bird has been kept in poor company. A screeching amazon can completely ruin an otherwise excellent jocko in a short time, because the bird learns to mimic the screeching just as readily as the spoken word. There is almost no way to cure such a bird of the habit of screeching.

I am frequently asked the question whether I can recommend purchasing an amazon or a jocko. Someone like me, who has lived in close contact with jockos for decades, would find very little that is appealing in an amazon. I have never owned an amazon that could even approach a jocko in talking ability.

9. Breeding

Breeding the nominate form. Dates of first breedings: France: probably in 1799 (world first-breeding); England, 1843; Germany, 1899; Portugal (Island of Madeira), 1908; India, 1920; U.S.A., 1931; Denmark, 1956; Czechoslovakia, 1968/69; Sweden, 1973.

Our discussion of the breeding of the nominate form will recount a complete, normal breeding episode. The birds do not appear to reach sexual maturity before their fifth year of life; most of the birds breeding in aviaries are usually older. But this should not be taken as conclusive proof that Grey Parrots do not become sexually mature at an earlier age. At the end of their third year of life, pairs have already formed, and courtship dances can already be observed. Grey Parrots then run with drooping wings along branches or other perches and seem to be very excited. The birds seem to be almost embarrassed when they preen each others' heads (this behavior has also been observed in other species of parrots) and rub their bills together. The male feeds the female when he is in breeding condition. The male bird is also the one that searches for a nest site and first examines it. The nest sites chosen vary so much that one cannot make generalizations. The height of the nest cavity is between 50 and 190 centimeters; the inner diameter is between 25 and 30 centimeters, and the entrance hole has a diameter of approximately 10 to 12 centimeters. A nest box can be built from thick boards, or a natural tree trunk can be used. It seems that nest holes that are too deep are not well liked. In rare cases the birds will also breed in cages (85 centimeters long), as well as in small or large indoor and outdoor flights. The nest site should not be exposed to strong light. As a rule, the female lays three or four eggs; the laying interval is two to three days, and the female usually starts incubating after the second egg is laid. Clutches of as many as five eggs and as few as two have been reported. It is extremely rare for four young from one clutch to reach maturity; three is the usual number. One can assume that incubation will last thirty days. The first young to hatch are always dominant, and when young do die, it is always the youngest birds.

The female always broods alone, and the male feeds her at the entrance hole or outside the nest. During the breeding season the birds are very aggressive, ruffling their feathers when anyone approaches their nest. Even birds that previously had been completely tame lose their tameness, but after breeding, this usually returns. Breeding has taken place at almost every time of year, although it most often occurs in June and November. During the darker times of year, with the low light level, one must lend a helping hand by increasing the length of day, so that the young are fed sufficiently. This can be quite easily accomplished with fluorescent tubes connected to an automatic timer. In the dark winter months my birds are awakened early (around 4 A.M.) by turning on the light, so that the birds go to sleep at the normal time and are able to take nourishment beforehand. If the lights are left on in the evening, there is always the possibility that if the lights suddenly go out, the female will not be able to find her way back to the nest hole. Even in complete darkness, the female again feeds the young from her crop.

The newly hatched young do not receive anything at all for many hours after hatching; then they are fed with so-called crop milk. The little ones have a flesh-colored body; the bill and feet are the same color.

During the first eight days, feeding proceeds approximately as follows: Since the young are not capable of lifting their comparatively large heads during the first week, the female grabs the nestling with her curved upper mandible and lays it on its back (this observation was also reported to me by J. Kennings from Australia, who observed this process in Budgerigars and

At six days of age, a Grey Parrot nestling cannot yet lift its head, has its eyes closed, and the upper mandible is not yet curved.

was even able to film it). There is definitely a possibility that this method of feeding is practiced by many, if not all, species of parrots.

After about a week, the male also goes into the nest to feed the young. The eyes of the young birds open very slowly, and are at first shaped like slits. The eyes open fully some time between the tenth and the eighteenth day. It takes approximately another four weeks until the female is seen outside the nest frequently, and both parents start taking food to the young continually. The first feathers appear after four weeks. The female spends the night with the young birds for approximately eight weeks, and after ten to eleven weeks the young birds start venturing from the nest occasionally. At first they are somewhat clumsy. For a while longer they return to the nest cavity at night or at any sign of danger. The tails of the young are not such a bright red as the parents, and the iris is blackish. In the first months the upper mandible is hardly longer than the lower mandible. The young do not start to take seed on their own for another two weeks. It stands to reason that the young should be given softened, or, better yet, hulled sunflower seeds, for example. Preferably, the food bowls should be placed up near the perches, so the still awkward young can easily see and reach them. Fresh ears of maize can also be fastened high up in the cage. These are very well liked, particularly when they are still milky and juicy, so that they are easier for the young birds to handle. Herr Langenberg of Copenhagen chanced upon the trick of giving the young birds pieces of maize ears and softened sunflower seeds when they were only eight weeks old, before they left the nest. In so doing, he found that the nestlings actually learned to feed themselves faster and also became independent earlier.

A young Grey Parrot that was only seventeen days old had to be reared by hand because the parents no longer brought food. Every two hours until 11 P.M., porridge had to be given with a spoon. When the bird was five weeks old, it was fed only five times a day. After more than six weeks the bird learned to shell softened sunflower seeds, but this took a very long time, and the food intake was correspondingly small. Since the bird no longer wanted to take any "baby food," it was fed lean, cooked, shredded meat. This bird weighed 130 grams at the age of seventeen days, and 420 grams at six months.

As was already-mentioned at the beginning of the book, the iris is at first black, then over a period of months it turns dark gray, light gray, whitish, pale yellow (usually at an age of six to eight months), and finally becomes either deep yellow or straw yellow. The development of the color takes a variable amount of time, which suggests that process may be affected by the diet.

The first breeding attempts in Germany were reported in 1876; they were unsuccessful, however. The one bird that hatched died the next day.

Another attempt was made by Frau J. Gorgot in 1896. The female laid three eggs around the end of October and the beginning of November, but all three eggs died shortly before hatching. At the time, Dr. Russ regretted this loss very much and said: "We can in fact only hope desperately that a successful breeding will take place in Germany." The three eggs had the following measurements: 41.0 × 28.5 millimeters, 42.0 × 28.5 millimeters, and 41.0 × 29.0 millimeters; they were white, oval, and had no sheen. In February the female laid another egg, but this one did not hatch either.

Finally, in the year 1899, Fritz Lotze reported the first successful breeding. The written report of this breeding appears below, along with accounts of other breedings, to provide a complete picture. Today it is more important than ever to breed these parrots, since their breeding range is continually being reduced by environmental changes and fewer Greys are being imported. This will certainly lead to their becoming scarce.

Breeding the *timneh* race. Dates of first breedings: Nigeria, 1974; West Germany, 1976. Since the birds were first bred in West Germany in 1976, successful breedings have also been reported in various other countries as of 1982. It has been determined that there are no great variations in the course of breeding. As a rule, two to four eggs are laid, and these are incubated for thirty days. After approximately ten weeks the young birds leave the nest. Herr Wewering weighed some of the young birds: four weeks after hatching: 140 grams; six weeks: 250 grams; eight weeks: 310 grams; ten weeks: 310 grams. It is normal for a nestling to lose weight, or at least not gain any, shortly before leaving the nest, so that its flying ability does not suffer because of excess weight.

There also seems to be little difference in the taming and mimicking ability of young animals, compared to the nominate race.

Bird-keepers' reports. The first breeding was reported in detail by the fancier Lotze, as follows.

As reported previously, I have been able to accomplish two complete breedings with Grey Parrots. I will attempt in the following to describe the course of breeding in detail.

I made the first attempt at breeding early in 1899 with a pair of Grey Parrots, of which I obtained one (Jocko) in 1890 and the other (Lulu) in 1895 in Hamburg. Both of the birds were very young when

If Grey Parrot nestlings become accustomed to handling at an early age—these are six days old—they will be tame and trainable as adults.

I purchased them, and were therefore ten and five years old, respectively, last spring. I will continue the use of their names, Jocko and Lulu, in the following discussion.

For this first breeding attempt I built a compartment of wire mesh in my bird room, which was 1.50 meters wide, 0.75 meters deep, and 1.26 meters high. Then, using large pieces of peat, which were held together by wire mesh, I built a nest box. After a short time Lulu examined the nest box, crept through the entrance hole, and began to gnaw the inside enthusiastically. Jocko, who seemed to take less of an interest in the affair, also soon took part in the demolition from the outside, and after two days all that was left of the box was a pile of peat moss. After this I prepared a nest box from a little barrel made of fir, but this was also gnawed so thoroughly that it quickly fell apart.

Now I prepared a much stronger box from oak boards, which still had bark on one side. This was 0.50 meters high and had an inside width of 0.25 meters. The entrance hole, which had a diameter of 11 centimeters, was located 15 centimeters above the floor of the box. For nesting material I placed a few handfuls of peat mold in the box. Lulu soon tried to destroy this structure as well, but without success. Jocko also tried out his gnawing talents a few times, but after these attempts miscarried, he no longer concerned himself with it. After the birds had been together for about fourteen days, I noticed that they started feeding each other. After another eight days, I saw Jocko sitting on the box, while Lulu danced around him below, with the most unbelievable bodily contortions. During this display, both of them made sounds which were almost identical to the whimpering of young dogs; all sorts of human words, which they had frequently used earlier, could also be heard. These capers, which were repeated almost every day, lasted approximately five minutes. I had assumed that Lulu was the male, because the sexes of Grey Parrots cannot usually be ascertained from external characteristics. I changed my opinion a few days later, however, when I had the opportunity to observe a mating attempt.

Lulu now spent a great deal of time in the nest box, broke up the pieces of peat, and prepared a cup-shaped depression. Jocko also visited the box a few times but never stayed inside long. Lulu now started to spend almost every night in the box.

The birds' diet consisted of cooked maize, hemp, cooked potatoes, bread, and a few peanuts every day.

I must also mention that Lulu now almost never fed herself, but instead allowed herself to be fed almost entirely by Jocko. At noon on March 17, I saw Lulu, who had been quite active even that morning, crouching on the floor of the cage with drooping wings, fluffled feathers, and clenched claws. I took the animal from the compartment and found that her lower body was greatly distended and inflamed. I feared she was egg bound, and I attempted to introduce a feather dipped in oil into the vent. The bird seemed to be in a great deal of pain, her breathing was very rapid, and tears were in both eyes. On the advice of a trusted bird lover, I took her to a veterinarian, who wanted to perform an operation to remove the egg. I did not agree to this, because it would almost certainly have killed the bird. Then the attempt was made to squeeze the egg, which had no shell, from the bird. This was successful, and after the contents of the egg came out, the bird looked noticeably better. Food was not accepted, however, and the bird was so weak that she could not even hold herself on a perch. In the evening I placed Lulu back in the compartment, and Jocko immediately started his duty as male nurse; he certainly knew much better how to handle Lulu than I did. I left this business up to him, and the next morning I was overjoyed to find that Lulu was again active and lively.

Ten days later I noticed that Lulu was again egg bound, to the same degree as the first time. After several attempts to lay the egg were unsuccessful, to help her I again crushed the egg inside her body. Five days later Lulu was able to lay an egg on her own. But this was somewhat elongated because it had such a thin shell, and was not suitable for incubation. I removed the egg from the nest box, which was no easy task, since the two of them defended their nest with unbelievable bravery. Lulu now refused to be disturbed in her brooding activities, sat four more weeks in the empty nest box, and let Jocko continue to bring food to her in the nest.

After this time had passed, Lulu must have finally realized that sitting in the empty nest served no purpose, for she left the nest box and seemed to have lost the urge to breed. A short time later I again noticed copulation attempts. I now added ground egg shells to the soft food to forestall the laying of eggs with thin shells, and fed them a piece of bacon daily to prevent egg binding. On May 21, I was overjoyed to find a well-formed egg in the nest box; a second followed on the twenty-fourth, and a third on the twenty-seventh. Lulu began incubating after the second egg was laid. On the morning of June 23, I heard a peeping sound, like the meowing of a kitten, coming from the nest. When Lulu left the nest for a short time, I saw that an egg had hatched. Throughout the next day I frequently heard the voice of the little one, but in the evening everything was quiet. On the following morning I did not hear any sound, and on closer inspection I found that the nestling's head had been bitten off. I suspected that this had been done by Jocko, because he cast such furtive glances at the nest box and appeared not to have a clear conscience. Since I felt certain he was the "child murderer," I placed Jocko in a cage in the compartment, in the hope of preventing any additional murderous deeds.

On the following day another jocko hatched. This one was diligently fed by Lulu. But Lulu still received almost all of the food from Jocko, who offered it through the bars of his prison. Young Grey Parrots certainly cannot claim to have an attractive body shape; the plump body with the short little legs and the monstrously long neck could not be less attractive. I could see how Jocko could have mistaken the first-born for a monster, and I could understand how he might have wanted to get rid of this intruder in the simplest way. The fashion in which the young are fed is noteworthy. In the first six to eight days, the young are not capable of lifting their heads, and it is quite difficult to feed them. But the parents know how to do this. With the curved hook of the upper mandible the nestling is held and turned over on its back. The bill, which looks like a thick black muzzle, is placed on top, and the food, which is at first thoroughly chewed, is given to the nestling. After the feeding, the nestling is again turned over with the aid of the hooked bill, and the task is finished. While they were being fed, the nestlings made a continuous meowing sound, which continues to become louder as they grow older, until it gradually changes to a croaking. Since the young during the first days were turned over in exactly the same way in this breeding attempt as in the earlier one, I assume that this is always done the same way by jockos, and possibly by other species of parrots as well.

The nestlings are almost completely naked immediately after hatching; only isolated downy filaments can be seen. After approximately ten to fourteen days they open their eyes, but this is done gradually, and little by little the whole eye is exposed. This is completely dark, as is well known. After three to four weeks a thick covering of down appears on the yellowish green, shiny skin, and at the same time on the wings and on the top of the head. A few days later, on the rest of the body the larger feathers break through. Whether the young birds need a considerable amount of warmth I cannot confirm, because the average temperature in the room was 15 to 20 C., and in the morning as low as 7 to 10 C., since the room became much colder during the long, cold nights. But I never noticed that the young birds suffered in any way on account of this.

When the first nestling was four weeks old, I let Jocko, who had been locked up until now, out of his cage. But I watched him closely, because I was afraid that he still wanted to injure the little one. Lulu was very pleased with Jocko's freedom; she even forgot to feed the youngster. Since I saw that Jocko visited the youngster in the nest without injuring it, I allowed him to remain free. In the evening, however, I found that the nestling now had an empty crop, whereas it had alway been stuffed before. I locked Jocko back in his cage, and Lulu immediately started feeding the nestling again. On the following day I again let Jocko out of his cage, and this time he assisted in feeding the youngster, so I did not lock him up anymore.

Since the compartment seemed to me to be too small, I built a larger enclosure for the family. The floor of this one had an area of 3 square meters, and the space extended from the floor of the room to the ceiling. I furnished this area with several perches and transferred the family into it. The young bird left the nest at the age of ten weeks, but it was still quite awkward when climbing on the perches and spent most of its time on a small wooden platform I had placed

191

in the compartment. The young bird now started eating on its own; at first it took soaked white bread, and cooked maize and baby peas in the pod later. The adults still did some feeding.

After the youngster had been out of the nest for a few days, I had to take a short trip. At noon, just before I left, I saw the young Grey Parrot climbing on one of the highest perches. Unfortunately, I had seen it alive for the last time, because when I came back that evening, I found only its body. Shortly after I had left, my wife entered the room and found the young bird lying dead on the floor. The only possible cause of death that I can think of is that the animal, which was quite fat and heavy but could not yet fly, had fallen from a considerable height to its death. I now returned both of the adults to their former cages, in order to separate them temporarily, but I noticed that both of them seemed to be very unhappy, as they were no longer cheerful or active. In the middle of October I again placed the pair in the compartment, where I had installed a prepared beer barrel and a partially hollowed-out willow log, so that the birds could have a choice of nest sites. Now they started working industriously on the willow log, widening the parially hollowed-out interior. At the beginning of November, I again noticed attempts at mating, and on December 6, Lulu laid the first egg. On the ninth she laid the second egg, and on the twelfth the third—not in the willow log, but in the beer barrel below it. The incubation period proceeded exactly as before.

On January 9, 1900, after exactly thirty days of incubation, I again heard the call of a young Grey Parrot, and by noon a second had hatched. The third egg, which I opened after a few days, contained a fully developed bird which was dead, unfortunately. I was afraid that Jocko would again have murderous thoughts, but, as it turned out, he took great pleasure in the appearance of the little ones and diligently helped to feed them, even on the first day. Their diet consisted mainly of cooked maize, hazelnuts, stale white bread, and some hard-boiled egg. Hempseed was not taken during the first ten days, even though they had shown a special liking for it before.

The nestlings developed splendidly. The feeding method was the same as was practiced with the first brood, in that the young were laid on their backs. The first plumage is almost identical to that of the adult Grey Parrots, so that one can barely tell the young birds and adults apart once they are fully grown. In the first few months the upper mandible is only slightly longer than the lower.

Ten-day-old Grey Parrot siblings. The development of feather pigmentation is by now visible in the pink skin.

Since the adults gave no indication that they were going to raise another brood, the young birds were allowed to stay with them, although later they were driven away from the food bowls by the adults. For this reason I placed them in separate cages. The birds must have been badly frightened by this experience, because they behaved very fearfully and made a considerable racket every time I approached the cage during the next several weeks, and also tried to escape through the bars of their cages. My wife and the children were allowed to approach the cage boldly; the food was even taken from their hands. Gradually they did lose their fear of me after all, and now appear to be completely confiding toward me.

Only in the last few weeks, now that the young birds are almost eleven months old, have they started to practice talking and whistling. As a rule, they never become annoying by whistling or screeching loudly, which is frequently the case with imported Grey Parrots. At this time, the adults are still in their compartment in the bird room, while the youngsters are in the living room. For some time now, the adults have been occupied again with their nesting preparations. Apparently they are ready to raise another brood.

193

So much for the report concerning both the 1899 and 1900 broods of the pair, which created quite a sensation at the time. Two wonderful photographs appeared, in which the parents could be seen with the young; one of the photographs was awarded first prize in a competition.

Also worth noting is another communication in which the first eggs were laid after the bird spent twenty-eight years (1910) in captivity. It states:

My Grey Parrot, which I have kept in a cage for twenty-eight years, laid an egg for the first time on October 8 of this year. Eggs were also laid on November 19, 22, and 26. The first egg was laid in apparently considerable pain, since the animal whimpered the entire day and gave out loud cries of pain, and also sat constantly at the water dish and drank continually. The first egg was somewhat larger than a pigeon egg; the other three were smaller and were laid without any particular indication of pain. The long interval between the first and second egg (six weeks), and the short interval of three to four days between the other three eggs is also noteworthy.

For a long time no progress was made in the breeding of the Grey Parrot, and no reports appeared in bird publications; in fact, in the last twenty-five years, very little information of any kind concerning Grey Parrots has been reported. The next detailed breeding report came from Walter Langberg of Copenhagen. For over twenty years the author has known Herr Langberg, a knowledgeable fancier and breeder, who possesses a considerable understanding of birds and has bred many other psittacine species. In 1959, he finally succeeded in breeding the Grey Parrot after years of trying. This is described in the following report.

About nine years ago (around 1950), I decided to attempt to breed the larger talking parrots, the Grey Parrot in particular.

My first Grey Parrot was not a success in any way; the bird was very shy and was a screecher. I hoped that it would become tame with time, but it died suddenly of food poisoning. My next Grey Parrot was a wonderful bird. The bird dealer from whom I purchased the bird had obtained it when it was very young. The bird had spent a couple of years in his shop and was now completely tame and a good talker. I estimated that it was about three years old when I purchased it. The bird was soon a highly prized member of the family and brought us considerable joy. Countless times I answered because I thought my wife had called, and found that it was the bird—we named it Jocko—imitating her voice. We assumed that the bird was a female, so I now started to look for a male.

As expected, this was by no means an easy task. The selection was not large, but any Grey Parrot that I could get hold of and that I thought was a male, I tested. Usually the birds could not tolerate each other. To allow them to get used to each other, I built a large metal cage with a removable mesh partition. I placed Jocko in one compartment and the latest acquistion in the other. When the birds had apparently grown accustomed to each other, I removed the partition. The result was usually discouraging: either the birds fought, or one chased the other.

Someone advised me to try wild parrots, real screechers, since it seemed hopeless to continue trying to breed tame birds. I would certainly not recommend this method to anyone with weak nerves. In my experience, parrots captured when they are old never become tame. They never lose their fear of people, but instead immediately start screeching as soon as anyone approaches the cage. This overpowering outcry is something of a cross between the squealing of a pig and the lowing of a cow, and it is continued until the intruder goes away.

Young Grey Parrots have a gray iris; somewhat later the iris becomes whitish gray. It has been my experience that if a Grey Parrot with a whitish yellow iris happens to be shy and starts to screech as soon as someone approaches the cage, then it will be difficult to tame such a bird. A young bird with a gray iris will gradually become tame and will stop screeching, assuming that it is handled correctly.

After various unsuccessful attempts, from which I had, however, learned a number of interesting things, I one day found myself in the fortunate position of choosing from among a large shipment of Grey Parrots. I chose a large, dark gray bird with a heavy bill and large feet, since I had the idea that a male should look just like that. (The late Duke of Bedford, in the first edition of his book *Parrots and Parrot-like Birds,* also advances the theory that male Grey Parrots are larger than females.) For some reason, many more female than male Grey Parrots are imported. Coloration cannot be used to distinguish the sexes, since the birds' native range is very large, and the birds in different parts of the range can vary a great deal in color as well as size.

The newly acquired presumed male was placed in the usual parrot cage, approximately 45 × 45 centimeters and 80 centimeters high

Except while being hand-fed, these fifteen-day-old Grey Parrot chicks spend their time in a box lined with paper towels in a brooder, as homoeothermy is as yet underdeveloped.

(this model is the most common cage for larger parrots here in Denmark, but is actually too small to serve as permanent housing for this bird). The new bird was somewhat shy and screeched from time to time, but since the iris was still somewhat gray, I presumed it was a young bird and that it would become tame with time. This actually did occur, but it never became as trusting as Jocko. We named it Coco, and though it did learn this name, its speaking talent has never become as great as Jocko's.

Jocko was placed in a cage right next to Coco's, and throughout the winter the two birds perched next to one another. The next spring, I endeavored to place the birds together in a cage and was overjoyed when they appeared to get along well. I built a nest box, which I hung outside the cage, but the birds appeared to have absolutely no interest in it. Unfortunately, all of my outdoor flights were being used, so the Grey Parrots had to spend the entire summer in the cage.

196

I had kept one of the males that Jocko had rejected, and I bought a companion for him. The birds got along very well from the start, and I now believed that I had two legitimate pairs.

In the spring of 1955, I placed all four parrots in an outdoor flight with an attached shelter. The flight was approximately 2.00 meters long, 1.25 meters wide, and 2.00 meters high; the shelter was approximately 1.25 × 1.25 and 2.00 meters high. The floors of both the flight and the shelter were made of wood treated with creosote, and the flight was raised about 30 centimeters above the ground. The hatchway was almost as wide as the whole breeding chamber, and was approximately 75 centimeters high. The four birds got along tolerably well, but always stayed together in pairs. After a time it was apparent that Coco and Jocko did not enjoy the company, since the two others appeared to be too dominant. I therefore took the other two out and put them back in the large cage indoors. Here they showed a great deal of interest in the nest box, but nothing came of it.

During the course of the summer, Coco and Jocko attempted mating numerous times, but again there was no issue. In the fall I took them inside and placed them in a cage with nest boxes; it was exactly the same size as the one in which they had been kept during the winter.

At the end of the winter it appeared that Coco and Jocko showed a greater interest in one another. Jocko was fed by Coco daily, and they performed courtship dances with drooping wings and also attempted to mate. For this reason I decided to place this pair in the outdoor flight as soon as the weather permitted. I hung two nest boxes, each 30 × 30 centimeters and 50 centimeters high, in the shelter right under the roof, and on the floor of the shelter I placed a small barrel without a cover. In the flight I hung a box that was approximately the same size as the others but somewhat deeper. On the floor of the flight I placed wood chips and a piece of peat moss, so the birds would have something they could chew to pieces.

Coco and Jocko were placed in the outdoor flight on May 1. They soon felt right at home, since they recognized it from before. They soon started performing courtship dances. At the beginning of June, Jocko showed a great deal of interest in the box that hung on the rear wall of the shelter. She spent a lot of time inside the box, and spent the entire day in the box on Saturday, June 16. Sunday morning, when I was feeding the birds, I noticed that Jocko was outside the nest box. I therefore took advantage of the opportunity and looked in the box, where I saw the Grey Parrot's first egg. My assumption had proved to be correct: Jocko was definitely a female. She returned to the box and sat on the egg, which had apparently been laid on the sixteenth. I now inspected the box daily: on the nineteenth there were two eggs, on the twenty-fifth, three; and on the twenty-seventh, four. As far as I could determine, the eggs were laid at intervals of three days. Jocko now incubated almost constantly. I naturally wanted the opportunity to inspect the eggs to see if they were indeed fertile, as I did not believe they were, since the mating attempts had not appeared to have been very successful. On July 14, I had the opportunity to inspect the eggs. They were all infertile. Now I was again in doubt: maybe both of them were females.

In the course of the next few days, the birds again started mating, but in the same casual fashion as before. They ran back and forth along the branches with drooping wings and appeared to be very excited. Copulation then took place from the side, and it seemed that it had not been an effective mating, but only an attempt.

On August 4, Jocko again sat in the box and had laid another egg. This time, four eggs were laid at intervals of three days. She started incubating after laying the first egg. On August 21, I inspected the eggs. I could hardly believe my eyes; they were all fertile. It seemed to me, however, that the air spaces in all of the eggs were too large, and I feared that the embryos would consequently dry out. Jocko, however, sat tight and did not seem to mind too much that I occasionally looked in the box.

Until now their diet consisted of canary seed, hemp, spray millet, and sunflower (white and two kinds of striped). In addition, I gave canary seed, hemp, oats, sunflower, and maize in sprouted form. For soft food the birds received white bread soaked in milk, to which glucose and various vitamins had been added. I thought that something special would be necessary to feed the young birds, and since fresh, half-ripe ears of maize were available, a natural food for parrots, these were added to the menu. I also gave peanuts, which are well liked by Grey Parrots. They barely touched any green food but did eat some apple, albeit without any particular enthusiasm. The ears of maize appeared to be the correct food for rearing the young, and more than 200 were used by the end of the season. My wife had bought a large number of them, which were stored in plastic bags in the freezer; in this way, we had this excellent food for a very long time. We almost had a catastrophe just before the eggs were supposed to hatch. The birds had gnawed on the box a great deal, particularly the roof, so that a large piece fell down, luckily not into the box but to the floor.

Daily weighing during the course of hand-rearing monitors the chick's development and provides the best indicator of incipient problems.

On Sunday, September 2, I inspected the eggs and saw that the air space had filled up in all of the eggs. To my delight, I saw small cracks in one egg, a sign that the shell had been pipped and that the chick would soon hatch. On September 8, when Jocko was outside the box, I looked in and saw two apparently well-fed young and a third that was in the process of hatching. On September 18, when I again looked in the nest box, a fourth bird was in the process of coming out of the shell. Since the youngster was apparently having difficulty in freeing itself from the egg, I stuck my hand in the box to help it. But Jocko ruffled her feathers and tried to bite me, so that I had to remove the half-hatched youngster with a spoon. The youngster seemed to be very weak, so I tried to help it by carefully breaking off the largest part of the shell. With the spoon I placed the youngster back in the nest box and hoped it would survive. However, when I again looked in the box that evening, the youngster was dead, apparently bitten to death. It is possible that I did not place it far enough under the female, so she may have mistaken it for another animal.

The newly hatched young were flesh color, thinly covered with long down, had light bills and feet, and looked like gigantic baby lovebirds. The incubation period is apparently thirty days.

So long as the young were very small, the female rarely left the nest, being fed by the male, who slipped into the box. On September 18, the bills of the young started to turn black. The female now started leaving the nest more frequently and also began to feed herself again. In contrast, the male now went in the box often to feed the young. They were now hostile toward me when I inspected the nest. When the young were approximately one month old, they were covered in gray down, and the female now left the nest for longer and longer periods of time.

On October 6, I noticed that the smallest youngster did not keep up with the others in development and apparently did not receive enough food. On October 8, it was obviously ill, lying in a corner of the nest; there seemed to be no doubt that it was badly fed. For this reason, I decided to take the youngster into the house and to try to rear it by artificial means. It was placed in a nest box on a bed of sawdust and peat moss, with a 50-watt infrared lamp as a source of warmth. The youngster was fed breakfast roll soaked in milk, to which glucose and a protein-rich preparation (called Recoven) was added. Various vitamins were also added. Later, crushed grapes, bananas, and other soft fruits were given. The lukewarm food was fed via a food syringe. Things went surprisingly well; the youngster recovered very quickly and appeared to be feeling well. As it grew older, we had to feed it very often, up to ten times a day. This was a lot of work for my wife, who cared for the youngster, but it had to be done. The young bird of course became very tame and dependent and loved to be held in our hands.

About the time the weak youngster was removed from the nest, the other two started to grow feathers; even the red tail was visible. It took considerably longer for the weaker youngster to grow the red tail feathers, but later it developed very quickly. October 15 was a black day. When my wife went to the flight to feed the birds, she found one of the young birds lying dead on the floor. The nestlings, which were six weeks old, were already well developed. I suspect that the youngster had climbed up to the entrance hole, lost its balance, and had fallen from the nest. When I examined the bird, I could not

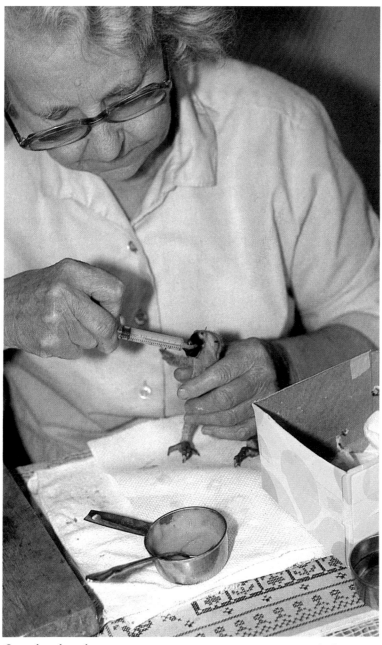

Some breeders choose to use a syringe in rearing quite young chicks. Here, Oregon breeder Vi Ipsen feeds a fifteen-day-old Grey.

201

find any sign of injury, so I presumed that the youngster had died of exposure, since the day had been quite cold. I was understandably alarmed and decided to bring the whole family into the house. The large cage was made ready, and the nest box was hung inside. It took up a lot of space, but the birds soon felt comfortable in the familiar surroundings, and after a while I could hear that the nestling was being fed. Now there was only one young bird with the parents, and on November 7, when it was about two months old, I noticed it feeding on a maize ear, which the parents had dropped in the nest. I now placed maize ears and sprouted sunflower seeds in the box daily, and these were accepted by the youngster. It was also still being fed by the parents, of course.

On November 23, the youngster climbed up and perched on the edge of the box. On November 25, it left the box for the first time and climbed around on the wire of the cage, but immediately disappeared back into the box when we approached. The parents took up a defensive posture with ruffled feathers. I noticed that this young bird was a light color and had a light tongue and light claws, as opposed to the darker color, black tongue, and black claws of the one reared artificially.

After the young bird had left the nest (although it did go back in whenever someone approached, as well as at night), it was mainly fed by the male. But it also ate some on its own, mostly sprouted sunflower seeds and a few small, hard nuts (cembra-pine nuts). But even on January 4, when the young bird was four months old, I saw that it was still being fed by the male.

I, of course, do not wish to be separated from these two young birds. I will attempt to determine at what age the iris turns yellow in Grey Parrots, and, if possible, at which age they become sexually mature. I believe that a hand-raised bird is hardly suitable for breeding, because it is so used to people. In any case, it will be interesting to try to solve these problems.

It is difficult for me to determine the age of the parents exactly. Based on the information I was given, I suspect that the male was about five or six and the female was about ten or fifteen years old when they bred for the first time.

Coco and Jocko spent the winter of 1956/57 in the large cage in the house. In the spring, the aviary was prepared, and the nest box was hung in the same place in the shelter as the last time. I did have to repair the entrance hole, however, since almost the entire front

Sturdy, firmly fixed perches in the aviary will increase the likelihood that copulation will be successful.

side had been gnawed away. On April 7, the birds were released into the aviary, and they soon felt completely at home.

After some time, Coco started feeding Jocko, and we could see occasional attempts at mating. At the beginning of June the female went in the box from time to time, but never stayed inside long. On June 17, she spent almost the entire day in the box, and when I had the opportunity, I saw that she had already laid an egg. On June 20, there were two eggs, and on the twenty-sixth four. When I inspected the eggs on July 6, I determined that at least one had been fertilized.

Unlike the previous year, this time it was very difficult to inspect the nest, because Jocko was very hostile and did not wish to allow me to look in. When she was in the flight and saw me approaching, she immediately flew back to the shelter, so that I was rarely able to open the door to the shelter before she was back in the nest. Nevertheless, on July 22, I was able to look in the box before she came back, and I saw that one of the young had hatched. On July 25, I was again able to check the nest, and I now saw a second live nestling.

Until now, the male had taken bread soaked in milk in addition to the usual sprouted and dry seeds, which led me to hope that he would feed this to the young in place of the maize ears, which were not available at the time. But as soon as the young had hatched, he stopped taking the bread, and neither of the parents took the sunflower, hemp, or canary seed placed in the shelter. I then tried hanging some bowls of canary and hemp on the wire of the flight. This apparently appealed to the birds, because they immediately went to them. While the young were being reared, the dry sunflower seeds were hardly touched. The birds mainly fed dry hemp and canary, as well as sprouted canary, hemp, and sunflower seeds, and later the soaked bread again. As far as I can remember, I obtained no maize ears until the young were three weeks old.

The young birds thrived, and on September 29, one perched on the edge of the box; but it was not until October 13 that one of them sat on one of the perches in the shelter. The feathers of the wings and tail were fully developed, but the youngsters were somewhat slimmer than the parents, and the iris was of course gray. On the following day, both of the birds were out of the nest, and sat in the flight the whole morning. They were quite similar in appearance, but over the course of the next few days I noticed that one apparently did not feel completely well and was not fed as much as the other. The youngsters now started to eat food on their own, but in this respect too the one seemed to be less advanced than the other.

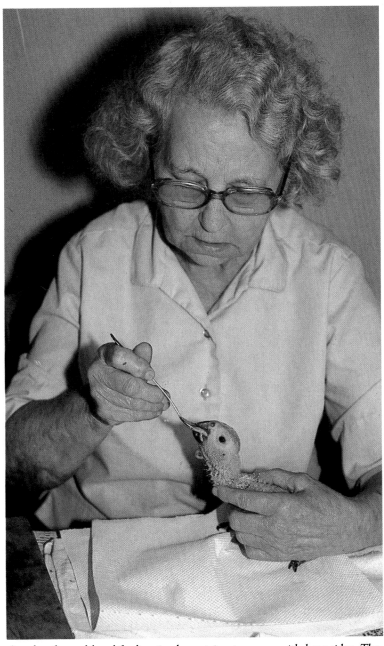

Another favored hand-feeding implement is a teaspoon with bent sides. The chicks themselves will prefer to receive food from one tool or another.

On October 22, the weaker youngster sat on the floor of the shelter room and seemed to be freezing. Since the evening was quite cool, I decided to take the bird inside, and I placed him in a large nest box under a 50-watt infrared lamp. My wife fed the youngster with a food syringe, and it quickly recovered. When I brought it inside, it was wild and shy and screeched whenever we approached. But within three to four days it was already tame, and after only two weeks it started to mimic human voices. On October 14 it said *jocko* quite clearly. The other young bird stayed with the parents in the aviary. I will try to keep the adults in the aviary all winter and will bring them inside only if the winter is very cold or they do not look well. In the winter of 1956/57, I kept two wild-caught Grey Parrots in a similar aviary the entire winter, and they seemed to do quite well. Of course, that was an unusually mild winter.

At the moment I have nine Grey Parrots, and I hope in the course of time to be able to breed the second generation.

The second youngster remained with the parents in the aviary, but some time after he had become independent, I brought him inside and placed him in a cage in my bird room. He was very shy and did not become confiding as quickly as the first one. After a very long time he became calmer, and he is now completely tame and can say a number of words.

I attempted to keep the breeding pair in the aviary over the winter, because Coco frequently had severe attacks of asthma when she was kept inside, whereas these attacks never occurred in the aviary. For the first part of the winter the two Grey Parrots did very well, were in the best of condition, and had beautiful plumage. The winter of 1957/58 was not particularly cold here in Copenhagen, but toward its end an extended period of cold set in. The temperatures were not that low, but the cold weather lasted well into the spring. One day I discovered that one of Coco's claws was bleeding. I thought that he could possibly have torn it in some way, although I of course did not rule out the possibility that the cold was responsible. A few days later I discovered that one of Jocko's claws was bleeding too. I was now no longer in doubt about the cause, so I immediately brought the birds inside. They now received cod-liver oil mixed with their seeds, and vitamins in the drinking water. After a few days the bleeding stopped.

At the beginning of April, Coco and Jocko were returned to their old outdoor aviary, and at the end of the month I saw Coco feeding Jocko for the first time. I now thought that they would start the brood early, but the first egg was not laid in the nest box until July 19. This

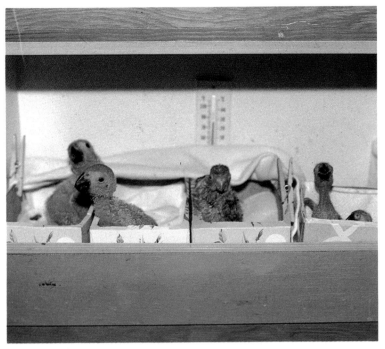

*Between five and six weeks old, the Grey chicks have by now outgrown a single box. Their companions in the brooder are two younger Greys and a Barraband's Parrot (*Pionopsitta barrabandi*).*

time a total of three eggs were laid, at intervals of three days, as usual. Jocko incubated the eggs, and on August 18 the first youngster hatched. A nest inspection on August 23 revealed two young; the third egg was infertile. After the young hatched, nest inspection became very difficult, because the female immediately went back in the box whenever I approached.

I had planned to identify the young birds with closed bands, since I was interested in finding out how old Grey Parrots can get. For this reason I ordered two metal bands with the year 1958 inscribed on them. One hears and reads from time to time that these large parrots can live more than a hundred years, but the evidence has so far been inconclusive. With the aid of the closed bands with the engraved dates, this can be determined with certainty. If none of us will be able to make the determination, at least our descendants will. On Sunday,

Grey Parrot parents, with their youngster perched at the nest box entrance.

August 31, when the female was outside of the nest, I found it relatively easy to place the bands on the two young birds.

I was of course nervous that the female would try to remove the bands from the nest—which is reported to occur with some birds—and in so doing injure the young, but everything went well. On September 24, I was able to inspect the nest again, and to my dismay I found that one of the young birds was dead. It had some blood on its bill, but as far as I could determine, it had not been bitten. It had plenty of food in its crop, and I unfortunately could not determine the cause of death.

The other young bird was apparently doing well; I heard it calling now and then when it was being fed. On October 13, I noticed that Coco and Jocko were showing more interest in each other than they had previously when they were feeding young. It appeared that they were preparing to breed again. When I looked in the nest, the last youngster was lying there with an empty crop. There was no doubt that the parents had stopped feeding it because they wanted to nest again. But since the time of year was already past, it remained only an attempt.

Both of the birds from 1956 have been together in the same cage for the last two years and seem to be strongly attracted to each other. When we placed them together for the first time, the bird my wife had raised by hand was horror struck, so afraid of the other, that we thought that it would never get used to others of its own kind. But now, fortunately, it behaves like a normal Grey Parrot. My wife and I have observed on a number of occasions that one feeds the other and that both perform courtship displays on the perch. Perhaps we will be fortunate enough to have another pair, and will be able to breed Grey Parrots of the second generation before too long.

By the summer of 1976, over fifty young have grown up for Herr Langberg. But so far Grey Parrots of the second generation have not bred.

B. Wenners of Heide, whom the author has known for many years, has bred the most Grey Parrots in Germany. Herr Wenners wrote about his breeding successes only once, in 1964. From 1962 until the summer of 1976, twenty-three of his birds were reared, although forty-two were hatched and forty-nine eggs were laid—an unparalleled achievement by a Grey Parrot pair! It is hoped that many more fanciers and Grey Par-

A clutch of infertile Grey Parrot eggs.

rot owners will try to breed these birds. The number of birds imported will certainly not increase; it will grow smaller, and prices will rise. The breeding pair mentioned in the following account usually laid eggs in the months of June, July, and August, but also in November and December; one brood also came in March. This shows that in our climate the birds can breed successfully in almost any month. Three or four eggs were always laid, and as a rule, they were incubated for thirty days. The young birds stayed in the nest for eleven to twelve weeks. In almost every clutch of this breeding pair, one of the young was not viable. The reason for this could not be determined. What follows is Herr Wenners's report of his experiences and thoughts.

The unexpected behavior of my first jocko, which I received through an exchange of birds in March 1960, convinced me to place the bird in an outdoor flight and to buy another bird for companionship, which I acquired in April 1960.

These jockos had nothing in common with the tame, devoted, intelligent jockos usually written about; on the contrary, their foolish and excessively mistrustful behavior surpasses that of all other species of parrots and is even capable of bringing even a bird fancier used to disappointments to despair.

The flight of Grey Parrots is heavy and is even more awkward than that of amazons. When frightened—and that is what they are at the sight of any person—they fly blindly and soon fall to the ground, where they continue to produce the most unbearably loud screeches and shrieks. They react with mistrust to any even minor change in their surroundings, and they would prefer to go hungry for several days rather than sit on a new perch or eat from a different food bowl; even a change in the way their food is offered can meet with their disapproval.

Their fear of humans has declined somewhat over the years; however, it has not changed when dealing with strangers, and we count as strangers even family members who are wearing different clothes than usual or are no longer separated by wire mesh from the birds. On weekends the disagreeable task of cleaning the Grey Parrots' flight is mine. One seldom sees jockos that are more attracted to women and children than to men; but here again, these birds are an exception. For instance, they take peanuts from my mother's hand (but only if

210

At five weeks of age, the little Grey Parrot is quite well behaved.

she appears in her apron); but when I offer them, they would rather do without the otherwise prized nuts.

My Grey Parrots' habit of destroying everything in sight with their powerful bills, which almost brought me to despair, disappeared immediately when I gave them a more suitable or more appealing nest box. The roof of the nest box and the wooden frame of the flight, both of which had been constructed of wood soaked in creosote and wood preservative, were always the targets of their powerful bills, as were the perches. On the other hand, fresh willow and fruit-tree branches remained untouched. Since then I no longer believe in the theory that parrots need certain nutrients found in fresh bark; this is also based on my observations of my amazons and Sulphur-crested Cockatoos. Except while the nest hole is being excavated, I think the birds gnaw only for pleasure and to whet their bills. Normal bird wire, even in double or triple thickness, will not withstand this powerful tool, and I was quickly forced to cover all the wood with heavy galvanized sheeting, and also to build a flight with a metal frame and strong wire mesh. The usual bird wire is also not recommended, because parrots often catch their claws in it while climbing, and they could be injured as a result.

One should never cut the flight feathers of parrots to prevent them from flying. My male, which had cut wings when I bought him, even now has gaps on his wings and is severely hampered in flight. Only after two molts—even though I offered everything possible for feather growth—was he able to fly the 1.2 meter distance between perches.

The flight in which I keep my Grey Parrots is located in an large, unheated stable, and measures 2.0 × 1.3 × 2.5 meters. The birds have withstood temperatures as low as − 10 C. without showing any signs of discomfort. I believe that they can withstand temperatures below zero better in a flight than temperatures above zero in a cage.

The diet of my Grey Parrots consists of peanut kernels, sunflower seeds, hemp, maize, and wheat, as well as apples and the green tops of carrots. They refuse to eat anything else, particularly soft food, even when they are rearing young.

The sexes of my Grey Parrots are easily told by anyone with an eye for that sort of thing. The difference was so obvious to me even in the beginning that I thought I had birds from two different geographical areas. The bill, head, and body of the male are more massive. The unfeathered area around his eyes seems to be larger than in the female, which also has noticeably lighter plumage than he, partic-

A young Grey Parrot is fed baby food from an eyedropper. Parrot breeders inclined toward hand rearing make extensive use of the wide variety of foods available in this form.

213

ularly when viewed from above. I could also detect a clear difference in coloration in the youngsters, so that I now believe that it is possible to tell the sexes apart even when the birds are very young. The calls of males and females also differ; on the whole, the calls of the female are higher and shriller. I have not heard her sing the pleasant song that the male sings to her—even in the coldest weather, but never in a cage. The male's song has certain similarities with that of the thrush, but I am not completely sure if he has learned it in parts or as a whole, because he has also learned with astonishing accuracy to mimic the way I whistle for my pigeons. I have never noticed the pair exchange caresses, as is done by parakeets and lovebirds. To be sure, the male does perform a courtship dance for the female, when she leaves the nest box, for example. He ruffles his feathers, flaps his wings, hops from one leg to the other, and makes a growling sound with lowered head, as well as the pleasant-sounding whistling. The female reacts by also flapping her wings. The jockos also behave in a similar way when I speak to them from a certain distance, but instead of the song, they instead make a loud clacking, and the female sounds brief fear and alarm calls. Molting takes a long time, and the feathers are replaced, as with my other parrots, between April and July. After the molt is completed, sometime in August, they begin breeding.

This Grey Parrot was not raised by its parents, but instead hand-reared using a baby bottle.

214

Grey Parrots in the Cameroon, feeding on oil-palm fruits.

If one owns a suitable pair and is able to offer them an acceptable nest box, then, in my opinion, successful breeding is not that difficult. I could probably have bred them even in 1961 had I guessed that the Grey Parrots would chew to pieces the nest box that was used for large parakeets. In only a few days, starting with the bottom, these boxes were reduced to small pieces. The realization that Grey Parrots require a deep nest hole occurred to me later. The female started laying within two weeks after I installed a nest box made of strong boards, with a depth of about 60 centimeters below the entrance hole, in the flight. They would almost certainly prefer an even deeper nest cavity. Incubation began on November 15, 1962, at temperatures around the freezing point, with a clutch of three eggs. This brood unfortunately fell victim to the cold, after the three young, which hatched on Christmas, had reached a length of 7 centimeters. Even though the female stayed in the nest box almost constantly, flying into it as soon as the door of the bird house was opened, I did not find that she had again laid two eggs (with one more to follow) until August 15. The incubation period lasted thirty days. During this time, the female rarely left the nest, presumably only to drink and to defecate. The male assumed the task of feeding the female entirely. The female sat

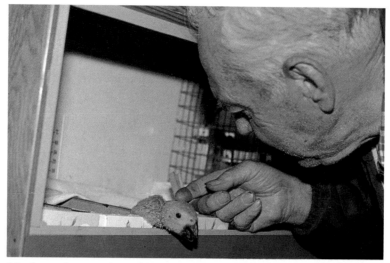

Hand-reared parrots have the opportunity to become accustomed to visitors as well as the people who take care of them. This chick is between five and six weeks old.

tightly on the eggs and then the small young, the presence of which was indicated by the loud begging calls. Two young hatched on September 15, 1963, and were, like the eggs, only slightly larger than those of the large parakeets. The young are covered with thick, long, yellowish down. Their rate of growth was quite slow. At an age of four weeks, when the young birds were approximately the same size as a small fist, the first feather sheaths started to sprout. The course of feather development is almost exactly the same as in the young of Budgerigars: that is, flights, head, tail, back, and finally the breast and belly. The growth of the plumage was complete at an age of ten weeks. Even so, the first young bird did not leave the nest for the first time until it was twelve weeks old. Apart from the still awkward movements of the young bird, it could be told apart from the adults only by the black iris and the shorter upper mandible. In the second week after it left the nest, I observed the young animal feeding on its own. Unfortunately, the second bird had developed more slowly and was not vigorous enough, compared to the first. When I took it out of the nest in the middle of December, because it was already noticeably cold, and tried to feed it with a baby bottle, it was already so weak that it died very soon after. Meanwhile, the first youngster had developed very well and was able to survive the winter with no trouble. The upper mandible had reached its normal length, and the iris had already gotten noticeably lighter by three and a half months after leaving the nest. It remains to be seen how long it will take before the iris has the yellowish white color of the adults and, above all, at what age Grey Parrots reach sexual maturity. Based on its characteristics, the bird, now fully grown, is almost certainly a female.

In 1967, after a considerable amount of effort and patience, H. Schmitt of Lampertheim had a successful breeding that took a different course. An abandoned egg was placed under a Cockatiel to be incubated; the Grey Parrot hatched. The Cockatiels fed the youngster too little, however, and the little Grey Parrot was reared by hand. The author also had to undertake this tiresome task once with Eclectus Parrots, when, after several days, they did not feed the young ones enough. H. Schmitt's report follows.

I have owned a Grey parrot for approximately ten years. Even though Reichenow (in *Vogelbilder aus fernen Zonen—Papageien*) writes that males cannot be told apart from females, I have for many

At three months of age, these chicks are eager to eat from a spoon.

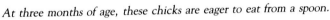

years held the position that the sexes can be distinguished clearly. Male Grey Parrots have large, massive heads, while those of females are smaller—which is also true of many other species of parrots. The male's bill is also significantly more massive than that of the female. But the sexes can be distinguished most easily by the length of the tail. The red tail of the male extends approximately 3 to 4 centimeters beyond the wing tips, while the female's wing tips are at about the same point as the tip of the tail. In our local club, some members have owned Grey Parrots for many years, and we have always been able to show a number of jockos (which is what Grey Parrots are called) at our exhibitions. In conversations with fanciers, it has always been confirmed that my jocko is a female, while the other Greys owned by our members are all males. One of our AZ members, Herr Langberg of Copenhagen, wrote in the *Die Gefiederte Welt* in 1958 about his successful breeding of the Grey Parrot, and advanced the opinion that the majority of imported Grey parrots were females. I am of a different opinion, and believe that we have more males than females in our possession.

One evening in February 1967, my female jocko made an unusual sound, which I had not heard from her before. I believe that the speaking talent of males and females is equal. At least all of the members of my local club report that all of their Grey Parrots can speak well. My jocko made a sound just like a hen does when laying an egg. At that time Jocko was in a familiar cage in the living room. She suddenly moved to one of the lower perches, and I could see that an egg was coming out. I immediately held my hand underneath and caught the egg. Free of her burden, Jocko immediately started talking again, as she has for years. The next day I visited the vice-president of our local club, Herr Daniel, who has also owned a Grey Parrot for nine years and which we assumed was a male because of its large size. We placed them together in a somewhat larger cage and quickly built a large nest box, which we hung outside the cage. The dimensions of the cage are 85 centimeters long by 50 deep and 60 high. Jockle, which was the name of my friend's Grey Parrot, at first took little interest in his new "bride." On the other hand, the female ruffled her feathers and assumed an aggressive posture. It took about two weeks before the two Grey Parrots got together. One could frequently observe the two birds feeding each other, a behavior we were already familiar with from breeding parakeets, with the male regurgitating food from his crop and giving it to the female. Mating was observed for the first time in the second week of March. The birds were in the

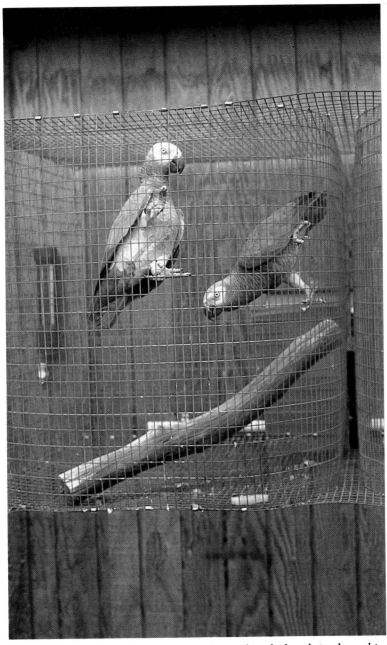

At Golden Egg Aviary in Oregon, Grey Parrots benefit from being housed in cages outdoors as the weather allows.

It is very unusual for four Grey Parrots to hatch and also to survive to maturity. Almost ready to fledge at 11–12 weeks old, they still have dark eyes, but otherwise they look almost like their parents. They belong to W. Langberg.

house and took little notice of their surroundings. At first the male often stayed in the next box, and also talked a great deal while inside, which sounded like a telephone conversation. A few days later the female disappeared into the box as well.

We were surprised to find the first egg in the nest on Easter Monday, March 27. The second egg was laid on March 30, and the third and last egg followed on April 2. From this time on, the female stayed in the box continually; the nest was also extremely difficult to inspect, since both birds were very ill natured, even though they had previously both been finger tame. The talking was also considerably reduced, and the birds were dedicated to the business of incubating. Both sat together in the nest box at times. On April 25 we planned to inspect the eggs, so we lured both of them from the nest with spray millet, which had been accepted greedily since the start of incubation. Our inspection revealed that two eggs were fertile. The female rarely came out of the nest; the male fed her through the entrance hole. He now took large amounts of green food (chickweed, dandelion, lettuce)

Fruits and vegetables have helped to make the transition from the hand-rearing pap to independent feeding, including dry seed, at three and a half months of age.

and also soft food, which consisted of soaked rolls, CéDé egg food, and baby cereal.

On May 4, exactly thirty days after the start of incubation, the first Grey Parrot hatched. It was about the same size as an eight-day-old Cockatiel. The bill was black, the feet were rose red, and the down was whitish yellow. Our joy was great, as any fancier could imagine. Unfortunately, our joy was not long-lived, because the next morning we discovered that the young bird had been killed by the female and bitten to pieces. Three days later, on May 7, the second young bird hatched. Loud peeping alerted us to the presence of the bird, but after we lured both adult Grey Parrots from the nest, we found to our sorrow that the female had also tried to kill this young bird, because its right foot bled heavily and the claws had been chewed off. We immediately removed the young bird to save it from death. We fed the young Grey Parrot and placed it with a pair of Cockatiels. Unfortunately, they refused to feed it, so that five days later, on May 12, even this last hope failed, and the little Grey Parrot died. We now removed the last, infertile egg and placed the two Grey Parrots, Jockle and Jocko, in a large flight, which they are examining even as I write this (May 15), and are visiting a nest box as well.

It is also intresting to note that the eggs were laid in the months of February to April, though Herr Langberg reported that his Grey Parrots laid eggs between June and September. I also agree with Herr Langberg that Grey Parrots in captivity have to be perhaps eight to ten years old before they are ready to breed, since both my friend Daniel and I bought our birds in 1957 and 1958 when they were very young birds. We have not forgotten the sight of the eggs and the incubating birds, and hope to have real success in breeding in the coming summer.

Already on May 25, 1967, after the Grey Parrots had been placed in the large flight, they built a new nest in a tree stump. At intervals of two to three days the eggs were laid, and on June 7 we determined that a total of three eggs had been laid. Jocko immediately started incubating, which again took thirty days. On July 11, the first young bird hatched, but was killed by the female after only a few hours and again torn to bits. The second bird hatched on July 13, apparently at night, because when we inspected the nest in the morning it was already dead.

The one remaining egg had been pecked at from the inside, so we immediately removed it and placed it with a pair of Cockatiels that already had young that were several days old. The next morning, a

Outside the breeding season, Grey Parrots—especially youngsters—may be housed in spacious indoor cages such as this.

Of the Greys in the cage, two are a proven breeding pair. They belong to Oregon breeder Carol Hinterbrandt.

young bird lay in the nest and was being fed along with the parakeet young. Daily inspection showed that even though the Cockatiel pair were feeding the youngster, this was not enough to maintain it. A friend gave us a syringe from his pharmacy, and my friend Daniel's wife filled the crop of the young Grey Parrot three or four times a day with a special soft-food mixture. After only a few days, the young Grey Parrot no longer struggled, and willingly let the mixture (consisting of baby cereal, CéDé egg food, Matzinger dog chow, grated apple, and carrot juice) be squirted in. The bird is now three weeks old and is already larger than the young Cockatiels, which are about the same age and with which it shares the nest. We are optimistic that we will be able to rear this little Grey Parrot successfully. Its parents are now, at the end of July, entering the nest box again, so it is not impossible that they will breed again in this high-summer weather.

George Bock of Furth was also able to report a successful breeding in 1970: two young grew to maturity from three eggs. In November the fledged young left the nest. Herr Bock provides the following report:

For many years I have owned and cared for parakeets and parrots and have always tried to tame the birds I owned. In the beginning, I kept lovebirds and smaller parakeets, and later I concentrated more on the larger species of parrots. I obtained two Grey Parrots a year and a half ago; both were tame, but not in good condition. After I brought them home, I discovered that one of the two could not fly, which certainly detracted from the joy of the purchase. The previous owner had told me that he was ninety-percent sure that they were a pair, but this was questioned by various fanciers.

I now began to provide loving care for my Grey Parrots, and their initial shyness, which is usual in these parrots, was soon overcome. It is interesting that the birds differ considerably in size. Under the assumption that the larger bird was the male, I named him Jacob, while the smaller animal was named Lora. Their urge to gnaw kept me very busy at first, and even the glass pane of the food hopper was destroyed in a very short time. The normal wire mesh presented no problem to them, and the wood frame and door also fell victim to their need to gnaw. A friend gave me the sturdy trunk of a pear tree, which I hollowed out with great effort to make a nest box. In the autumn of 1968, I placed the nest box in a corner of the flight. After some time the birds started working on the nest box, and they were able to dismantle the strong roof, which I had nailed on. But at least they no longer showed an interest in the now unrecognizable food hopper.

In the spring of 1969, I observed that Lora was busily working on the entrance hole, but for a time this was the only response to the nest box. In May, I once in the morning saw the female being fed by the male. A few weeks later, Lora started examining the nest box from the inside, but as soon as I approached the flight she left it immediately. From this point on, she did not treat me with affection as before, although I could still feed her by hand.

Fortunately, they also continued to exercise their speaking and whistling talents. By the beginning of July, progress was such that the female no longer left the nest box, and I avoided disturbing her. So far, their diet consisted of spray millet, sunflower seeds, walnuts, green food, carrots, and apples. Very little was heard from the male from this time on. One day, when Lora left the nest for a while, I inspected it and, to my joy, saw three eggs inside. At the beginning of August the male was very lively and appeared to be excited, so I assumed that one of the eggs had hatched. About thirty-two days had elapsed since the female had disappeared, so that there certainly was a possibility that one of the eggs had hatched. On August 12, I noticed that Jacob was spending a great deal of time in the nest box, and I also thought I could hear faint peeping. For this reason, I immediately changed their diet, offering instead hard-boiled egg, egg biscuit, sprouted sunflower seeds, sprouted spray millet, and half-ripe ears of maize, as well as bananas and apples, which were now accepted readily. On August 20, my curiosity got the best of me, and, removing the lid, I looked into the nest chamber from above. Quite astounded that Lora did not cause me any particular trouble, I could see two young Grey Parrots lying in the nest. From then on, I inspected the nest once a week, during which the female only ruffled her plumage, though Jacob became very aroused and showed his anger by screeching loudly. On August 28, I removed the infertile egg from the nest, during which the female bit me vigorously on the hand. It seemed to me that the development of the young birds was very slow in comparison to parakeets, since at the beginning of September the young were still naked, with only a few feather sheaths. I was afraid that the parents had been plucking the feathers, but after the middle of September the plumage suddenly started growing rapidly: first the head and tail feathers and flights, and later the feathers of the back, breast, and belly. By the end of October the young birds were completely feathered. The first young bird left the nest box after thirteen and a half weeks, on November 10, while the second did not leave until ten days later. Apart from their awkward behavior, the only differences between the young animals and their parents are that they have black irises and somewhat shorter bills. In my opinion, the young birds are a pair, and I am anxious to see how long it will take before the iris takes on the yellowish white color of the adults.

A few other successful breedings have taken place. Particularly fortunate were the breedings of Kurt Oehler of Friedrichshafen: his pair raised two broods in one year. Breeding has also taken place in zoos, such as, for example, in Leipzig in East Germany.

Herr V. Humpl of Czechoslovakia in 1970 reported on various attempts at breeding in his country, not all of which were successful, as follows:

The Grey Parrot is without a doubt one of the most beloved of all parrots. The ease with which this bird is tamed, as well as its ability to talk and to imitate various sounds, is well known. Since this species can almost always be found on the price lists of importers, interest in breeding it is not great, even though we do find reports of successful breedings in specialist journals from time to time. These experiences are even more valuable because we have very little reliable information about the reproductive behavior of this species in its homeland.

In years past, we have also had various partially successful breedings of Grey Parrots in our own country. But complete success was first realized in the circumstance which I will describe in more detail below. An additional breeding success by the breeder Bernasek was reported in both the domestic and the foreign specialist press. In his case the young Grey Parrot died at the age of six weeks. The bird was found in the nest box only after it had been dead for several days, so the cause of death could not be determined. His breeding pair later started feeding each other again and also mated, and both birds frequently visited in the nest box. But, unfortunately, no more eggs were laid.

Further attempts were made by the breeder Cerny in Prague. His breeding pair is made up of a female approximately eight years old and a five-year-old male. The older bird had been kept in the kitchen for three years. The bird was friendly toward the breeder's wife but was quite unfriendly toward the breeder himself. The bird also distrusted all other visitors. For this reason, it was assumed that the bird was a male. But this assumption was placed in doubt when the bird found a

227

dark corner of a cabinet after wandering through the house. Before it was discovered, the bird had destroyed a leather coat and various articles of clothing, and had built a nest from the remnants. The bird frequently spent long periods of time in this cabinet.

Cerny purchased two more Grey Parrots from a recent import shipment and placed them in small flights located in a small overwintering room. Located on one side of this heated room were four flights, each having dimensions of 100 × 130 × 200 centimeters. On the other side of the room were more cages and flights also used for overwintering birds. The new Grey Parrots were very wild, nervous, and shy. They became tame only very gradually. To speed up this process, the tame bird from the house was placed with one of the wild birds in the autumn of 1968. The birds got along well. In the spring of 1969, the wild bird was observed feeding the tame one, which flapped its wings and begged for food. Then the birds were given a nest box measuring 40 × 30 × 60 centimeters. The small size of the flight left no room for the box except on the front side.

For several weeks the pair completely ignored the nest box; later they gnawed at it so much that only scraps remained. A new nest box was constructed, this time made of boards 5 centimeters thick. The new box was also ignored for a long time, but finally, in the autumn of 1969, the tame bird was observed entering it frequently. The second bird sat in front of the box, and at the approach of the breeder or a stranger it growled like a little dog. The bird had never made a sound like this before. Later, the birds spent a considerable amount of time in the nest box. Since both birds were now very shy, no nest inspections were made for fear of damage to the eggs. After approximately five weeks, both birds perched outside and no longer showed an interest in the box. Inspection was made through a side door, and two white, completely cold, infertile eggs were found. They were discarded, and the nest box was repaired.

In the winter of 1969, a new attempt was made. For the same reasons given above, inspection was again not attempted, so that the date of egg laying was not known. After some time, an increased food intake was noted, and the hope that young were in the nest increased. Later the calls of a young bird were heard. The breeder estimates that the tragedy occurred six weeks later. The breeding pair sat on a perch, ignoring the nest box. The subsequent inspection revealed a dead bird and an infertile egg. The young bird had a full crop, the wing and tail feathers were relatively well developed, and its age was estimated as six to seven weeks. After this failure, the birds showed no further interest in breeding. The nest box was again repaired.

Early in the winter of 1970 another breeding attempt was made. In this case as well, the exact dates are not known, because after all the failures the breeder had no desire to perform any kind of inspection. After some time, faint voices again could be heard coming from the nest. At an age of four to five weeks, the young birds were separated from the parents and an attempt was made to rear them artificially. This was not successful; after two to three weeks, the young birds died with full crops in the usual way.

To us, of course, the deaths of the young birds always at approximately the same age (with the breeder Bernasek as well as with Cerny) was a mystery. But everyone, looking at these events from the outside and theorizing, agreed that some kind of mistake was being made. The diet seemed to be adequate and appropriate, so the reason had to lie in some external cause.

At the beginning of June 1971, the breeding pair again started to visit the newly repaired nest box. By the end of the month the female was no longer seen. No inspections were made in this case either; on the contrary, the breeder left the birds alone as much as possible. In fact, the only time he saw them was when he fed them once a day. Besides him, no one else entered the room. At the end of July he again heard faint sounds coming from the nest box. Even more attention than usual was paid to the diet. In addition to good sunflower seeds, hulled oats, millet, niger, canary, and rice, sprouted oats were also given. The birds also received grated carrot with white bread and egg. Chopped apples and carrots were fed daily, and occasionally slices of banana and orange as well. They also received the following green foods: chickweed, dandelion (also with flowers), and half-ripe seeds; later, they were given half-ripe maize, half-ripe sunflower seeds, and ripe peas.

The rearing of the young bird proceeded normally; even the critical time at six to seven weeks, which we feared, passed without incident. The specialist literature at this time indicated a rearing time of ten weeks. The ten weeks went by without worry, but our anxiety increased as the rearing period became protracted. The young bird was still alive though, and the breeder Cerny found the young Grey Parrot in the flight together with its parents for the first time on November 25, 1971, which is a length of time that has never been reported in the literature. Despite the uncertainty that remains because of the lack of inspection and the incomplete information, at least we are able to say that we have had a successful breeding.

I have no satisfactory explanation for the long length of stay in the nest. In breeding circles it is well known that a single young bird stays in the nest longer than when several are present. But in this case we are dealing with weeks, not days. On the other hand, it is also possible that the bird had left the nest earlier but that this had gone unnoticed by the breeder in his efforts to disturb the birds as little as possible.

Another interesting question is why the male stayed in the nest with the female the whole time. This behavior is unnatural. But it is also possible that the male actually perched on the box the whole time and went inside only at any disturbance. The constant destruction of the nest box is also interesting. The birds always had fresh branches from fruit trees at their disposal. I feel that all of these uncertainties are the result not only of the lack of inspections; the unsuitable flight also played a role. The flight was located directly under a skylight, so that the sun shone in the room the whole day. Even though exact information about nesting in the wild is lacking, one can presume that the Grey Parrot nests in the dark virgin forest and that the well-hidden nest hole is certainly not struck directly by the rays of the sun. Perhaps additional breeding successes will clarify this point.

The breeder will hardly agree to make any changes in the breeding facilities, and in view of his experiences, this is not difficult to understand. One can also take the position that any changes might lead to more trouble and that further nesting would only be delayed. At this point I wish to reiterate that we in our breeder's club finally have the first attested and recorded breeding of a young Grey Parrot of our own.

10.

Plumage and Skin Problems

Molting. I do not mean to anticipate the chapter on illnesses here, particularly because in many cases molting is caused by psychological disturbances and not by any physical disease. These observations are based on practical experience in keeping parrots and will be conveyed to the fancier in simple terms.

While molting is a natural process in which worn feathers are replaced, molting disorders also do occur. For example, there is continual molt ("stuck in the molt") in which the completion of the molt takes much longer than usual. The causes of this are various: lack of essential nutrients; humidity that is too high or too low; disorders caused by diseases or parasites.

An abnormal loss of feathers can also be caused by stress ("fright molt"). In this case the bird loses its feathers suddenly. This process can be caused by severe fright or shock. Although I have never personally seen a fright molt in Grey Parrots, it certainly can occur. In other species of parrots, and in gallinaceous birds and pigeons especially, fright molt is not uncommon.

The first complete molt occurs at approximately twelve months of age, and is usually completed in six to eight weeks. Though it frequently occurs in July and August, it can take place at any time of year. With this molt the tail feathers become a clear red for the first time.

Feather plucking. Usually neither of the unnatural processes described above are involved when bare spots appear on the underparts of a Grey Parrot or when the bird is completely bare except for feathers on its head. This plucking of a bird's own feathers or those of other birds is an anomaly that must be taken seriously; unfortunately, it is a malady that is not rare in Grey Parrots. One finds both occasional pluckers and chronic pluckers. It has also been demonstrated with some degree of certainty that talented birds especially, the ones that are tame and are good mimics, are more likely to engage in this activity; but it seldom occurs in apathetic Grey Parrots, or ones that are not tame. Based on my twenty years of contact with various species of parrots the following causes certainly come under consideration (there may be other causes as well):

1. Very low humidity in the room, particularly in the winter. This is easily ascertained with a hygrometer (humidity tester). It is best to use a precision hygrometer, which is more expensive but also more accurate. In the wild, the Grey Parrot lives in very humid forests, and one must therefore maintain a humidity of at least 60% in heated rooms. Otherwise, the bird's skin will become too dry, which can lead to a kind of skin irritation and to feather plucking sooner or later. Water evaporators placed on radiators will provide the necessary humidity. There are also automatic humidifiers, which can be set accurately with a humidistat. These devices, which can be obtained in various sizes, all run on electricity.

2. Another important factor is boredom. Intelligent birds which have grown very accustomed and attached to the companionship of people are particularly susceptible. The Grey Parrot discovers plucking by accident and then becomes more and more habituated to it. Owners should take their bird to work with them if possible, since this is better than leaving the bird alone the entire day. This will, of course, be possible only with very trusting birds, since otherwise fear can lead to injuries. Since in most situations it will not be possible, one should at least place a chain, a strong piece of rope, or a piece of wood in the cage. One can also leave a radio on, or at least turn it on from time to time with an automatic timer.

3. A strong breeding drive can also lead to plucking. The au-

thor was also able to observe this incontestably in other large parrots as well. It makes no difference whether a male or a female is involved. The females then frequently lay eggs, or both sexes regurgitate food, although this is less common in females. A mate would be the ideal solution, of course, but it is also possible that the new bird would not be accepted. One must ask the seller to be allowed to take the bird home on trial for a few days, until it is clear whether the two will get along. For the seller this certainly is an act of great generosity, but if one explains the reason for the request, or is a good customer, perhaps the seller will agree to it.

4. A Grey Parrot can also start plucking after a change in surroundings—not so much a change of location within the house, but when it comes under the care of other people. And it is just as common for a feather plucker to give up this vice when it is placed in different surroundings. It is difficult to say what causes such symptoms in a parrot.

5. Some kind of jealousy of another bird or animal could also be the cause.

The points listed above are some of the known causes of feather plucking. It is important that an owner does not dismiss a bare spot as simply molting, but instead immediately takes the appropriate steps, as far as possible (see the chapter on illnesses).

Even in days past, these same problems with plucking occurred. It sometimes starts with the playful plucking of a few feathers, and ends with an "oven-ready" plucked bird! The author has received photographs showing that only the bird's head feathers were present, and the people still believed it was a normal molt! One fancier proposed the following:

My jocko, after indulging in this vice for a year and a half, has not plucked or bitten any feathers for a long time. Whether one or another of my many attempts at curing him had any effect, I cannot say, but I can claim with certainty that the plucking stopped after I placed a swing in his cage. It is a horseshoe-shaped round iron bar with eyelets, which is hung on a chain so that it can move freely in

A large indoor flight cage on casters can easily be rolled outside, so its occupant can enjoy fresh air and sunshine.

all directions. A piece of wood the thickness of a perch is clamped in the eyelets, and the bird not only performs gymnastics on it but from time to time thoroughly gnaws on it as well. Both are difficult for the bird because of the swing's great freedom of movement. Even talking is difficult, because if he makes the slightest movement, he will be forced to get off the contraption. He hangs on it, swings himself around, and flaps his wings; for this, of course, only a large cage is suitable, so that the parrot cannot injure himself.

B. Mayer of Hamburg, who is deeply involved with Grey Parrots, told me of a Grey Parrot that plucked itself for five years but was finally cured by him. For a week the bird was given, by prescription, Federol-Antipick in his drinking water. After this he was treated with Federvit, according to the instructions. This is a viscous substance which is also added to the water. It contains carotenoid (a plant pigment), chlorophyll (leaf green), and xanthophyll (yellow pigment found in plant cells). After approximately six weeks, the Grey Parrot again had normal plumage and also behaved normally thereafter. Such happy results cannot, of course, be expected in all cases, but it does show a course of action that should be attempted.

Feather eating. The very unattractive appearance results from the bird biting off its own feathers. Frequently the bird concentrates on the large flight or tail feathers. The feather is always bitten through at the blood-containing sheath; usually only the shafts remain, and these protrude until the next molt, when they fall out and are replaced—but the newly growing feathers are again bitten off immediately. Here too there are various causes, which were already discussed above. A deficiency of certain amino acids (the building blocks of proteins) could be the cause. Such birds can seldom be treated successfully.

In another case, a Grey Parrot became a feather eater after its flights were trimmed, biting through the cut feathers and later the tail feathers as well. One should not generalize from this case either. Finally, all of the feather stumps, some of which bled, had to be pulled out. As terrible as this torture was at the time, it did help, since the bird left the newly growing feathers alone and its plumage remained normal. In this case, at least, wing trimming led directly to biting the remaining shafts. This is another example of how individual Grey Parrots can behave and react differently.

Cannibalism. The author will never forget a certain Salmon-crested Cockatoo that literally fed on his breast, eating small pieces of its own skin and flesh. The wounds were treated and stitched, and for a while everything went well. But then the situation grew worse and worse, so that the animal finally had to be destroyed. With a macaw that did likewise, defective kidneys were found to be the cause, for substances in the urine led to skin itching.

As the veterinarian Dr. Kronberger says, the cannibalism was probably caused by feeding meat to this bird. He states that "by providing a food so rich in protein, which is true of all meat, any reduction in excretion can produce a sharp increase in the nitrogenous metabolic products in the animal's system, which can lead to severe inflammation of the skin and to intensive gnawing. The increased amount of protein in the diet was completely contraindicated for this bird." Here again we see the danger of feeding meat, or of any diet too high in protein; it should always be given in moderation.

Illnesses

by S. Mundt, DMV

Preface. The following discussion of the illnesses and diseases of the Grey Parrot has the following goals:

1. After the bird keeper is provided with detailed information about the physiology of the Grey Parrot, he should be able to quickly recognize behavior in his animal that indicates illness.
2. Through the description of symptoms that frequently occur, the author will provide aid in the diagnosis of disease.
3. As far as possible, advice on therapy will be provided; but information concerning specific dosages will not be given, because this must remain the province of the veterinarian (because of drugs available only by prescription).

In the interest of the parrot keeper, the diseases which will be discussed in greater detail are those which are more significant for him because they meet the following criteria:

1. Frequent occurrence.
2. Ease of diagnosis.
3. Possible transmission to humans.

The number of infectious diseases that can be transmitted from parrots to people is very small. We must deal here with ornithosis (so-called parrot fever, or psittacosis), salmonellosis, tuberculosis, mycosis, and colibacillosis. The danger posed by these diseases to people in contact with parrots is considerably less than is generally believed. The typical Grey Parrot that has frequent contact with family members hardly presents a poten-

237

tial source of infection. Knowledge of these diseases should therefore not encumber the hobby of keeping birds with exaggerated fears, but, even so, the basic principles of hygiene should be observed when keeping any kind of animal.

My presentation of parrot diseases is preceded by a brief procedure for performing an examination, so that no visible symptoms necessary to make a diagnosis will be overlooked. The special tests that should be performed only by a veterinarian (such as blood tests, tissue analysis, virological identification, bacteriological and mycological tests, x-ray examinations, and parasitological tests) will not be discussed in any detail.

With most of the diseases, the diagnostic aids, as well as the briefly described therapeutic recommendations, will not diminish the necessity of a visit to the veterinarian.

The Examination Procedure

Because similar symptoms often occur in different illnesses, when examining parrots it is important to note all of the symptoms of the illness so a correct diagnosis can be made. A systematic procedure is the best way to ensure that no symptoms are overlooked. In practice, the following examination procedure has proven useful:

1. *Scrutiny of behavior:* Movement, activity, compulsive behavior, feeding, drinking, talking and whistling, respiratory sounds, flying ability, ruffled plumage, liveliness, receptivity to contact, fleeing distance, perching behavior (such as standing on one leg or lying on the breast).
2. *Assessment of living conditions:* Kept in aviary or cage, scattered feathers, consistency of droppings (with possible traces of blood), condition of food (with possible fungus growth), vomiting food, parasitic infestation of wooden parts.
3. *Observation of the bird from a distance:* Nutritional state, plumage condition (soiled and matted), eye inflammations, nasal discharges or encrustations, bill encrustations, coloration of the tail feathers, soiled upper and lower mandibles, deformities of the toes.

Since many avian diseases are insidious in their onset, the parrot owner should cultivate the habit of observing his pet closely whenever the opportunity presents itself.

4. *Examination of the bird in hand:* Soiled or matted plumage; reddenings, swellings, pain reactions; nutritional condition (particularly noticeable in the breast musculature); examination of the eyes, nostrils and mouth, belly, wings and wing veins, limbs and anal region, and feather structure.

I. Diseases of Body Systems

1. Diseases of the plumage. The symptoms of plumage diseases are itching, feather loss, and feather plucking. The most frequent cause is infestation by ectoparasites (mites and various kinds of lice). Identification of the parasite leads to the diagnosis. Other possible causes are, for example, allergies, hormonal imbalances, vitamin and mineral deficiencies, amino-acid deficiencies, and psychological disturbances. A diagnosis can be made only after making an exact analysis of diet, care, and living conditions.

One particular illness that occurs frequently in Grey Parrots is so-called feather eating. Principally in the areas of the primaries, the bend of the wing, the breast, and the lower belly, the feathers are plucked and chewed, and sometimes also bitten off, so that the stumps remain imbedded in the skin. In some cases, newly sprouted feathers, in which the sheaths are still filled with blood, are also plucked, which then leads to heavy bleeding. In some cases, the birds pluck themselves bare.

The causes that lead to this abnormal animal behavior have not yet been determined, but a series of contributing factors are known: Dietary deficiencies, faulty diet and care; insufficient contact with, or even aversion to, the human keeper; parasitic infestation; environmental conditions; the company of another plucking bird. Sometimes the cause is a psychological disturbance, similar to nail biting in people. Initial successes in therapy frequently prove to be only apparent, so that we must come to the conclusion, unfortunately, that feather eating is a special form of self-mutilation that is curable in very few cases.

The attempt at therapy begins with the optimization of diet and care. The diet should be rich in vitamins, mineral elements, and protein sources (particularly the amino acid arginine). Temperature, humidity, lighting conditions, and bathing facilities, as well as opportunities for keeping the bird occupied, must be improved. A possible aid is the fitting of an elizabethan collar, which is removed only after the new feathers have grown. The use of other coercive measures, which are not allowed by humane regulations (such as keeping the bird confined so that no movement is possible, or extracting the bitten feathers) must be cautioned against. If the feather sheaths do bleed, this can quickly be stopped by brief compression with ferrous chloride on a cotton ball. In some cases, giving the bird to a different keeper has proved to be a very effective therapy. The purchase of a conspecific (even an amazon) can have a positive influence on behavior.

Just as complex as the causes of feather eating, so it would seem, are the various patented remedies to cure feather eating that are offered to inexperienced bird keepers. Let me repeat it one more time clearly: there is no panacea for feather eating. The recently experimentally developed treatments with cytoplasmatic preparations (so-called fresh cells) or with the treated blood of the animal in question (desensitization) appear to be promising. Nevertheless, it remains uncertain whether these treatments will be effective in all cases.

2. DISEASES OF THE SKIN. The symptoms of skin disease are as follows: itching, redness, self-inflicted wounds, thickening of the skin, discoloration, scabrous deposits, bill deformities, and feather loss. The known causes are:

a) Red mite infestation (*Cnemicocoptes* mites)—treated by brushing with Odylen every third day until healed.
b) Fungus infection—diagnosis is difficult but is possible with the aid of the Woodsian lamp and by analyzing skin scrapings.
c) Dermatitis—can be treated with Decoderm trivalent salve, which will cure most bacterially caused local inflammations.
d) Diptheria—a viral disease which is transmitted through contact with animals (be careful when buying or boarding!). Often with this disease, only eye inflammations are observed, which makes diagnosis difficult.

3. DISEASES OF THE LIMBS. The symptoms are lameness, pain, swelling, and reddening. Numerous causes are possible:

a) Inflamed joints—caused by external injury or by bacterial infection. The treatment consists of restricting movement (bandaging) and the use of salves to reduce swelling.
b) Inflammation of balls of feet—recognized by a swelling of the foot pads, in the center of which are found yellowish masses and craterlike depressions. The treatment consists of 10% Ichthiol (icthammol) salve or Unguforte PBS.
c) Coccal infection—recognized by yellow nodules on the feet

and legs. The cause is a bacterial infection, which can be treated with a broad-spectrum antibiotic.

d) Gout—recognized by yellow nodules on the legs, swelling of the joints, and stiffness. In this illness, the white portion of the droppings is watery because of increased water intake. The cause of gout is often a kidney disease, which can be treated with antibiotics and vitamins.

e) Hyperkeratosis—recognized by a thickening of the horny scales on the legs. The cause is frequently mite infestation, which is treated with Odylen or salicyl salve.

4. DISEASES OF THE SENSORY ORGANS (EYE, EAR). Conjunctivitis (inflammation of the lining of the eyelids) is a common eye disease. If only one eye is involved, a foreign body may be the cause. Conjunctivitis of both eyes is frequently caused by a draft, and is therefore a sign of a cold. Inflammation of the eyelids and of the conjunctiva can also be a symptom of a general infection (such as psittacosis, pox, or mycoplasmosis). Since these are diseases which must be taken very seriously, any treatment undertaken with just any human eye drops at hand, without first consulting a veterinarian, is foolish. Inflammations of the cornea, ulcerations on the eye, and clouding of the lens should also be treated by a veterinarian.

Diseases of the ear occur infrequently. Otitis (inflammation of the auditory canal) should be suspected when secretions are discharged from the canal. At times this may be accompanied with holding the head to the side and a loss of balance.

5. DISEASES OF THE RESPIRATORY SYSTEM. Illnesses of the respiratory tract are rare in parrots. Principal symptoms that are common to various pervasive illnesses—such as wheezing, difficulty in breathing, or coughing—lead to a premature diagnosis of "lung inflammation." The anatomical and physiological peculiarities of the avian lung make it clear, however, that in this class of animals lung diseases occur much less frequently than in mammals, for example. In birds the gas exchange between air and blood takes place in the lungs, as it does in mammals; however, the movement of air between the outside world and the inside of the body occurs with the aid of the air sacs, which even extend into the large, hollow bones. In addition, the avian lung, relatively small in comparison to that of mammals, is rigidly attached to the rear wall of the body cavity. Thus birds cannot cough up foreign bodies or exudate from their lungs.

A. *Diseases of the nose and the nasal cavities.* In illnesses of this kind, accumulated secretions will be seen in the nasal openings. The horny substance of the nostrils is then frequently covered; there can also be a swelling between the nose and eye (*sinus infraorbitalis*), as well as catarrh (*coryza*).

B. *Diseases of the lungs, bronchi, and air sacs.* Diseased parrots often exhibit labored or irregular breathing (often with open bill), rattling or squeaking breath sounds, rapid fatigue when flying, coughing, discoloration of the cere, etc. The most frequent causes, besides colds, are so-called mycoses (fungal infections). But thyroid-gland diseases, abdominal tumors, and possibly *Syngamus* (gapeworm) infestation can lead to diseases of the respiratory tract. The author has, however, never observed gapeworm in Grey Parrots.

Besides the causes already mentioned, we also recognize the following: diseases of the heart and circulatory system, diseases of the sexual organs, bacterial infections (*Cocci, Diplococci, Streptococci, Staphylococci, Pasteurella, Salmonella, Escherichia coli, Listeria, Mycoplasma*), and tuberculosis. The following can also lead to illnesses of the respiratory tract: pox, ornithosis-psittacosis, filariasis, mites; mycoses such as aspergillosis and candidiasis, as well as tumors in the body cavity; carcinomas of the skull, leukosis, and metabolic diseases such as fatty degeneration, liver degeneration, and gout. Injuries such as the rupture of an air sac or lung can also be the cause.

This still incomplete list indicates the difficulties in diagnosing respiratory diseases in parrots. In all such cases the opinion of an expert must be sought. In every instance, infrared radiation has proved to be a beneficial supportive therapy.

6. DISEASES OF THE DIGESTIVE ORGANS. Dysfunction of the digestive organs and the resulting refusal to eat can quickly lead to death, since birds have a much higher metabolic rate than mammals (their body temperature is 5–6 C. higher). A one-sided diet can be a significant factor contributing to an illness. Parasitological and bacteriological analysis of the droppings should be used to aid in diagnosis.

A. *Diseases of the crop.* Diseases of the crop are manifested by regurgitation, vomiting of viscous, mucinous substances, matted feathers, and difficulty in breathing. Possible causes that should be considered are crop inflammation caused by bacteria or trichomonas, diseases of the thyroid gland, foreign bodies, abcesses, and tumors. Treatment can be undertaken only by a veterinarian.

B. *Intestinal disorders.* The conspicuous symptoms are watery, greenish, and sometimes bloody diarrhea. The increased loss of liquids must be balanced by increased water uptake. The causes of intestinal diseases are bacterial infections, viral infections, tumors, liver and kidney diseases (gout), poisoning, and others. In addition to countering the cause of the intestinal disease, a number of supportive measures have proved useful. Among these are infrared therapy and a multifarious diet, which should include soft food such as cooked rice (its absorbency removes excess liquids) or baby food. Only well-versed and experienced fanciers should attempt gavage, because of the danger of asphyxiation.

7. Diseases of the nervous system. Visible signs of nervous disorders include lameness of legs or wings, convulsions, and uncoordinated movements. The diverse causes are very difficult to differentiate. The following come into consideration: nerve damage, traumas (external injuries), infectious diseases, tumors, and dietary deficiencies (B-complex and E vitamins). In parrots, the diagnosis and treatment of illnesses of the nervous system, like those of the circulatory system, must be left to veterinary specialists. For this reason, these subjects will not be covered in further detail here.

8. Diseases caused by parasites. We must distinguish between the gastro-intestinal parasites, those which live inside the host

animal (endoparasites), and parasites that live on or in the feathers or on the skin of the host animal (ectoparasites). Symptoms of ectoparasitic infestation are: itching, feather loss, and skin flaking. The following are found in parrots:

A. *Ectoparasites:* Red mite (*Dermanyssus gallinae*), scaly-leg mite (*Cnemidocoptes pilae*), and various *Ornithonyssus* mites, which are becoming more widely distributed. Of considerably less incidence in parrots are feather mites, quill mites, and food mites, which feed only on dead organic substances on the bird's body and inconvenience their hosts only by causing itching. Less common are fleas and feather lice (Mallophaga).

The therapy for any parasitic infestation focuses on healing skin wounds and on the extermination of parasites in aviaries and cages, to prevent reinfestation. It is important to replace the floor covering, to disinfect the cage, and to boil all wooden parts thoroughly. The bird should be treated with an appropriate insecticide, such as Odylen, Pervalenum, Glutox, or pyrethrum.

B. *Endoparasites.* Signs of illness are emaciation, watery feces, discolored feces, general weakness, and matted plumage. The diagnosis can be made only by performing a parasitological analysis of the feces. The droppings should be fresh and should be brought for examination in a watertight container. The larger the amount of feces available for analysis, the more exact the result will be. In addition to very rare protozoan infections (trichomoniasis and coccidiosis), roundworms (ascarids) and threadworms (*Capillaria*) are also found in parrots. Many other kinds of worms that occur in aviary birds, such as gapeworms (*Syngamus trachea*) and tapeworms (*Cestodes*), are very rarely found in parrots, because the intermediate hosts, such as snails, earthworms and other live animals, are as a rule not eaten by parrots. None of the parasites of parrots are transmissible to people. The most commonly found endoparasites of parrots and parakeets are roundworms. Their growth cycle takes place wholly inside the bird, without an intermediate host. The microscopic eggs are very hardy in the outside world and can survive for a very long time. Thorough cleaning of the feeding utensils and frequent changes of the floor covering can hinder their dispersal. The following preparations have proved useful: piperazine solution, Concurat, and Panacur.

II. Infectious Diseases

Infectious diseases can occur in singly kept birds as well as in large collections. Since a diagnosis is frequently possible only after a necropsy, the statement made by T-W-Fiennes in 1969 should not be dismissed out of hand: "Avian medicine is primarily a matter for the pathologist." The symptoms of the infectious diseases are all very similar, and the diseases frequently run their course so rapidly, that only very limited success may be expected from treatment. But even without an exact diagnosis, the veterinarian will be able to combat a large number of infectious agents, since a wide choice of polyvalent medicines (broad-spectrum antibiotics, for instance) is available. An additional and essential component of the therapy in any infectious disease is to isolate the infected bird and to practice strict hygiene. Changes in location, diet, and care, as well atmospheric conditions, can trigger infectious diseases that may be latent (that is, showing no clinical symptoms) in the organism for long periods of time.

1. FUNGAL DISEASES. Infections caused by fungi (mycoses) have increased in leaps and bounds in animals and man, in part at least because the extensive use of certain antibiotics is conducive to the spread of fungi. The following are arranged according to the frequency of incidence: aspergillosis, candidiasis, and mycoses of the skin.

A. *Aspergillosis.* The pathogen *Aspergillosis fumigatus* is widely distributed in the environment. For an infection to occur, a number of related factors must be present. Warmth and moisture are particularly favorable for the growth of the pathogen. Infection most often spreads via rotten and moldy food. Caution is advised in feeding nuts that are no longer fresh. The principal symptom of disease is abnormal breathing. Also, fungal plaques in the vicinity of the palate are not unusual. Transmission of aspergillosis from animal to animal or from animal to man does not occur. No effective treatment is known. Attempts with Pimafucine inhalation, Daktar injections, and applications of Ampho-Moronal have brought only partial success.

B. *Candidiasis.* This fungal infection, caused by *Candida albicans*, usually leads to inflammation of the crop. In conjunction with this, deposits appear on the mucous membrane of the mouth, which are easily removed. The membrane below them becomes severely inflamed. Clinical symptoms include vomiting, reduced appetite, and, at times, diarrhea and difficulty in breathing. The pathogen is ingested with food. Therapy entails vitamin-A preparations and Monoral.

C. *Skin mycoses.* Skin mycoses can be diagnosed only by using mycological analysis. Skin areas on the head are particularly susceptible to infection: the feathers fall out, the skin becomes wrinkled and thick, and at times appears to be dusted with flour. Infection spreads through contact, and even people can be infected. Treatment consists of trypaflavine solutions and griseofulvin preparations.

2. VIRAL INFECTIONS.

A. *Parrot fever (ornithosis, psittacosis).* The pathogen is *Bedsonia psittacosis*, which apparently cannot be included among the viruses proper. It belongs in a special category, because *Bedsonia*, as an obligate intracellular parasite, is sensitive to certain antibiotics that can control its growth and reproduction. The pathogen is also communicable to people. For this reason, this illness will be discussed in more detail.

Based on the latest findings, parrots are not the only carriers of this disease, which originally was given the name *psittacosis*. In fact, almost all birds can be carriers. Sparrows and pigeons in particular must be considered a latent reservoir of this disease. The various strains of the pathogen are distingushed in part by their pathogenic effects on people. In the interests of protecting human health, legislators have ordered that newly imported parrots be detained in so-called quarantine stations under veterinary supervision. There, by means of medication, even latent carriers of *Bedsonia* will be cured of this infection. Detailed stipulations are made in the German federal law on

247

contagious disease dated 18 July 1951 and in the ordinance for protection against psittacosis and ornithosis of 18 July 1975. In Section 11 of the contagious-disease law, ornithosis is designated a reportable disease (even if it is merely suspected). In view of the quarantine regulations, the obligation to be familiar with the symptoms and to notify the authorities, along with the veterinary supervision of breeders and animal dealers, an exaggerated fear of ornithosis is certainly unfounded, as long as the fundamentals of hygiene are practiced with parrots and all other pets. But persons who ignore the regulations and smuggle parrots into the country or engage in other shady practices are grossly negligent—and not only in terms of the zoonotic legislation.

The course of illness in psittacosis is extremely variable. As a rule, systemic septicemia is the end result, following somnolence, loss of appetite, emaciation, watery droppings, catarrh with sticky exudates, conjunctivitis, and disturbances of the central nervous system. The illness is usually accompanied by an extreme enlargement of the spleen.

Diagnosis is carried out serologically using blood tests or microbiologically through fecal analysis, with a final test using animals (mice). These tests are usually done by the larger institutions, such as the Insititute for Maritime and Tropical Diseases in Hamburg. They are very time-consuming, and therefore expensive (over DM100). But if the veterinarian consulted has reasonable suspicion of the presence of this disease, then he can contact the authorized state veterinarian, who will undertake appropriate veterinary measures as stipulated, as well as the testing, at no cost to the animal keeper.

All newly purchased birds with diarrhea, conjunctivitis, and nasal discharge should immediately be suspected of having parrot fever. The infection is communicated to people by aerosols of droppings, exudates, and feather down, which can still be infectious even after drying for some time. In people, all degrees of severity of the illness have been observed, from a subclinical course to extremely severe pneumonia and death. The illness manifests itself in people mostly as influenza and pneumonia, which can be cured relatively quickly with broad-spectrum antibiotics. The following broad-spectrum antibiotics have proved useful in parrots: chlortetracycline, oxytetracycline, and chloramphenicol. The treatment of choice, which has been proven effective when given for long periods of time (a minimum of five weeks) is Psittacin (Wilhelm Hopermann GmbH). Unfortunately, this pelleted food is accepted very reluctantly, particularly by very weak birds.

B. *Avian pox.* This viral disease is introduced via new acquisitions. In the establishments of dealers and breeders, the virus spreads by contact, from animal to animal. Pox usually begins with a thickening, an edema, of the edges of the eyelids. Through lacrimation and scratching, an inflammation of the eyelids ensues, with severe thickening and encrustations, which spreads to the rictus, the lower mandible, and the mucous lining of the mouth. From there, the infection spreads to the respiratory organs, which often leads to death within four to ten days. No effective treatment is known.

C. *Newcastle disease.* The principal symptoms of this disease are anomalies in movement and carriage, with occasional S-shaped twisting of the neck. In quarantine stations, this disease leads to unusually high losses in parrots. Diseased Grey Parrots can be recognized by dilation of the pupils, twisting of the head, trembling, spasmodic breathing, convulsions, lameness, and all sorts of disturbances of the central nervous system. Associated symptoms include discharges from the eyes and nostrils, diarrhea, and crouching on the floor. Sudden, almost symptomless deaths occur just as frequently as do spontaneous cures subsequent to the appearance of the symptoms just described.

In large quarantine stations, it is frequently observed that at a given time only amazons or only Grey Parrots become infected. This indicates that the virus is very species-specific and adapts only slowly to another group of birds.

No effective therapy is available at the present time, but as a preventive measure, the bird can be inoculated with an inactivated vaccine. It would be encouraging if these inoculations were carried out in the homeland of the Grey Parrot; the birds would then be immune to the disease within a week.

3. BACTERIAL DISEASES.

A. *Coli infection.* In parrots these infections occur often as so-called multifactor diseases: that is, for them to appear and spread, a whole series of factors must simultaneously be present. *Escherichia coli* is one of the most common pathogens that cause enteritis (diarrhea) in parrots. It is the result of improper hygiene, particularly where parrots can come into contact with the feces of carnivores (including people). Diagnosis can be made only through a bacteriological analysis of the feces. Broad-spectrum antibiotics have proven useful in treatment.

B. *Salmonellosis.* Various *Salmonella* species account for certain bacterial illnesses that lead to high losses in birds. The pathogens shed can also endanger other animals and people. Water and food—particularly egg-white concentrates—can contain *Salmonella*. Also, rodents, flies, and other birds can spread *Salmonella*, particularly through their feces. Stressful situations of all kinds are favorable to the appearance of the infection. In young animals the incidence is extremely high. The symptoms are diarrhea, respiratory difficulty, increased thirst, and convulsions. Diagnosis is made by performing a bacteriological analysis of the feces. The most frequently encountered *Salmonella* strain is *Salmonella typhimurium*. With a single animal, treatment with sulfonamides and broad-spectrum antibiotics is frequently begun too late to be effective.

C. *Tuberculosis.* This disease has become extremely rare in parrots. The pathogen (*Mycobacterium avium*) is spread through the droppings, and even people can be infected. The pathogen can be detected in the blood and in all secretions and excretions. In addition to the skin appearing peculiar, emaciation and diarrhea can also occur. Usually, diagnosis can be made only from tissue sections from a dead animal. No treatment is possible for a diseased animal, and, in the interest of safety, none should be attempted by the bird keeper.

Surgical Procedures.

With parrots, the majority of surgical procedures can be performed only by a veterinarian, particularly because only then is there a possibility of eliminating pain through the use of anaesthetics. Wounds are treated in the same way as in mammals. Large, fresh skin and flesh wounds must be stitched. Small wounds, old injuries or abrasions, and hematomas can be treated with externally applied preparations (cod-liver-oil salve, Hirudoid, Mobilat, etc.). Tumors are treated surgically or conservatively depending on their site. Fractures are either placed in splints, pinned, or fixed percutaneously, depending on the site.

Leg bands can cause engorgement or pressure necrosis. The removal of the band in such cases should only be done by an expert, with the bird completely restrained beforehand; otherwise, fractures or other serious injuries may occur.

Trimming the claws is necessary when a parrot's claws become too long because of lack of exercise. Using suitable nail clippers or scissors, any bird keeper can learn to trim the claws after some practice. Any bleeding that may occur is not dangerous and can be stopped quickly by compresson with a swab soaked in ferric-chloride solution.

Reshaping the bill should be left to an expert. Polishing the cutting surfaces using a dental drill with a grinding attachment has proved successful.

It can be beneficial for parrots kept singly, and not kept in aviaries, to have their wing feathers trimmed so they cannot fly. By cutting the primaries of one or both wings, the bird will no longer be able to do so. Trimming both wings is preferable so that the bird can still manage shorter distances (about 2 meters); if the feathers are cut on only one wing, it will spin to the ground each time it tries to fly. The shortened flights will grow back at the next molt.

Therapy for Parrot Diseases.
Even veterinarians experienced in the treatment of parrots have great difficulty in making a diagnosis, because of the great number of possible illnesses and the frequently similar symptoms. Because birds have a much higher metabolic rate than mammals, the feathered patients are frequently moribund after having an illness or going without food for only twenty-four hours or so. An intensive and multifaceted therapy is therefore neces-

sary. When a diagnosis has not been made, the illness must be-treated symptomatically.

In addition, the administration of medicines has proved to be problematical with parrots because pulverized medicines are not taken by seed eaters in effective amounts, because of inadequate adhesion. The same is true of water-soluble medicines, which affect the taste and smell of the water and so are avoided by parrots. Also, in comparison with other bird families, parrots drink very little. With the exception of certain vitamins, amino-acid complexes, tinctures of iodine, and glucose, administering medicines in the food or water makes little sense. Administration directly into the mouth is recommended only in exceptional cases, despite the more precise control of dosage, because of the danger of asphyxiation. Handling the bird daily can also lead to shock. The effectiveness of this course must be questioned also because some of the medicine spills from the lower mandible.

It should be obvious that for all the manipulations that the veterinarian undertakes with a parrot, a trained technician employed by the veterinarian—not the animal's keeper—should hold the bird still. The veterinarian can rely on the grip of his assistant, and the bird will not hold this handling against his master or mistress. For the same reason, I consider it to be important that the bird should remain covered in its enclosure while the owner is asked to supply all of the observed symptoms of illness and all the relevant data, before the actual examination is performed.

The most advantageous method of administering medicine is injection done by the veterinarian. For this, the following possibilities exist: (1) subcutaneous (nape skin); (2) intramuscular (upper thigh and breast); (3) intravenous (wing veins); (4) intracutaneous (upper thigh and nape); (5) intratracheal (in the windpipe).

Additionally, medicines can be administered as follows: (1) intranasally (with a cannula); (2) via inhalation; (3) orally (for example, Psittacin pellets or antiparasitic medicines); (4) percutaneously (with salves and lotions); (5) externally (as a powder or rinse, or a spray, if necessary).

As a rule, several treatments over a period of at least three days will be necessary to ensure a therapeutically effective level of the medicine in the blood. Since parrots are particularly susceptible to shock, it must be pointed out that any handling of a patient weakened by illness involves a definite risk that the patient will die spontaneously, despite all precautions, before the medicine given can take effect.

The following measures to initiate or support therapy can be undertaken by the bird keeper himself.

1. Infrared radiation, with the source placed approximately 0.75 meters from the cage, should be left on for about three days and nights. Half of the cage toward the heat source must be covered, so that the bird can either seek the light or the shadow. The top of the cage must be left uncovered to prevent heat buildup. Additionally, the increased fluid requirement of the bird during irradiation must be taken into account.

2. With weakened birds the perches should be placed about 5 centimeters above the floor of the cage, which should be padded with gauze napkins, so the bird can also rest on its belly. The food and water utensils should also be placed near the floor of the cage.

3. The diet should be as varied as possible; that is, in addition to seeds, soft food such as baby food, cooked rice, and the like should also be given.

4. The bird should be transported to the veterinarian only in a cage wrapped against drafts or in a separate transport container. The cage should be kept in a draftfree location at all times.

5. A fecal sample should be brought along to the consultation with the veterinarian. The sample should be placed in an airtight container, since the feces are more difficult to examine if they have dried out. The amount of dropping should not be too small, since some will also be needed for a flotation test to detect parasites.

6. In the event that the bird's illness leads to death, a necropsy should be performed at a qualified institution (for ex-

ample, the Institute for Poultry Disease at the veterinary school in Hannover).

The following medicines have proven useful in the treatment of parrots:

1. *Nutritive and fortifying agents:* Aminotrat Liquid (Nordmark) is a hydrolized egg white containing all the essential amino acids. Hepsan Syrup (Chem. Werke Minden). Mineral-salt Mixture Bayer and Calcistin (Boehringer) both provide minerals. Vitacombex (Parke Davis), Tricrescovit (Rentschler), Crescin (Friesoythe), Vitatropin (Asid), and Trigantol (Bayer) are vitamin preparations. Trafulon (Rentschler) is a glucose preparation.

2. *Antibiotics:* Chloromycetin (chloramphenicol; Parke Davis). Elanco M50 (tylosin). Erythromycin (Abbott). Spectam (spectinomycin; Abbott). Terramycin (oxytetracycline; Pfizer). Oxytetracycline (Chevita). Ampicillin (Albrecht). Refobacin (gentamicin; Merck). Vetoprim 120 (trimethoprim, sulfadimidine, and sulfathiazole; Friesoythe).

3. *Antimycotics:* Mycojellin (fluocinolone acetonide and chlormidazol-HCl-salicyl-acid; Grünenthal). Multifungin (5-bromo-4'-chlorsalicylanilide; Knoll). Moronal V (nystatin; Heyden). Pimafucine (natamycin) solution. Daktar iv (miconazole). Ampho Moronal (amphotericin-B).

4. *Ophthalmic preparations:* Terracortil (oxytetracycline HCl and hydrocortisone; Pfizer). Corti-Biciron salve (dexamethason-21-isonicotinate, oxytetracycline-HCl, polymyxin-B-sulfate, and tramazoline-HCl). Also, various Baeschlin preparations.

5. *Respiratory disease:* Biosolvon (bromhexin-HCl; Boehringer). Zoo-Frenon (expectorant with essential oils; Hydro Chemie). Puraeton cough medicine (Dolorgiet).

6. *Hemostatics:* Arterinol (norepinephrine-HCl; Hoechst). Ferric-chloride solution. Haemoscon (sodium salt of naphthalic acid; Vemie). Revici (citric acid in butanol; Schwarzhaupt).

7. *Disinfectants:* Desinfectans (organic stannous aldehyde combination in a mixed-alcohol vehicle; Chevita). Mikrozid (Schülke & Mayr).
8. *Ectoparasites:* Alugan (brommethylhexachlorbicyclohepten; Hoechst). Glutox (carbaryl, pyrethrum, and piperonyl butoxide). Pluridox (bromine-phosphorous compound; Cela). Pyrethrum. Odylen (mesulphen; Bayer). Pervalenum (chlorcresol, biphenol, glycerol, saponfier, and isopropyl alcohol; Asid).
9. *Endoparasites:* Concurat (levamisole; Bayer). Piperazine solution (WdT). Thibenzole (thibendazole; Therapogen). Panacur (fenbendazole; Hoechst).
10. *Hormones:* Deltacortril (prednisolone; Pfizer). Voren (dexamethasone-21-isonicotinate; Boehringer). Testoviron, Testoviron T (testosterone; Schering). Laurabolin (nandrolone; Vemie). Primobolan (metenolone; Schering).
11. *Iodine preparations:* Lugol's solution. Tincture of Iodine DAB 7.
12. *Circulatory and respiratory analeptics:* Crataegus Miniplex (Hydro Chemie). Digimerck Tr. (digitoxin 0.1 mg/ml; Merck). Cedilanid (lanatoside; Sandoz). Respirot (crotetamide and N,N-dimethyl-2-butyramide; Ciba-Geigy). Veriazol (pentetrazole and pholedrinsulfate; Knoll).
13. *Sulfonamides:* Duoprim (trimethoprim and sulfadoxine; Friesoythe). Borgal (trimethoprim and sulfadoxine; Hoechst).
14. *Wound treatment:* Unguforte PBS (cod-liver oil with a sulfonamide; Heyl). Althosol (cod-liver oil and wood tar; WdT). Salicyl salve 2%.
15. *Cytoplasmic preparations ("fresh cells"):* Revitorgan Stärke II, Nr. 5, 26, 63, 64, 65, 67, 98. Lingualtropfen Nr. 61, 64, 65, 98. Desensitization according to Theurer (modified own-blood treatment).

Index